# READING REVELATION RESPONSIBLY

# reading **REVELATION** responsibly

Uncivil Worship and Witness:
Following the Lamb into the New Creation

MICHAEL J. GORMAN

CASCADE *Books* · Eugene, Oregon

READING REVELATION RESPONSIBLY
Uncivil Worship and Witness: Following the Lamb into the New Creation

Cascade Books
An Imprint of Wipf and Stock Publishers
199 W. 8th Ave., Suite 3
Eugene, OR 97401

www.wipfandstock.com

ISBN 13: 978-1-60608-560-8

*Cataloguing-in-Publication data:*

Gorman, Michael J.

Reading Revelation responsibly : uncivil worship and witness : following the lamb into the new creation / Michael J. Gorman.

xviii + 212 p. ; 23 cm. Includes bibliographical references and indexes.

ISBN 13: 978-1-60608-560-8

1. Bible. N.T. Revelation—Criticism, interpretation, etc. I. Title.

BS2825.52 G55 2010

Manufactured in the U.S.A.

To my students of Revelation
at St. Mary's Seminary & University in the School of Theology
and the Ecumenical Institute of Theology,
Duke Divinity School,
Community United Methodist Church,
and many other churches

# Contents

# Acknowledgments

There are many people to thank for their contributions to this book. I am grateful to Chris Spinks and Jim Tedrick at Cascade Books of Wipf and Stock Publishers for the invitation to write it. They are good friends and theological conversation partners as well as editors and publishers. I am also thankful for the privilege, many years ago, of studying Revelation with Bruce Metzger, and then assisting him in teaching it. I am very grateful to friends who read a portion of this manuscript and offered helpful comments: New Testament colleagues Andy Johnson and Nelson Kraybill; former student Jason Poling; current student and research assistant Kurt Pfund; and the students in my St. Mary's Ecumenical Institute of Theology seminar "The Book of Revelation and its Interpreters" in June 2010. They read the entire book in draft form, giving both positive feedback and helpful critique. Thank you, Jaki Hall, Betty Kansler, Brian McLoughlin, and Tom Tasselmyer.

Of all those who saw the book in draft form, Kurt Pfund deserves my heartiest thanks. His careful attention to the book's style, argument, and indexes improved it in myriad ways. I look forward to reading more of his own work one day, no doubt in published form.

I express my gratitude as well to other students, both academic and ecclesial, for their interest, questions, and contributions, especially those who have accompanied me on the five study tours to Turkey and Greece over the last decade. I also wish to mention the stimulating class of students I taught at Duke Divinity School while there as a visiting professor in the spring term of 2009.

I also gladly acknowledge my debt to many other interpreters of Revelation, above all Richard Bauckham, Eugene Peterson, and Christopher Rowland. Others who have influenced me significantly include David Aune, Alan Boesak, Ian Boxall, Wes Howard-Brook and Anthony Gwyther, Richard Hays, Craig Koester, Mitchell Reddish, Pablo Richard, Elizabeth Schüssler-Fiorenza, and Ben Witherington, plus visual artists and musicians William Blake, Albrecht Dürer, George Frideric Handel, Paul Manz, Pat Marvenko Smith, and many hymn writers.

I am grateful as well to my son Brian, who helped prepare the Scripture index. Finally, I thank my wife Nancy, who is always happy to talk about Revelation, and our long-term Friday night Bible study group, with whom we patiently walked through Revelation during the better part of a year. These wonderful friends have also endured many slide shows of places like Ephesus and Laodicea. (The photos in this book were all taken by the author.)

Sixth Sunday after Pentecost, 2010

# Prelude:
# Reading Revelation Responsibly

This book is for those who are confused by, afraid of, and/or preoccupied with the book of Revelation (not Revelations plural). My aim is to help rescue it from those who either completely misinterpret it or completely ignore it. It is the product of twenty-five years of serious reading, reflecting, teaching, and traveling related to the Apocalypse, as Revelation is also known. This term is the English form of the first Greek word in the book, *apokalypsis*, meaning "revelation." It does not mean "destruction," "end of the world," or anything similar.

This book is not a detailed commentary.[1] It is rather a guide to reading Revelation in a responsible way and a theological engagement with the text, with chapters 1–4 stressing the former and chapters 5–10 the latter. Both for emphasis and for the benefit of those who do not read the entire book, the chapters deliberately repeat certain key points. The approach I take is hardly unique to me, at least in its broad strokes. But perhaps, nonetheless, a little self-revelation is in order.

Recently I read a *Washington Post* story about a 12-year-old boy whose favorite reading material was the "kids version" of the "Left Behind" books, an imaginative, dramatic, and sometimes violent account of the world's last days and the return of Christ based on a particular way of reading Revelation and other biblical texts. My first reaction to that newspaper story was sharply critical: of authors who write such books, publishers who market them to children, parents and churches who purchase them, and even the youth who are enticed by them.

Then I recalled the Hal Lindsey era of my own 1970s youth. As a teen with a recently invigorated Christian faith, I too was briefly capti-

---

1. I especially recommend (for various reasons) the short volume by Talbert; the mid-length contributions of Boxall, Koester, Peterson, Reddish, and Witherington; and the three-volume work of Aune.

vated by the hopes—and fears—outlined in *The Late Great Planet Earth* and similar books, the predecessors to the "Left Behind" phenomenon. Fortunately, our youth group was blessed with one leader who offered a different way of reading Revelation. My fears alleviated, I was able to put Revelation on the back burner through most of college, despite having a resident assistant who regularly camped out in the college woods to hone his survivalist skills before the Great Tribulation. (His preoccupation did, however, cause me considerable distress for a short period of time.)

My interest in Revelation resurfaced at Princeton Seminary, where I took a course on the book with the late, great professor Bruce Metzger, whose lectures became the basis for a popular book called *Breaking the Code*. Later, as a Ph.D. student, I helped him teach the same course. Thanks to Dr. Metzger, I developed a strong interest, not only in the book of Revelation itself, but also in the many ways it has been interpreted. When I in turn became a New Testament professor, I began regularly teaching a course called "The Book of Revelation and its Interpreters." I also started giving talks on Revelation to church groups, college and seminary students, and others. And I began leading study tours called "The Cities of Paul and John" that include most of the seven cities—all located in modern Turkey—addressed in Revelation.

While I was writing this book several other events provoked interest in the End. One was the election of US President Barack Obama. Almost immediately the blogosphere and airwaves were full of commentary suggesting that he could be the antichrist (a term that does not appear in Revelation[2]). One concerned woman contacted a good friend of mine, who teaches New Testament at another seminary, asking for his perspective on this question, the book of Revelation, and the "last things" more generally.[3] He graciously responded in a way that was quite consonant with this book.

More recently, a well-known radio Bible teacher, Harold Camping, once again predicted the date of Jesus' second coming—May 21, 2011— and the end of the world as we know it. Despite the clear words of Jesus that no one except God the Father knows that date, not even the Son himself (Mark 13:32; Matt 24:36), and despite Mr. Camping's earlier

2. The word (singular and the plural) appears only in 1 John 2:18 (twice), 22; 4:3; 2 John 1:7.

3. The technical theological term for the study of the last things is "eschatology."

erroneous prediction—September 6, 1994—both he and his follow-ers ardently believe(d) that the Scriptures, when properly interpreted, clearly indicate this date. Such predictions are normally coupled with an escapist eschatology and a mentality, similar to what my college resi-dent assistant manifested, that can have significant effects on oneself and others. A colleague had a family physician in the 1990s who was such a devout follower of Harold Camping, and was therefore so convinced that Jesus would return in 1994, that he talked ceaselessly about it with his patients, spent his free time getting ready for the end, and eventually let his entire staff go, since they clearly would have no work to do after September 1994.

The times during which I have written this book have felt quite "apocalyptic" (a term we will need to define later) to many people. There have been wars and rumors of wars. There was the great economic crash of October 2008, which seemed to many like it happened "in one hour" (see Rev 18:10, 17, 19), and its aftermath. Then, in January of 2010 a devastating earthquake struck the impoverished island-nation of Haiti. Some religious leaders deemed this tragedy the punishment of God and the beginning of the End. Apparently, some Haitians had been told for years that such an event would be the start of the earth's destruction. Immediately after the quake, some women ran around, tearing their clothing and screaming, "The Apocalypse is here." Not long afterwards, the Gulf Coast oil disaster occurred, leaving an impression on some that the death of a third of the living creatures in the sea (Rev 8:9) was not a far-fetched fantasy. Another sign of the End?

Finally, though far more trivially, a slip of the finger at the keyboard while trying to order a movie led me to a website called nexflix.com, one of thousands predicting the fulfillment of Bible prophecy, the imminent rapture (another term—and even concept—absent from Revelation), the appearance of the antichrist, and the unfolding of Revelation's "script." The site was meant to inculcate fear and repentance. Had I been a non-believer, however, I would have found the whole thing ridiculous, add-ing its strange perspective to my list of reasons not to take Christianity seriously.

All this is to say the following: *How one reads, teaches, and preaches Revelation can have a powerful impact on one's own—and other peo-ple's—emotional, spiritual, and even physical and economic well-being.* Therefore, interpreting the book of Revelation is a serious and sacred responsibility, not to be entered into lightly. Furthermore, although Scripture is a *living* word from God that can bring a fresh message to people in changing contexts, with respect to Revelation it must be clearly stated that some readings are not only inferior to others, they are in fact unchristian and unhealthy.

This last sentence may concern readers who are expecting a responsible reading of Revelation to be unbiased. But by "responsible" I mean *theologically* responsible, which entails paying attention to the book's original historical and literary contexts, its relationship to the rest of Scripture, its relationship to Christian doctrine and practice, and its potential to help or harm people in their life of faith. As a biblical scholar who strives to interpret Scripture theologically and missionally, I do not find it appropriate to separate exegesis (analysis of the historical and literary aspects of the text) from theological reflection or application.[4] This is not a license for sloppy scholarship, but an invitation to lively and life-giving engagement. Otherwise, as Mitchell Reddish warns about the symbolism in Revelation, "[o]ne may dissect the text to such an extent that one ends up with a cadaver rather than a living text that continues to inspire, challenge, and embrace the reader."[5]

Perhaps more than any other biblical book, reading Revelation responsibly is greatly aided by knowledge of how people in other times and places have interpreted, and do interpret, the Apocalypse: in sermons and books, yes, but also in paintings, music, films, and other media. (However, we can only reveal the tip of the iceberg in this book.[6]) Responsible reading builds on the strengths of other readings of the book while seeking to avoid others' weaknesses and errors. Responsible engagement with Revelation ultimately pays attention to Revelation's theological message as a word from God for the twenty-first century that is analogous to what its message was for the first century. Moreover, when we read the Bible as Scripture, we pay attention to the ways it has had real effects in the world, both good and bad, and how it ought to affect us, especially in our calling to participate in God's work in the

4. On this, see my article "A 'Seamless Garment' Approach to Biblical Interpretation?" and my book *Elements of Biblical Exegesis*.

5. Reddish, *Revelation*, 230.

6. On the history of interpretation, see especially Wainwright, *Mysterious Apocalypse*; Kovacs and Rowland, *Revelation*; and (for overviews) Rowland, "Book of Revelation," 528–56; Koester, *Revelation and the End of All Things*, 1–37; and Murphy, "Revelation."

world, the *missio Dei* (mission of God). Reading Scripture responsibly, therefore, entails embodying or even "performing it," like actors with a script. In the case of Revelation, performing Scripture must be done *very* carefully indeed.

What are the implications of this approach? Revelation is not about the antichrist, but about the living Christ. It is not about a rapture out of this world but about faithful discipleship in this world. That is, like every other New Testament book, Revelation is about Jesus Christ—"A revelation of Jesus Christ" (Rev 1:1)—and about following him in obedience and love. "If anyone asks, 'Why read the Apocalypse?', the unhesitating answer must be, 'To know Christ better.'"[7] In this last book of the Christian Bible, Jesus is portrayed especially as

- the Faithful Witness, who remained true to God despite tribulation;

- the Present One, who walks among the communities of his followers, speaking words of comfort and challenge through the Spirit;

- the Lamb that was slain and now reigns with God the Creator, sharing in the devotion and worship due God alone; and

- the Coming One, who will bring God's purpose to fulfillment and reign with God among the people of God in the new heaven and earth.

Revelation is therefore also about being true to God and heeding the Spirit by following Jesus, specifically in

- faithful witness and resistance;

- attentive listening;

- liturgical (worship-infused) living; and

- missional hope.

As we will explore in detail, Revelation's liturgical and missional spirituality (that is, a life of worship and witness) is the antithesis of religion that idolizes secular power. Because such religion is usually referred to as *civil* religion, the subtitle of this book is "*Uncivil* Worship

---

7. Prévost, *How to Read the Apocalypse*, 11.

and Witness," that is, "Following the Lamb into the New Creation." This reading of Revelation challenges many values and practices people simply take for granted. I do not expect everyone to agree with every part of this book, but I do hope that all will approach it with an open mind and a serious desire to wrestle with Revelation.

Because of my own journey, I can identify with a young adolescent's fascination with the end of the Bible and the end of the world. I understand a layperson's curiosity about the antichrist. While I have no sympathy with those who set dates, or tell the poor that natural catastrophes are obviously signs of divine judgment, I feel pain for those who are victims of such misguided biblical interpretations. This book is therefore intended for the boy fascinated with the "Left Behind" series (even if he does not read it immediately); for his parents and peers, present and future; for his youth leaders and pastors; and for college and seminary students who will one day interpret Revelation for others.[8] It is written for those unnecessarily worried about the identity of the antichrist or the date of the second coming. It is intended as well for those looking for an alternative to readings of Revelation that promote fear about being left behind at the rapture or narcissistic preparation for the end times.[9]

An early fascination with Revelation is not necessarily harmful. Another teenager read Revelation from beginning to end at school one day. He writes about the experience:

> The funny thing is I am quite sure I didn't understand what on earth it was all about, but I can still remember the explosive power and beauty of it, the sense that the New Testament I held in my hands had a thunderstorm hidden inside it that nobody had warned me about.

Some years later, that young man became an Anglican bishop and the world's most prominent contemporary biblical scholar: N. T. (Tom) Wright.[10]

I write with the conviction that Revelation can be understood, and that, as Tom Wright realized even as a teenager, it speaks a beautiful,

---

8. The notes throughout the book are primarily for students who may wish to follow up on a subject.

9. Eugene Peterson rightly notes, "The Bible warns against a neurotic interest in the future and escapist fantasy into the future" (*Reversed Thunder*, 21).

10. The quote is from Wright, *Following Jesus*, 54.

powerful message of prophecy and promise to us, if only we have ears to hear.[11]

## Questions for Reflection and Discussion

1.  What have been your experiences, whether positive, negative, or neutral, with the book of Revelation?

2.  Why do you think that some people seem to have an obsession with Revelation?

3.  What has been the role of Revelation in the church(es) in which you have been involved?

4.  What do you hope to gain from the study of Revelation?

---

11. This does not mean that reading Revelation responsibly will be easy. As John Wesley said, "The Revelation was not written without tears; neither without tears will it be understood" (*Explanatory Notes*, on Rev 5:4).

# 1

## The Puzzle, Problem, and Promise of Revelation

What comes to mind when "The Book of Revelation" is mentioned? Here are some words and phrases that are often heard in association with it: the end . . . the rapture . . . 7 . . . four horsemen . . . the antichrist . . . 666 . . . judgment . . . vengeance . . . the second coming . . . heaven.

Interestingly, two of the words in this list most associated with Revelation—rapture and antichrist—do not even appear in Revelation. Some of the most important words in Revelation, such as witness, throne, and lamb, do not come to mind as quickly, yet they are central to Revelation and will be central to this book, too. Others words that often come to mind reflect emotional reactions to the book: scary . . . alarming . . . confusing. Revelation can indeed be a perplexing and difficult book; some would even call it dangerous. Here are some characterizations of it from a variety of critical perspectives:

- "neither apostolic nor prophetic. . . . I can in no way detect that the Holy Spirit produced it. . . . Again, they are supposed to be blessed who keep what is written in this book; and yet no one knows what that is, to say nothing of keeping it. . . . Christ is neither taught nor known in it." (Martin Luther, 1483–1546, writing in 1522)[1]

- "a book of riddles that requires a Revelation to explain it" (American pamphleteer Thomas Paine, 1737–1809)[2]

1. "Preface to the Revelation of St. John [I]," 398–99 (1522). Luther later found both polemical and theological value in the book.

2. Cited in Wainwright, *Mysterious Apocalypse*, 111.

- "the most rabid outburst of vindictiveness in all recorded history" (Friedrich Nietzsche, 1844–1900)[3]

- John the Divine's "grandiose scheme for wiping out and annihilating everybody who wasn't of the elect . . . and of climbing up himself right on the throne of God"; a book that "has in it none of the real Christ, none of the real Gospel" for "just as Jesus had to have a Judas . . . so did there have to be a Revelation in the New Testament" (D. H. Lawrence, 1885–1930)[4]

- the "curious record of the visions of a drug addict" (playwright George Bernard Shaw, 1856–1950)[5]

- a "retreat from ethical responsibility" such that "its existence and its place in the canon are, in the fullest sense of the word, evil" (New Testament scholar Jack Sanders, writing in 1975)[6]

- a "misogynist male fantasy at the end of time" (feminist New Testament scholar Tina Pippin, writing in 1992)[7]

- a book that transforms the "nonviolent resistance of the slaughtered Jesus into the violent warfare of the slaughtering Jesus" (New Testament scholar John Dominic Crossan, writing in 2007)[8]

Jack Sanders's reference to the canon, the collection of Christianity's authoritative writings, or Scripture, may sound extreme, but it is true that Revelation barely made it into the Christian canon (more on this later). And today, while Revelation remains in the canon, it seldom appears in the lectionary (list or collection of readings for worship) of the Roman Catholic Church or the Protestant churches that use one. Lectionaries tend to avoid the hard passages and omit certain verses of the passages they use to make Revelation "a more acceptable book."[9] Furthermore,

---

3. Cited in Hays, *Moral Vision*, 169.

4. *Apocalypse*, 63, 66, 67.

5. Cited in Johns, *Lamb Christology*, 4.

6. *Ethics in the New Testament*, 115.

7. *Death and Desire*, 105.

8. *God and Empire*, 224.

9. Kovacs and Rowland, *Revelation*, 222. The Revised Common Lectionary has only six readings from Revelation: 1:1–8; 5:6–14; 7:2–17; 21:1–6; 21:10—22:5; 22:12–21.

Revelation *never* appears in the lectionary of the Orthodox Churches, though it is read in toto in some Orthodox churches on the Saturday before Pascha (Easter). For many Christians, Revelation has been functionally de-canonized. As one woman commented on one of my blog posts on Revelation, "My own Bibles might as well have omitted Revelation for all the attention I've given it."

Even the great reformers, Calvin and (the early) Luther, were suspicious of Revelation, fearing that its symbolism veiled Christ and confused the average Christian. Early on Luther grouped it with James and a few other New Testament books that he deemed inferior to the Gospels and Paul, and it is the only New Testament book on which Calvin did not write a commentary.

Fear and suspicion of Revelation are almost as old as the document itself, in part, at least, because from the beginning Revelation has been used and abused—we might say "hyper-canonized"—by people on the fringes of the Christian church and by fanatics. Already in the second Christian century a group called the Montanists used Revelation to support their charismatic prophetic and visionary experiences, as well as their belief that the New Jerusalem would soon descend into Phrygia (part of modern northwestern Turkey). In more recent times, some members of an offshoot of the Branch Davidians, inspired especially by visions of coming judgment against Babylon (for them, the U.S. government), secluded themselves in a compound near Waco, Texas under the leadership of Vernon Howell, who had taken the name David Koresh. Koresh saw himself as the second coming of the Lamb (Messiah) who would lead the violent conflict against Babylon, which tragically culminated in many deaths when U.S. officials laid siege to the compound in April of 1993.

As one scholar has put it, "Throughout history, certain groups of believers have elevated the importance of Revelation as their 'canon within the canon' either to promote a sectarian sociology or to justify an extreme interest in eschatology."[10] Another rightly says that "no other part of the Bible has provided such a happy hunting ground for all sorts of bizarre and dangerous interpretations."[11] Yet another, noted New Testament specialist Luke Timothy Johnson, says this about Revelation:

---

10. Wall, *Revelation*, 29.

11. Boring, *Revelation*, 4.

> Few writings in all of literature have been so obsessively read with such generally disastrous results as the Book of Revelation (= the Apocalypse). Its history of interpretation is largely a story of tragic misinterpretation, resulting from a fundamental misapprehension of the work's literary form and purpose. Insofar as its arcane symbols have fed the treasury of prayer and poetry, its influence has been benign. More often, these same symbols have nurtured delusionary systems, both private and public, to the destruction of their fashioners and to the discredit of the writing.[12]

That is to say, there have been many *irresponsible* readings of Revelation.

Despite these problems and concerns, there have been many admirers of the book of Revelation, Christians (and others) who have read the book sensitively and creatively, stressing especially its aesthetic dimensions, or its ability to excite the imagination in the contemplation and worship of God, or its offer of hope for the oppressed. The influence of these aspects of Revelation has been not merely benign, but inspiring, especially in music and art.[13]

One thinks, for example, of great Christian hymns such as "Holy, Holy, Holy!" (Reginald Heber, 1826) and "Crown Him with Many Crowns" (Matthew Bridges, 1852):

> *"Holy, Holy, Holy!"* (second verse; see Revelation 4 and 1:4, 8)
> Holy, holy, holy! All the saints adore Thee,
> Casting down their golden crowns around the glassy sea;
> Cherubim and seraphim falling down before Thee,
> Which wert, and art, and evermore shalt be.[14]

> *"Crown Him with Many Crowns"* (first verse; see Revelation 5;
> 7:17; 19:12; 22:1)
> Crown Him with many crowns, the Lamb upon His throne.
> Hark! How the heavenly anthem drowns all music but its own.
> Awake, my soul, and sing of Him who died for thee,
> And hail Him as thy matchless King through all eternity.

12. Johnson, *Writings*, 507.

13. Koester (*Revelation and the End of All Things*, 31–37) suggests that "mainline" Christians know Revelation primarily through music.

14. The last line is sometimes modernized to read "Who was, and is, and evermore shall be."

No less well known or inspiring is some of the music in G. F. Handel's 1742 oratorio *Messiah*. The words (prepared by Charles Jennens) of two of its most famous pieces come from Revelation (Authorized Version):

- "Hallelujah! For the Lord God Omnipotent reigneth / The kingdom of this world is become the kingdom of our Lord and of His Christ; and he shall reign for ever and ever / King of kings, and Lord of lords. Hallelujah!" (Rev 11:15; 17:14; 19:6, 16)

- "Worthy is the Lamb that was slain, and hath redeemed us to God by his blood, to receive power, and riches, and wisdom, and strength, and honor, and glory, and blessing / Blessing, and honor, glory and power, be unto him that sitteth upon the throne, and unto the Lamb, for ever and ever / Amen." (Rev 5:12–14)[15]

The first of these triumphant choruses ends the second of *Messiah*'s three parts, while the other concludes the entire oratorio.

One of the best known American choral anthems is the beautiful "E'en So Lord Jesus, Quickly Come" (1953). Drawing on various texts in Revelation, but especially chapter 22, the distinguished Lutheran church musician Paul Manz (1919–2009) and his wife Ruth wrote the piece as their young son lay very ill in a hospital bed. (He later recovered.) Its hauntingly beautiful combination of text and music is a fitting introduction to the interpretation of Revelation (see 1:4–5; 4:8; 22:5, 7, 12, 20):

> *"E'en So Lord Jesus, Quickly Come"*
> Peace be to you and grace from Him
> Who freed us from our sins,
> Who loved us all and shed His blood
> That we might saved be.
>
> Sing Holy, Holy to our Lord,
> The Lord, Almighty God,
> Who was and is and is to come;
> Sing Holy, Holy Lord!

---

15. The "Amen" after "Worthy is the Lamb" is actually a separate chorus.

Rejoice in heaven, all ye that dwell therein,
Rejoice on earth, ye saints below,
For Christ is coming, is coming soon,
For Christ is coming soon!

E'en so, Lord Jesus, quickly come,
And night shall be no more;
They need no light nor lamp nor sun,
For Christ will be their All!

Not all the music inspired by Revelation is traditional sacred music. Several contemporary Christian artists have drawn from Revelation; perhaps the best known is Michael W. Smith's *Agnus Dei* ("Lamb of God"; 1990), rooted in the same texts from Revelation that inspired the choruses in Handel's *Messiah*. The well-known words include "Holy are you, Lord God almighty" and "Worthy is the Lamb." Also indebted to Revelation (22:17, 20) is the popular song of invitation "All Who Are Thirsty," by Brenton Brown and Glenn Robertson (1998). That song begins, "All who are thirsty, all who are weak / Come to the fountain," and it includes "Come, Lord Jesus, come" repeated several times.

Besides musicians, many visual artists have also produced works inspired by Revelation, from the fantastic drawings of multi-headed beasts by Joachim of Fiore (ca. 1135–1202), to a series of detailed woodcuts of key scenes by Albrecht Dürer (1471–1528), to the vivid color images of William Blake (1757–1827), to more recent renditions of similar scenes by modern artists such as 1950s cartoonist Basil Wolverton (1909–78) and contemporary Blake-like illustrator Pat Marvenko Smith.[16]

These musical and visual artists would perhaps be sympathetic to the words of pastor-theologian Eugene Peterson, whose spiritual commentary on Revelation, *Reversed Thunder*, focuses on its poetic and sensory power to stir up the imagination and direct the soul toward God. After lamenting his and others' condition of being "thick-skinned to the Spirit's breeze, dull-eared to the heaven-declared glory of God," he asks:

Is there no vision that can open our eyes to the abundant life of redemption in which we are immersed by Christ's covenant? Is

16. http://www.hollywoodjesus.com/wolverton01.htm for Wolverton and http://www.revelationillustrated.com/default.asp for Smith. See also http://www.biblical-art.com and http://www.textweek.com/art/art.htm for hundreds of art images related to Revelation.

there no trumpet that can wake us to the intricacies of grace, the profundities of peace, the repeated and unrepeatable instances of love that are under and around and over us? For me, and for many, St. John's Revelation has done it.[17]

*"St. John before God and the Elders," by Albrecht Dürer, ca. 1497–98*

17. Peterson, *Reversed Thunder*, xi.

Similarly, the late New Testament scholar Bruce Metzger wrote that Revelation is "unique [in the Bible] in appealing primarily to our *imagination*—not, however, a freewheeling imagination, but a disciplined imagination."[18] In fact, it would be appropriate to apply the words of Richard Hays, originally regarding Paul, to Revelation: the final book of the Bible is about the "conversion of our imaginations."[19] Its intent is "to purge and to refurbish the Christian imagination."[20]

In addition to the liturgical (worship) and aesthetic dimensions of Revelation, its inherently political character has also flamed imaginations. On the one hand there is the bizarre stuff—the identification of popes, political figures, and others as the antichrist—and the dangerous—pseudo-messiahs like Jim Jones in Guyana misleading the gullible, or politicians influenced by particular readings of Revelation shaping U.S. foreign policy in the Middle East.

On the other hand, however, there are those whose reading of the Apocalypse has inspired them to seek freedom for the captive and justice for the oppressed, whether in South Africa, South America, South L.A., or elsewhere. Why does the Apocalypse have such power to inspire? Because this liturgical, poetic (or, better, theopoetic) conclusion to the Christian canon also has a political (or, better, theopolitical) character. It can transform the imagination with respect to how we perceive and live in relation to God, others, and the world.

The present book, written in the conviction that Revelation is "not only one of the finest literary works in the New Testament, but also one of the greatest theological achievements of early Christianity,"[21] will seek to show how this conversion of the imagination can happen. Revelation invites us to imagine and then practice what we will call uncivil worship and witness, which means following the Lamb (Christ) into the new creation.

18. Metzger, *Breaking the Code*, 11. On imagination, see also Rowland, "The Book of Revelation," 503–13.

19. I refer here to Hays, *The Conversion of the Imagination*.

20. Bauckham, *Theology*, 159.

21. Ibid., 22.

**Questions for Reflection and Discussion**

1.  With which of the strong negative reactions to Revelation, if any, do you identify? Why do you think that Revelation evokes such strong feelings?

2.  Why do you think that Revelation has inspired so much music and visual art over the centuries?

3.  What would it take for you to believe that Revelation is "not only one of the finest literary works in the New Testament, but also one of the greatest theological achievements of early Christianity"?

# 2

## What Are We Reading? The Form of Revelation

In this chapter and the next we consider the kind of literature Revelation is: what are we reading when we read Revelation? I have chosen the term "form" to describe the focus of this chapter and "substance" to describe the next, but that is mostly to avoid having a very long chapter, because form and substance are in fact inseparable.

### The Question of Substance and Form

If we imagine that we are film producers and have chosen the text of Revelation as a movie script, we will need to give the movie a title. The titles and subtitles of some of the many books written about Revelation may give us some ideas. I reproduce here a few titles of works by biblical scholars and theologians (marked with *) as well as other authors.

Many books focus on Revelation's message about the future (eschatology) in some way: *The End** (Scott Hahn); *Revelation: Unlocking the Mysteries of the End Times* (Bruce Bickel and Stan Jantz); *Revelation and the End of All Things** (Craig Koester); *God's Grand Finale* (Hilton Sutton); *The Rapture Exposed: The Message of Hope in the Book of Revelation** (Barbara Rossing); and *Living Hope for the End of Days* (John MacArthur).

Other titles point to some aspect of Christ, especially to Christ as the Lamb (a key image in Revelation) or to his return: *The Book of the Risen Christ** (Daniel Harrington); *The Victorious Christ** (C. Freeman Sleeper); *The Returning King** (Vern S. Poythress); *Worthy is the Lamb*

(Sam Gordon); *The Power of the Lamb*\* (Ward Ewing); *The Lamb who is The Lion* (Gladys Hunt); and *The Message of the Book of Revelation, or The War of the Lamb* (William John Dey).

Still others focus on the apocalyptic and political conflict in Revelation, and/or its possible relevance to contemporary politics: *The Final Tale of Two Cities* (Paul Winkler); *The Book of Revelation: Apocalypse and Empire*\* (Leonard L. Thompson); *Unveiling Empire: Reading Revelation Then and Now*\* (Wes Howard-Brook and Anthony Gwyther); *Revelation: Vision of a Just World*\* (Elisabeth Schüssler Fiorenza); and *Comfort and Protest: The Apocalypse from a South African Perspective*\* (Allan Boesak).

Some titles focus on discipleship, sometimes in combination with politics: *Revelation's Rhapsody: Listening to the Lyrics of the Lamb*\* (Robert Lowery); and *Apocalypse and Allegiance: Worship, Politics, and Devotion in the Book of Revelation*\* (J. Nelson Kraybill).

Some spotlight danger and the message of repentance, explicitly or implicitly: "Escape the Coming Night" (series by David Jeremiah) and "Left Behind" (series by Tim LaHaye and Jerry Jenkins).

A few emphasize the book's fantastic images: *Spectacles of Empire: Monsters, Martyrs, and the Book of Revelation*\* (Christopher A. Frilingos); *Dragons, Grasshoppers, and Frogs* (Jerry L. Parks); and *The Chaining of the Dragon* (Ralph Schreiber).

Finally, some titles of books on Revelation hint not at its content but at its difficulty: *Unlocking the Book of Revelation* (Perry Stone) and *Breaking the Code*\* (Bruce Metzger).

These various titles raise serious questions about the content of the book of Revelation: Can Revelation be understood? Is it good news or bad news? Is it primarily about Christ or the antichrist? Does it concern the past, the present, or the future? Does it intend to instill fear or faith? Is it primarily about judgment or hope? Is it about a particular evil empire—whether past, present, or future—or about evil and empire more generally?

It is of course possible that such either-or questions are too simplistic and that the answer is frequently both/and. But which part of each "both/and" answer does Revelation stress, or should *we* emphasize? I am tempted on some days to focus on Christ and say "Worthy is the Lamb" or "The Lordship of the Lamb," and on other days to focus on discipleship and say "Lamb People, Lamb Power" or "Out of Empire."

Another attractive angle is highlighting the theological or even theo-political dimension in light of Christ: maybe "The Reconstruction of Divine Power," or perhaps "God's Politics." "The Commencement" has some appeal (after all, commencements always mark both an end and a beginning), and "God Wins" might also be appropriate. My point is twofold: first, that many of these possible answers to the question of a title view Revelation as something other than a detailed forecast about the so-called end times; and second, that Revelation is a rich, thick text with multiple layers of meaning.

The title for Revelation I actually prefer above all the candidates is what I chose as the second part of this book's subtitle: "Following the Lamb into the New Creation." This subtitle attempts to express my conviction that Revelation is fundamentally a book about Christ, worship and discipleship, and final hope for the world. But it is such in contrast to a kind of false religion and allegiance. The first part of the subtitle, "Uncivil Worship and Witness," is a thus a play on words; Revelation is "uncivil" in its rejection of civil religion, whether of the first or the twenty-first century.

So, to return to the either-or questions, Revelation is (primarily) good news about Christ, the Lamb of God—who shares God's throne and who is the key to the past, present, and future—and therefore also about uncompromising faithfulness leading to undying hope, even in the midst of unrelenting evil and oppressive empire.

But if this is the substance of Revelation, what is the carrier of that content? What kind of literature is it? To return to the filmmaker question, what kind of movie should one make of Revelation? A documentary or a fantasy film, perhaps a science-fiction flick? Something in between? Or maybe both! This is a challenging and important question.

### The Genre(s) of Revelation

To the question "What kind of book is Revelation?" the obvious answer is "a biblical book." But that will not suffice because there are various types of literature in the Bible, and we read and interpret different types (genres) in different ways. This principle is true for reading in general; we would be foolish to read a science-fiction fantasy in the same we read an academic history of the Roman Empire. So too with Scripture. For instance, we do not interpret the poetic writings of the Psalms in precisely the same way we interpret the narratives in the Acts of the Apostles, and we do not interpret Acts in the same way we interpret the rhetorical argumentation of the Pauline letters.

The question of genre is absolutely critical for proper interpretation of any writing, but especially a work like Revelation. If we get this question seriously wrong, we are likely to misinterpret the text in major ways; if we get it right, we will at least avoid the most fundamental error and should be steered, more or less, in the right direction.

The problem with determining the genre of Revelation is that it seems to possess features of several literary forms. It appears to be, in other words, a *hybrid* document, a mixed breed. The good news is that the text itself tells us this rather explicitly, while certain features of the book as a whole confirm this claim. One of the reasons Revelation elicits so many themes (as in the book titles above) and interpretations is its hybrid literary character.

Most scholars agree that Revelation is simultaneously an apocalypse, a prophecy, and a letter, "an apocalyptic prophecy in the form of a circular letter."[1] Revelation also seems to be a liturgical (or worship, or theopoetic) text and a political (or theopolitical) text. As Eugene Peterson observes in commenting on Revelation as a political work, "The gospel of Jesus Christ is more political than anyone imagines, but in a way that no one guesses."[2]

At both the beginning and the end of this last book of the Bible, all five of these interrelated dimensions manifest themselves. In this chapter and the next, we will consider in turn each of these five types of text that together constitute the one, hybrid book of Revelation. We will focus on the more traditionally identified forms of apocalypse, prophecy, and letter in this chapter. In the next chapter, under "substance," we will focus on the liturgical and theopolitical dimensions of Revelation. There will, however, be unavoidable overlap, since we are dealing with one, unified book of the Bible, not multiple documents.

1. Bauckham, *Theology*, 2.
2. Peterson, *Reversed Thunder*, 117.

*Apocalypse*

As noted earlier, the first word in the Greek text of Revelation is *apo-kalypsis*, meaning "unveiling" or "revelation." The text identifies itself as a "revelation of Jesus Christ," which might mean that it is a revelation about Christ, from Christ, or both. Although this word is not used in Rev 1:1 in a technical sense to identify a literary genre, students of Scripture and ancient literature use the term "apocalypse" to identify a kind of writing that was quite common among Jews and Christians for several centuries before and after Christ. The word "apocalyptic" can be used as either an adjective or a noun referring to the worldview expressed in this kind of literature.

More than thirty years ago, biblical scholar John Collins famously defined an apocalypse as

> a genre of revelatory literature with a narrative framework, in which a revelation is mediated by an otherworldly being to a human recipient, disclosing a transcendent reality which is both temporal, insofar as it envisages eschatological salvation, and spatial insofar as it involves another, supernatural world. [3]

Apocalypses appear in various sub-forms, such as visions, otherworldly journeys, and accounts of access to heavenly books.

Some other important examples of apocalyptic literature in the Bible are Daniel 7–12 and Mark 13 (parallels in Matthew 24, Luke 21), which is often called "The Little Apocalypse."[4] Examples of apocalyptic literature outside the Bible include Jewish works such as *1 Enoch* (a composite of several apocalypses from the third century B.C. to the first century A.D.) and *4 Ezra* (first century A.D., with many parallels to Revelation[5]), as well as Christian works such as *Apocalypse of Peter* and *Shepherd of Hermas* (both probably from the early second century A.D.). Before the canon of Scripture was finalized, some early Christians even thought that one or the other of these two Christian apocalypses should be included in the Bible.

---

3. Collins, "Introduction: Towards the Morphology of a Genre," 9.

4. See also Isaiah 24–27, Ezekiel 38–39, and Zechariah 9–14.

5. See the table in Howard-Brook and Gwyther, *Unveiling Revelation*, 80; and Rowland, "The Book of Revelation," 524–28.

Some biblical scholars have called apocalyptic literature "prophecy in a new idiom."[6] Apocalyptic has affinities with prophecy, but the idiom is really quite distinct. Scholars debate the origins of apocalyptic theology and literature, but its basic function seems fairly clear: to sustain the people of God, especially in times of crisis, particularly evil and oppression. Apocalyptic literature both expresses and creates hope by offering scathing critique of the oppressors, passionate exhortations to defiance (and sometimes even preparation for confrontation), and unfailing confidence in God's ultimate defeat of the present evil. Usually articulated in symbolic, even cryptic, language, this hope means that apocalyptic is also the language and literature of resistance. Richard Horsley contends that "[f]ar from looking for the end of the world, they [Jewish apocalyptic writers] were looking for the end of empire. And far from living under the shadow of an anticipated cosmic dissolution, they looked for the renewal of the earth on which a humane societal life could be renewed."[7]

Apocalyptic literature enables such hope and resistance by revealing the truth about unseen present realities, such as God, heaven, and hell, and about unknown future realities, such as judgment and salvation. An apocalypse can therefore be a vertical, or spatial, revelation about the present, or it can be a horizontal, or temporal, revelation about the future. Sometimes, as in the case of Revelation, an apocalypse is both. In the last book of the Bible, visions of God, Christ, and believers and martyrs in heaven (spatial, vertical) are intermingled with visions of coming persecution, judgment, and salvation within a new heaven and earth (temporal, horizontal). Sometimes an apocalypse includes journeys into, or even tours of, heaven and hell. In Revelation, for example, the seer is taken up into heaven (4:1). The following chapters are "something like a travelogue."[8]

Apocalyptic literature gives expression to apocalyptic theology. At the core of this kind of theology is a *cosmic* dualism, the belief that there are two opposing forces at work in the universe, one for evil (usually Satan and his demons) and one for good (usually God and the angels).

6. E.g., Russell, *Method and Message*, 92.

7. Horsley, *Revolt of the Scribes*, 207 (cf. 18, where he says apocalyptic texts are "statements of opposition to imperial rule"). See also Wright, who calls apocalyptic "the subversive literature of oppressed groups" (*The New Testament and the People of God*, 288).

8. Wall, *Revelation*, 13.

This cosmic dualism gets embodied in real-life struggles between good and evil on earth, resulting in a more *historical* dualism of conflict between the children of God or light and the children of Satan or darkness. The reality of this cosmic and historical struggle means that every human must choose sides; one is either on the side of good and God or of evil and Satan. We might label this *ethical* dualism.

Apocalyptic theology includes another kind of dualism, a *temporal* dualism. It divides history into two ages, this age and the age to come. The present age is characterized by evil, injustice, oppression, and persecution, while the coming age will be a time of goodness, justice, and peace. Since these two ages are so antithetical, and since the current age is so completely infested with the power of Satan and evil, apocalyptic theology is marked by *pessimism*; there is no hope for a human solution to the crisis of this age. Only God can—and will!—intervene to set things right. Therefore, apocalyptic pessimism does not have the final word; it gives way to *optimism*. This is not optimism based on human activity, but confidence in the coming triumph of God. Theologian Douglas Harink reminds us that the New Testament often portrays God's act in Christ as an apocalyptic act: the final, decisive battle with the cosmic powers that is an act of judgment on all people and nations but also a liberating "invasion" for all humanity and indeed for the entire cosmos.[9]

In apocalyptic literature, both Jewish and Christian, this way of thinking about God and the cosmic-historical-ethical struggle in which we find ourselves is often depicted in highly symbolic language and vivid images, though Revelation stands out among apocalypses for its sheer abundance of visionary material. As Mitchell Reddish says about Revelation as an apocalyptic book:

> [It] uses visions, symbols, and ancient myths to convey its message. The language of the book is primarily pictorial, symbolic language. It is *not the language of science or logic*. Rather, it is evocative, powerful, emotive language, at times *more akin to poetry than to prose*. Like the language of poetry, the language of Revelation sometimes is mysterious and slippery, teasing its reader to make connections and see possibilities that one has never made or seen before. The language of Revelation "works"

---

9. Harink, *Paul among the Postliberals*, 68.

*not by imparting information*, but by helping the reader to experience what John experienced.[10]

Animals, colors, numbers, and other everyday entities take on symbolic value as apocalyptic seers attempt to express the nearly inexpressible. Among the most frequent and important aspects of the symbolism in Revelation are certain colors and numbers.[11] The colors function more like images than adjectives, and the numbers more like adjectives than numbers.[12] The following table highlights values that often are assigned by scholars to key colors and numbers in Revelation:

Table of Symbolic Colors and Numbers in Revelation

| Color/ Number | Apparent Symbolic Significance | Textual Examples |
|---|---|---|
| White | Victory, resurrection, purity/cleanness, heaven/ divinity | Son of Man's hair (1:14); clothing of the faithful, martyrs, elders (3:4–5, 18; 6:11; 7:9, 13–14; 19:14); horse of judgment (6:2); horses of Christ and his armies (19:11, 14); throne of God (20:11) |
| Red | Blood, violent power | horse of judgment (6:4); riders' breastplates (9:17); dragon (12:3) |
| Purple, scarlet (similar to red) | Decadence, empire and imperial evil | beast (scarlet; 17:3); clothing of great harlot/city = Babylon (purple, scarlet; 17:3–4; 18:16); merchants' cargo traded to great harlot/Babylon (purple, scarlet; 18:12) |
| Black | Death, disaster | horse of judgment (6:5); sun (6:12) |
| (Pale) green | Death | horse of judgment (6:8) |

10. Reddish, *Revelation*, 29 (emphasis added).

11. In Revelation, things are counted more than 75 times. In addition to the explicit calculations, certain key words, phrases (e.g., "Lord God Almighty"), and other items (e.g., benedictions) appear four, seven, twelve or fourteen times. See Beale, *Revelation*, 58–64.

12. I owe the latter insight to my student Brian McLoughlin, an accountant.

| Color/ Number | Apparent Symbolic Significance | Textual Examples |
|---|---|---|
| Gold | Incorruptible wealth, beauty, royalty; actual or false divinity | lampstands (1:12, 20; 2:1); sash of Son of Man and of angels (1:13; 15:6); what Christ offers the church (3:18); elders' crowns (4:4); bowls of incense & censer = prayers (5:8; 8:3); bowls of wrath (15:7); locusts' crowns (9:7); heavenly altar (9:13); idols (9:20); Son of Man's crown (14:14); jewels and cup of great harlot/city (17:4; 18:16); measuring rod for New Jerusalem (21:15); New Jerusalem and its streets (21:18, 21) |
| 1/3, 1/2 | Limited scope or time | silence (8:1); destruction (8:7-12; 9:15, 18; 12:4) |
| 3 | A distinct group | angels (8:13), plagues (9:18), parts of the city (16:19) |
| | Divinity or false divinity | the one who was, is, is to come (1:4); triune source of grace (1:4-5) dragon + two beasts (chaps. 12–13); foul spirits emanating from them (16:13) |
| 3 1/2 | Limited time (half of fullness = 7) | 3 1/2 years = 42 months = 1,260 days, the time for: the trampling of the holy city and the two witnesses' prophesying (11:2–3); days between witnesses' death and resurrection (11:9, 11); years of woman's nourishment in wilderness (12:6, 14) and of the beast's blasphemy (13:5) |
| 4 | Universality, especially within creation | living creatures in heaven (4:6–8; 5:6, 8, 14; 6:1, 6–7; 7:11; 14:3; 15:7; 19:4); horses (6:1–8); angels, corners of earth, and winds (7:1-2; 9:15; 20:8) |
| 6 | Imperfection, false divinity (lack of fullness = 7) | number of beast = 666 (13:18) |

| Color/ Number | Apparent Symbolic Significance | Textual Examples |
|---|---|---|
| 7 | Fullness, perfection | spirits of God (3:1; 4:5; 5:6); stars in Son of Man's hand = churches' angels (1:16; 2:1; 3:1); churches/lampstands (1:4, 11-12, 20; 2:1); seals, angels and trumpets, and bowls of judgment (5:1, 5; 6:1; 8:2, 6; 15:1, 6-8; 16:1; 17:1; 21:9); Lamb's horns and eyes (5:6); thunders (10:3-4); dragon's heads and diadems (12:3); beast's heads (13:1; 17:3, 7); heads = mountains, kings (17:9) |
| 12 (and its multiples 24, 144) | (fullness of) God's people, God's chosen tribes and/ or apostles, God's presence; cosmic fullness | 12: woman's crown of stars (12:1); gates of pearl, angels, inscriptions of tribes, foundations, and names of apostles in new Jerusalem (21:12, 14, 21); kinds of fruit on tree of life (22:2) 24: heavenly thrones and elders (4:4, 10; 5:8; 11:16; 19:4) 144: 144,000 who are sealed (7:14) and the faithful with the Lamb (14:1, 3) |
| 1,000 and its multiples | Large number with enhanced symbolism in multiples | thousands of heavenly angels (5:11); the 144,000 who are sealed (7:4), with 12,000 from each of the 12 tribes (7:5-8); 7,000 killed in earthquake (11:13); 144,000 faithful with the Lamb (14:1, 3); dragon bound for 1,000 years while Christ reigns with the faithful (20:2-7) |

Some scholars have compared the images in Revelation to political cartoons,[13] full of symbolism, exaggeration, and fantasy. They are in vivid HD, 3D, big-screen color. Apocalyptic "employs a science-fiction-like idiom to describe events that exceed human capacities of expression."[14] The visions "expand his [John's] readers' world, both spatially (into

13. See, e.g., Beasley-Murray, *Revelation*, 16–17.
14. Mangina, *Revelation*, 25.

heaven) and temporally (into the eschatological future), . . . open[ing] their world to divine transcendence."[15]

This all works together, almost like a sustained single vision, to express deeply held convictions about God and the world-stage on which the forces of good and of evil are at odds with each other. Thus apocalyptic theology and literature are inherently theopolitical in nature, a point to which we will return in the next chapter. In Revelation, the cosmic struggle of God and the Lamb versus Satan (the dragon of ch. 12) manifests itself in the earthly struggle between God's people redeemed by the Lamb and Satan's agents, the beasts from the sea and the land—probably meant to signify the emperor and those who promote his cult.

Symbolic language is evocative and expressive; it is not the language of the newspaper but the language of poetry. Yet this symbolism points to actual, though transcendent, reality, so the language can be called "literal non-literalism."[16] "[T]he world created by symbols is not fictive; it is a non-literal but real world."[17] Furthermore, the "special genius of apocalyptic" literature, according to David Aune, is "its ability to universalize the harsh realities of particular historical situations by transposing them into a new key using archaic symbols of conflict and victory, suffering and vindication. Thus the beast from the sea [in Rev. 13] represents Rome—yet more than Rome."[18]

Most people in the West (or North), even many who are Christians, no longer operate within an apocalyptic universe in which visible powers and struggles correspond to invisible cosmic forces and conflict. Christians in other parts of the world, however, experience life in ways that are much more similar to the apocalyptic experience, and Westerners/Northerners may be able to learn something from such Christians. For example, James Chukwuma Okoye, a Nigerian biblical scholar living in the United States, writes that the "African attraction to apocalyptic is due to the fact that the fundamental worldview of apocalypse is similar to the worldview in Africa."[19] Moreover, the apocalyptic theology of Revelation is about power, worship, and hope, all fundamental aspects of African life, and in worship, especially in singing hymns

15. Bauckham, *Theology*, 7.

16. Attributed to John J. Collins (without reference) in Wall, *Revelation*, 15.

17. Wall, *Revelation*, 16.

18. Aune, "Revelation," 1188.

19. Okoye, "Power and Worship," 120.

like those in Revelation, Africans "enter the world" of Revelation to "celebrate the triumph of God in this mystical warfare."[20]

Understanding the book of Revelation as apocalyptic literature will encourage us to try to understand the real-world situations, depicted in cosmic terms, that it reflects and addresses. It will also encourage us not to take the symbolism "literally," that is, to think of actual pale-green horses or multi-headed beasts or thousand-year periods. *These are all symbolic, but that does not make the realities to which they point any less real.* In fact, even so-called literal interpreters of Revelation identify its symbols as symbols, positing that locusts are helicopters, the ten-horned beast is a reconstituted Roman Empire of ten European nations, and so on.

Like a good political cartoon or poem, an apocalypse appeals to the imagination to address the most profound realities that God's people can experience or hope for. As Peterson suggests:

> The task of the apocalyptic imagination is to provide images that show us what is going on in our lives. "If there are mysterious powers around," a character in a Saul Bellow novel says, "only exaggeration can help us see them. We all sense that there are powers that make the world—we see that when we look at it—and other powers that unmake it." . . . Flannery O'Connor, in answer to a question about why she created such bizarre characters in her stories, replied that for the near-blind you have to draw very large, simple caricatures.[21]

In this regard Peterson quotes yet another writer, Wendell Berry: "The imagination is our way into the divine imagination, permitting us to see wholly—as whole and holy—what we perceive as scattered, as order what we perceive as random."[22]

However, if we take John the Seer seriously, he is not just writing an imaginative apocalypse; he is recording visions and auditions (things seen and heard) that were given to him by God, just as God had done with biblical prophets (e.g., Ezekiel and the valley of dry bones in Ezekiel 37) and with other leaders in the early church, such as Peter (Acts 10). He has seen what others have not; indeed, he has seen Truth—invisible and

---

20. Ibid., 121.

21. Peterson, *Reversed Thunder*, 145–46.

22. Wendell Berry, *Standing by Words* (San Francisco: North Point, 1983), 90, quoted in Peterson, *Reversed Thunder*, xii.

future Truth—about the cosmos as it really is and really will be. The reports of what he has seen do what Old Testament scholar Ellen Davis describes prophets as doing: they "instruct our weak religious imagination by means of 'visual enhancement'; they enable us to see the present moment of history in divine perspective."[23] And Peterson notes that "[t]he power to wake us up is the most obvious use of the Revelation."[24]

As an apocalypse, Revelation is intended to reveal, not conceal. At the same time, like biblical prophecy, "its goal is not speculative *fore*-sight, but theological *in*sight."[25] This similarity between the prophets and John the Seer exists because John was himself a prophet.

### *Prophecy*

On five occasions (1:3; 22:7, 10, 18, 19), Revelation explicitly calls itself a work of prophecy, and it also characterizes the activity of John as prophecy (10:11; 19:10; 22:6, 9). Many people assume that Revelation is a prophetic book in the sense of predicting, in rather explicit detail, "the way the world will end." The most popular approach to Revelation, dispensationalism, both creates and reinforces this assumption. A theological movement that began in the 19th century, dispensationalism holds that history is divided into various ages, or dispensations, each characterized by different ways in which God deals with humanity. With respect to eschatology, it includes the doctrine of the rapture, or the removal of true believers to heaven before the return of Christ, an idea unknown in Christian teaching before the 19th century.[26]

Popular dispensationalism, disseminated by such best-selling sources as the *Scofield Reference Bible*, Hal Lindsey's writings (e.g., *The Late, Great Planet Earth*), and most recently the "Left Behind" series of books and movies by Tim LaHaye and Jerry Jenkins, interprets Revelation as portraying, in literal and linear fashion, the course of historical events.[27] Dispensational readers view Revelation as depicting the resurrection of Christ (ch. 1); the church age from the apostles to today

---

23. Davis, *Scripture, Culture, and Agriculture*, 10.

24. Peterson, *Reversed Thunder*, xii.

25. Schnelle, *Theology of the New Testament*, 752.

26. As we will see below, somewhat similar approaches to Revelation—without the notion of the rapture—may be found in certain early and medieval interpreters.

27. In addition to the books and films, see www.leftbehind.com.

(chs. 2–3); the rapture of the true church from the earth and out of history (4:1); the church in heaven (beginning with chs. 4–5); the seven-year tribulation on earth (chs. 6–18); the second coming of Christ, his literal thousand-year reign, and the last judgment (chs. 19–20); and eternity, the new heaven and earth (chs. 21–22).

But prophecy, in the biblical tradition, is not exclusively or even primarily about making pronouncements and predictions concerning the future. Rather, prophecy is speaking words of comfort and/or challenge, on behalf of God, to the people of God in their concrete historical situation. Old Testament prophets were called by God, sometimes in the context of a visionary experience (see Isaiah 6 and Ezekiel 1), to proclaim the message that God gave them, usually in the form of various oracles that were later written down, but also occasionally in visions, and often in poetic or symbolic language. Whatever the form, the message was one of judgment (on them or on their oppressors) or salvation—and usually both.

Similarly, John, as an apocalyptic prophet, is commissioned in a visionary experience on the Lord's day (1:9–20) to write what he has seen. He appears to have thought of himself as already commissioned to the prophetic role, like Ezekiel of old, an exile in the original Babylon (Rev 10:8–11; cf. Ezek 2:9—3:3). Because John has apparently been exiled by officials of the new Babylon (Rome) to Patmos on account of his faithful testimony (1:9), he is unable to proclaim orally the prophetic visions he is granted, but he can (and must!) write them down. Much of what he writes is indebted to the biblical prophets, in whose texts he was obviously steeped. Not surprisingly, John is particularly drawn to passages from the prophets that contain visions and/or narrate divine judgment, especially in apocalyptic images. Among his favorite prophetic books are Isaiah, Ezekiel, Zechariah, Jeremiah, Joel, and the quasi-prophetic (but technically apocalyptic) Daniel, to which he alludes very frequently. He is also fond of the Psalms. With both contextual sensitivity and inspired creativity, John weaves hundreds of scriptural allusions into a new, coherent prophetic vision.[28]

28. Estimates on the number of scriptural allusions vary from 200 to 1,000, depending on how and what one counts. Metzger (*Breaking the Code*, 13) claims that 278 of the 404 verses in Revelation contain one or more OT allusions. Wilson, *Charts*, has an accessible verse-by-verse table of scriptural and extrabiblical parallels and allusions (25–30). John's use of the OT includes individual verses, large blocks of texts, themes, people, places, etc. Revelation is therefore a thoroughly intertextual document, a mo-

Since Revelation is a word of prophecy in the biblical tradition, we must take care to understand that its primary purpose is to give words of comfort and challenge to God's people then and now, not to predict the future, and much less to do so with precise detail. Visions of the future, that is, are not an end in themselves but rather a means—both to warn and to comfort.

Prophets comfort God's people in crisis because they need assurance that, despite all signs to the contrary, God is God and will one day bring an end to all evil and oppression. On the other hand, prophets warn the people about the coming judgment because the people may be participating in, or be tempted to participate in, the very evil for which the oppressive system and its perpetrators will be judged. In fact, in the case of Revelation, we have clear evidence that John believes some in the churches to which he writes were engaging in forms of idolatry and immorality, the general categories for sins against God and sins against neighbor, that the human forces of evil were practicing. This is part of the fundamental and perpetual message of both Old and New Testament prophets: Flee idolatry! Flee immorality![29] Or, in Revelation's version of this message, "Come out" (18:4).

Earlier scholarship on the book of Revelation suggested that it was written to people undergoing intense persecution, probably sponsored by the emperor Domitian or his representatives in the province of Asia. In that situation, prophecy would focus almost exclusively on the promise of future salvation. More recent scholarship, however, has questioned the existence of evidence for pervasive, and especially official, persecution at the time Revelation was likely written (late first century; see discussion below).

At the same time, the evidence for some of the churches being less faithful than they should have been has been stressed. The result is that contemporary scholars of Revelation generally believe that Revelation is prophetic in its words of challenge as much as it is in its words of comfort. That is, Revelation as prophecy should probably be understood as anti-assimilationist, or anti-accommodationist, literature. It is also in this sense that Revelation is resistance literature—"a thorough-going

---

saic of biblical (and other) references. See especially Bauckham, *Climax of Prophecy*, 60–128, and Beale, *John's Use of the Old Testament*.

29. See, for example, the narrative of the golden calf in Exodus 32 and the admonitions of Paul in 1 Cor 6:18; 10:14.

prophetic critique of the system of Roman power" and "the most powerful piece of political resistance literature from the period of the early Empire."[30] This characterization overlaps, of course, with Revelation's apocalyptic and theopolitical character. This new perspective does not mean, however, that no persecution was occurring.[31] Indeed, as we will see, it is the complex relationship between the presence or absence of accommodation and persecution that drives the letter.

Calling Revelation "resistance literature" is appropriate because one of the primary prophetic purposes of Revelation is to remind the church, both then and now, not to give in to the demands or practices of a system that is already judged by God and is about to come to its demise. But Revelation is not just a document that stands against something. Like all biblical prophecy, it promotes true worship of the one true God, expressed not merely in formal liturgy but also in faithful living, the practice of having no gods besides God. Put more positively, then, Revelation is a summons to first-commandment faithfulness,[32] a call to faithful witness and worship in word and deed.[33] In other words, its character as resistance literature is actually secondary to, and derivative of, its more fundamental character as worship literature, as a liturgical text. We will return to these two aspects of Revelation in the next chapter.

### A Circular Pastoral Letter

The earliest Christian manifestations of prophecy, to the extent that they have been preserved, come to us wrapped in letter form and written by early Christian leaders who wrote to shape Christian communities. For example, Paul's treatment of the resurrection in 1 Corinthians 15 is seen by some scholars as a Pauline example of prophecy—an inspired word addressed to a specific congregation to comfort and challenge the people.

---

30. Bauckham, *Theology*, 38. Schnelle says that "the seer develops a powerful ethic, *an ethic of resistance and endurance*, which excludes every opportunistic accommodation to prevailing culture" (*Theology of the New Testament*, 764). deSilva even calls Revelation "a specimen of first-century (post)colonial resistance literature" (*Seeing Things John's Way*, 321).

31. "It is a large mistake to underestimate the context of persecution" in which John wrote (Witherington, *Revelation*, 101).

32. See Talbert, *The Apocalypse*, 11.

33. "Revelation is a document thoroughly oriented to ethics" (Schnelle, *Theology of the New Testament*, 762).

Similarly, the parallel, apocalyptically oriented texts in 1 Thessalonians 4–5 may reflect these two functions of prophecy, comforting (1 Thess 4:13–18) and challenging (1 Thess 5:1–11) believers in light of the gospel. Both the Corinthian text and the Thessalonian texts are obviously preserved within letters.

The visions and auditions recorded for us in the book of Revelation that constitute the apocalyptic prophecy John wishes to proclaim also come to us in the form of a pastoral letter. It is addressed to seven churches in the Roman province of Asia (Asia Minor, or modern Western Turkey): Ephesus, Smyrna, Pergamum, Thyatira, Sardis, Philadelphia, and Laodicea (1:4, 11). But John's Revelation begins with an announcement that it is indeed a revelation (1:1–2), following this with a benediction for those who read and keep "the words of the prophecy" (1:3), before shifting into ancient-letter mode. Then John finally writes in a style reminiscent of Paul and other New Testament letter-writers:

> John to the seven churches that are in Asia: Grace to you and peace from him who is and who was and who is to come, and from the seven spirits who are before his throne, and from Jesus Christ, the faithful witness, the firstborn of the dead, and the ruler of the kings of the earth. To him who loves us and freed us from our sins by his blood, and made us to be a kingdom, priests serving his God and Father, to him be glory and dominion forever and ever. Amen. Look! He is coming with the clouds; every eye will see him, even those who pierced him; and on his account all the tribes of the earth will wail. So it is to be. Amen. "I am the Alpha and the Omega," says the Lord God, who is and who was and who is to come, the Almighty. (1:4–8)

John, rather like another apostle writing to the Colossians and the Ephesians, appears unable to maintain pure epistolary form as he quickly ascends into the sphere of worship, composing (or perhaps reciting) first a doxology (1:5b–6), then an acclamation (1:7), and then a divine self-identification (1:8) that foreshadows the heavenly worship of God in chapter 4. This is no ordinary letter; it is a liturgical letter. It closes in similar fashion, with prophetic, apocalyptic, and liturgical elements (22:6–20) preceding the sort of final epistolary benediction (22:21) we find in other letters, which itself is also liturgical.

The presence of the names of the cities in ch. 1, however, keeps us anchored firmly in history, in concrete existence in the world (which is rather unusual for an apocalypse). The order of the cities listed in 1:11, and followed in chs. 2 and 3, constitutes a counterclockwise circle beginning in Ephesus and ending in Laodicea. Ephesus is the starting point probably because it was the home base of John's ministry prior to his exile and/or because it is the closest of the seven cities to Patmos. John writes to and for these seven churches, and thereby to and for the church universal.

But who is this "John," the author of this multifaceted writing?

## Author and Date

It is fairly clear that John (the author's name according to 1:1, 4, 9; 22:8) was a recognized teacher and leader of the churches in Western Asia Minor, the communities to which he writes. He tells his audience that he is their brother and that he has suffered persecution, like some of them, because of his proclamation of the word of God and his witness to Jesus (1:9). It is likely that his "crime" has been public testimony to and teaching about Jesus, which included as a necessary corollary his advocating against believers' participation in any activities devoted to the pagan gods, including the cult of the emperor (see the next chapter). What John thought of as bearing faithful witness looked to others—at first, perhaps acquaintances and associates, but later possibly religious and government officials, too—like threatening the political and social fabric by dishonoring the gods. John wanted the believers in the churches of Western Asia to follow his own example, even if it would cost them as it cost him.

John also considers himself inspired (22:6), one who has received and communicates the Spirit's message (2:7, 11, etc.), but, as noted above, this is the language of a self-described prophet, and John does not call himself an apostle or give any indication of having known the earthly Jesus. It is very unlikely, then, that John of Patmos is identical with the apostle John, son of Zebedee, even though many early Christian writers made that connection (though the reasons for doing so remain unclear).

Whether we think the Gospel of John is the work of the apostle, a community dedicated to him, or some other figure, Revelation is almost certainly not by the same writer(s). Although there are some similarities in themes and theology between the Fourth Gospel and Revelation, the differences in style and theology are dramatic. (This is no recent scholarly conclusion, the differences having been recognized already by Dionysius of Alexandria in the third century.)

The precise identity of John is therefore elusive. Yet Eugene Peterson rightly points out that in one sense his identity is clear. In addition to our recognition of John as witness and prophet, Peterson rightly calls him a theologian, poet, and pastor who is "God-intoxicated, God-possessed, God-articulate."[34]

Since the fourth century, when scribes copying the text of Revelation began labeling its author "the theologian," John has been known by that title, or as John the Divine (Middle English for "theologian"). Although his contribution to Christian theology has been highly controversial, it will become clear that, rightly understood, his theology is actually profound and significant.

Another epithet for the author of Revelation has been John the Seer. This is appropriate for someone Peterson calls a poet. He writes:

> A poet uses words not to explain something, and not to describe something, but to make something. Poet (*poētēs*) means "maker." Poetry is not the language of objective explanation but the language of imagination. It makes an image of reality in such a way as to invite our participation in it.[35]

As for the date of Revelation, most scholars situate it toward the end of the reign of the Emperor Domitian (ruled 81–96). A few would place it a little later, early in the reign of Trajan (ruled 98–117). Some have argued, however, that either the entire book or a briefer, earlier version of it originates in, or shortly after, the time of the Emperor Nero (ruled 54–68). The best guess, in my view, is the traditional dating to the time of Domitian, as stated by the church father Irenaeus of Lyon in the late second century. One chief reason many scholars hold to this date (rather than a date during or just after Nero's reign) is that it appears that Jews, and thereafter Christians, began calling Rome "Babylon" only after the fall of Jerusalem in 70. Furthermore, the situation of the churches in Asia Minor during the time of Trajan was probably different from that reflected in Revelation, if the famous correspondence between Trajan and Pliny, governor of Bithynia, is any indication. Thus a date for Revelation toward the end of Domitian's reign seems most likely.

---

34. Peterson, *Reversed Thunder*, 1–10; quote from 3.

35. Ibid., 5.

*Head and left arm from the statue of Domitian (Ephesus Museum)*

## Summary: A Hybrid Genre

We have seen in this chapter that the label "hybrid genre" is appropriate because of Revelation's own self-identification in the first few verses and because of its literary character, which Frank Matera summarizes for us:

> As an apocalypse, it reveals what "must soon take place" (1:1). As a prophecy, it *testifies* to the Word of God and Jesus Christ (1:2). As a letter, it *addresses* seven churches in the Roman province of Asia (1:4).[36]

We will therefore consider Revelation as a hybrid of these three—apocalypse, prophecy, letter—and more. This is what John the poet, prophet, visionary, and theologian has left us.

---

36. Matera, *New Testament Theology*, 402.

## Questions for Reflection and Discussion

1.  Which of the titles or subtitles of Revelation mentioned in this chapter (other than those chosen for this book) strike you as good summaries of Revelation's content?

2.  Do you think it is necessary to identify the genre(s) of Revelation to interpret it responsibly? Why or why not?

3.  How might understanding Revelation as apocalypse, prophecy, and letter—and as a hybrid of the three—affect our interpretation of it?

4.  Had you previously thought of Revelation as similar to political cartoons? As poetry? What do you think of these descriptions and their possible implications for interpreting Revelation?

# 3

## What Are We Reading? The Substance of Revelation

In this chapter we carefully consider two closely related aspects of Revelation: its liturgical and its theopolitical dimensions. We will explore these not merely as components of an ancient text, critical of an ancient superpower, but also as features of the living and active word of God that engages us today, especially those of us who live in or near the world's contemporary superpower.

We begin, however, with a continuation of the discussion that concluded the last chapter. What were the circumstances in which this word about worship and political witness was written?

### The Situation: Responding to Imperial and Civil Religion (A Theopoetical Reaction to a Theopolitical Crisis)

What has happened to the churches in Asia Minor, and to one of their prophetic leaders, that gave rise to this document? We may suggest the following scenario:

As Christian individuals and communities in Asia Minor interacted with family members, friends, business associates, and public officials who did not share their conviction that "Jesus is Lord," the basic early Christian confession (Rom 10:9), these believers were faced with hard questions and decisions. Should they continue to participate in social activities that have a pagan (non-Jewish, non-Christian) religious character? This would include most activities: watching or participating in athletic and rhetorical contests; buying and eating meat in the precincts of pagan temples; and frequenting trade guilds, clubs, and events in private homes, each with their meetings, drinking parties, and banquets. They would even have wondered, "Should we or can we go to pagan temples to do our banking or purchase meat? Should we acknowledge the sovereignty of the emperor when asked to do so at a public event in the precincts of his temple, or at another of the many events in his honor?"

Some believers continued to participate in such activities, while others did not. It was the latter group that created serious social conflict. Their confession of Jesus' lordship and their separation from normal Greco-Roman religious, social, and political activity was seen by pagan non-believers—that is, by most people in their cities—as unpatriotic and atheistic. Some of them were harassed unofficially, but some were likely excluded from guilds and others investigated by government officials. At least one of them (John) was exiled as punishment for his behavior. He says that his experience was not isolated, but part of a larger event of testimony and persecution. At least one of the faithful was actually killed, either by mob or by official action: Antipas of Pergamum (2:13). There may have been others.

These various sorts of localized persecution instilled fear in the Christian assemblies, resurrecting memories of the emperor Nero's persecutions of the 60s.[1] This natural fear led, in some assemblies, to increased accommodation with pagan practices in order to avoid the fate of John and Antipas. These people, understandably, did not want to "make waves." But John, living in exile as one probably accused of practicing and provoking atheistic sedition, that is (as John himself saw it), one who had borne faithful public witness both *to* Jesus and *like* Jesus, was given a series of messages to those churches. The common element in each message was a call to uncompromising faithfulness. "John sees himself as a witness in the succession of witnesses,"[2] beginning with Jesus as the first faithful witness and including all past, present, and future faithful witnesses like Jesus and John. John's call to faithfulness was tempered by the realistic expectation of increased persecution in the near future, but it was also buttressed by the certain hope of participating in

---

1. Nero accused the Christians of setting the great fire in Rome (A.D. 64), subsequently torturing and killing many of them, even burning some alive. According to some ancient Christian sources, Peter and Paul were among those murdered.

2. Schnelle, *New Testament Theology*, 764.

the new heaven and earth that will follow this temporary persecution. The new heaven and earth are indeed the culmination of God's plan, not only for the people of God, but for the cosmos. It was promised by the biblical prophets and guaranteed by Jesus' death and exaltation, and it is set to arrive as soon as the evil and blasphemous empire is judged and removed.

This perspective on the situation is important in many ways, not least because readers of Revelation sometimes think that the Roman empire (and perhaps its similar imperial descendents) is evil and worthy of opposition because it persecutes the church. But Richard Bauckham rightly insists that "it is not simply because Rome persecutes Christians that Christians must oppose Rome. Rather it is because Christians must disassociate themselves from the evil of the Roman system that they are likely to suffer persecution."[3]

The target of Revelation's prophetic critique is imperial idolatry (civil religion) and injustice (military, economic, political, and religious oppression), and specifically Rome's imperial idolatry and injustice. But since Revelation is almost certainly not a response to a systematic, state-imposed persecution or widespread mistreatment of Christians by the masses, it is better read as a response to "ordinary empire,"[4] to the everyday evils, injustices, and misguided allegiances that are daily with us. Revelation is a powerful wake-up call to those who have taken for granted beliefs, commitments, and practices that should be unthinkable. John did not write Revelation "to manufacture a crisis" for people complacent about empire, claim Howard-Brook and Gwyther. Rather, "complacency about Rome *was* the crisis."[5] Adds Craig Koester: "The visionary world portrays the clash of powers in extraordinary form in order to evoke the kind of faith and resistance needed to follow the Lamb in ordinary life."[6]

Furthermore, the target of Revelation's critique is not limited to Rome. "Babylon" means Rome, but it also means something more than Rome. Indeed, the absence of the word "Rome" from Revelation is significant, even if Rome is in view. The absence of the word forbids us, so to speak, from limiting Revelation's significance to the first century.

---

3. Bauckham, *Theology*, 38.

4. See Koester, "Revelation's Visionary Challenge"; Friesen, *Imperial Cults*, 150.

5. Howard-Brook and Gwyther, *Unveiling Empire*, 116.

6. Koester, "Revelation's Visionary Challenge," 18.

"Any society whom Babylon's cap fits must wear it."[7] Thus Revelation is also a critique of all idolatries and injustices similar to those of Rome, throughout history and into the present.

## Liturgical Text: A Call to Worship and Discipleship

The term "liturgy," or the public service of a people, has to do with worship. Worship, a word derived from Old English that means "worth-ship," or worthiness, can be defined as acknowledging the worthiness of God, and God alone, especially as creator and redeemer. No New Testament book does this more poetically or powerfully than Revelation, where the essential word spoken to God the creator and Christ the redeemer is "You are *worthy*" (4:11; 5:9, 12). The central and centering vision of Revelation is a vision of God and the Lamb, and specifically of the *worship* of God and the Lamb.

As a prophetic summons to first-commandment faithfulness, Revelation is both a call to worship the true God and a call to forsake all false deities. These two aspects are connected, and both appear in sharp relief at the beginning and the end of Revelation, as well as throughout the book. "Worship is so important in the book of Revelation," writes Mitchell Reddish, "because John rightly understood that worship is a political act. Through worship one declares one's allegiance, one's loyalty. . . . [Public worship] is a statement to the world that the church will bow to no other gods."[8] His words are echoed by Udo Schnelle:

> [I]n worship, the community of faith realizes its new identity under the lordship of the Lamb and under the conscious, intentional rejection of the claims to lordship made by Babylon/Rome. As the place where the new being is repeatedly practiced, worship is also a locus of resistance against the anti-God powers, and, since the Apocalypse was read out in worship, also a place of hearing, seeing, learning, and understanding/insight.[9]

The most obviously liturgical, or worship-related, aspect of Revelation is its ample supply of texts most likely drawn from early Christian hymns and identified as the music of heaven. "The text [of

---

7. Bauckham, *Theology*, 156.
8. Reddish, *Revelation*, 104.
9. Schnelle, *Theology of the New Testament*, 767.

Revelation] throbs with theopoetic energy, expressed in its numerous songs of praise and worship."[10] Revelation identifies for us six such hymnic texts:

- Holy, holy, holy, the Lord God the Almighty, who was and is and is to come. . . . You are worthy, our Lord and God, to receive glory and honor and power, for you created all things, and by your will they existed and were created. (4:8b, 11)

- You [Christ the Lamb] are worthy to take the scroll and to open its seals, for you were slaughtered and by your blood you ransomed for God saints from every tribe and language and people and nation; you have made them to be a kingdom and priests serving our God, and they will reign on earth. . . . Worthy is the Lamb that was slaughtered to receive power and wealth and wisdom and might and honor and glory and blessing! (5:9–10, 12)

- To the one seated on the throne and to the Lamb be blessing and honor and glory and might forever and ever! (5:13b)

- Amen! Blessing and glory and wisdom and thanksgiving and honor and power and might be to our God forever and ever! Amen. (7:12)

- We give you thanks, Lord God Almighty, who are and who were, for you have taken your great power and begun to reign. The nations raged, but your wrath has come, and the time for judging the dead, for rewarding your servants, the prophets and saints and all who fear your name, both small and great, and for destroying those who destroy the earth. (11:17–18)

- Great and amazing are your deeds, Lord God the Almighty! Just and true are your ways, King of the nations! Lord, who will not fear and glorify your name? For you alone are holy. All nations will come and worship before you, for your judgments have been revealed. (15:3b–4, called "the song of Moses, the servant of God, and the song of the Lamb")[11]

In addition to the hymns there are spoken doxological (praise) texts and acclamations:

10. Hays, *Moral Vision*, 184.

11. Some of these, especially the trisagion ("holy" three times) and the song of Moses/the Lamb, are in turn indebted to Old Testament hymnic texts.

- To him who loves us and freed us from our sins by his blood, and made us to be a kingdom, priests serving his God and Father, to him be glory and dominion forever and ever. Amen. (1:5b–6)

- Look! He is coming with the clouds; every eye will see him, even those who pierced him; and on his account all the tribes of the earth will wail. So it is to be. Amen. (1:7)

- Salvation belongs to our God who is seated on the throne, and to the Lamb! (7:10)

- The kingdom of the world has become the kingdom of our Lord and of his Messiah, and he will reign forever and ever. (11:15)

- Now have come the salvation and the power and the kingdom of our God and the authority of his Messiah, for the accuser of our comrades has been thrown down, who accuses them day and night before our God. But they have conquered him by the blood of the Lamb and by the word of their testimony, for they did not cling to life even in the face of death. . . . (12:10–12)

- You are just, O Holy One, who are and were, for you have judged these things; because they shed the blood of saints and prophets, you have given them blood to drink. It is what they deserve! . . . Yes, O Lord God, the Almighty, your judgments are true and just! (16:5b–7)

- Hallelujah! Salvation and glory and power to our God, for his judgments are true and just; he has judged the great whore who corrupted the earth with her fornication, and he has avenged on her the blood of his servants. . . . Amen. Hallelujah! . . . Praise our God, all you his servants, and all who fear him, small and great. . . . Hallelujah! For the Lord our God the Almighty reigns. . . . (19:1b–8a)

- Amen. Come, Lord Jesus! (22:20b)

Revelation also ends liturgically, with a benediction and a final Amen (22:21).

Together these texts glorify God, celebrating God's being, creation, reign, salvation, and justice, and they also glorify Christ the Lamb, celebrating his redemptive death, salvation, reign, and coming. They echo the themes of Psalms 96–98 that also sing a (new) song about the victorious salvation and coming of the Lord, the King. Revelation as a whole is fundamentally an apocalyptic variation on these three psalms. Encapsulating Revelation's entire message, its hymnic texts poetically take back claims to deity, sovereignty, power, and honor made by and about false deities and potentates and restore them to God alone. No matter what anyone says, Caesar is not Lord or God or Kings of Kings and Lord of Lords. Songs of worship reinforce and celebrate the visions of God, and of God's judgment and salvation. Such visionary worship can empower people in faithfulness and resistance.

Revelation, then is a "fusion of vision and prayer."[12] "By presenting a heavenly cultic reality within the framework of an apocalyptic vision of history, it [Revelation] provides a new interpretation of earthly events and experiences."[13] As a liturgical text, Revelation is not merely a call to prayer and contemplation, as important as they are. As a call to join the ongoing heavenly worship of God, Revelation is simultaneously a presentation of the divine drama that is celebrated in worship, and therefore also a summons to enter the story and mission of God, the *missio Dei*. We will return to the subject of mission later in this book; for now we consider briefly the story that is woven into John's vision.

### A Dramatic Narrative with a Liturgical Purpose

No one can read Revelation without sensing that it tells a story, even if that story does not have a merely linear progression.[14] There are major and minor characters, there is conflict and resolution, there is even a plot. Some have even likened Revelation to an ancient drama, complete with Greek choruses that burst into (liturgical) song, providing commentary on, as well as respite from, the dramatic action.

We get the sense of a story about to unfold from the very first verse of Revelation: "The revelation of Jesus Christ, which God gave him to show his servants what must soon take place" (1:1). Only a few verses later this same sense of anticipation reappears: "Now write what you have seen, what is, and what is to take place after this" (1:19). Unfortunately, most interpreters have used these two texts to start the decoding hunt

12. Peterson, *Reversed Thunder*, 87.

13. Schnelle, *Theology of New Testament*, 751.

14. For a commentary that focuses especially on the narrative character of Revelation, see Resseguie, *The Revelation of John.*

for one-to-one correspondences between images in Revelation and particular historical realities.

A better way to proceed is to recognize that Revelation actually consists of several overlapping, simultaneous, and inextricably interrelated stories. Five such narratives are particularly important, and they are all narratives of God's faithfulness and purpose, or mission:

1. *Creation and re-creation.* This is the story of the faithful, missional, creator God bringing humanity and all creation to its proper end: reconciliation, harmony, and eternal joy in the presence of God.

2. *Redemption.* This is the closely related story of the faithful, missional, redeemer Lamb living, dying, reigning, and coming again to carry out the creator God's mission and create a faithful, missional people.

3. *Judgment.* This is the story of the faithful, missional God and the Lamb bringing an end to evil as a necessary means for the purpose of re-creation and final redemption.

4. *Witness: the suffering pilgrim church.* This is the story of a faithful, missional people on earth who have been redeemed by the Lamb and empowered by the Spirit to worship and bear witness to God and the Lamb in spite of danger and persecution.

5. *Victory: the church triumphant.* This is the story of the faithful, missional people who worship God and the Lamb now and forever in their presence, the appropriate reward for their faithfulness even to death.

These five narratives reveal the major characters, the conflict, and the plot of Revelation that we find in the visions and other sorts of texts throughout the book. They constitute the complex set of dramatic narratives that provide a fitting canonical conclusion to the grand narrative of the entire Bible. We will explore this dramatic aspect of Revelation more fully in chapter 7.[15]

15. See also the discussion in Wall, *Revelation*, 29–32.

## A Book of Blessing

Seven (not surprisingly!) blessings or beatitudes appear in Revelation. They are a dimension of Revelation's liturgical character, but they are not merely aesthetic ornamentation. On the contrary, they lie at the heart of Revelation's message of faithful discipleship to Jesus the Lamb in anticipation of his return and the eschatological celebration: the "marriage supper" of the Lamb and his bride, the faithful church, in the New Jerusalem. In a word, Blessed are the faithful:

1.  Blessed is the one who reads aloud the words of the prophecy, and blessed are those who hear and who keep what is written in it; for the time is near. (1:3)

2.  And I heard a voice from heaven saying, "Write this: Blessed are the dead who from now on die in the Lord." "Yes," says the Spirit, "they will rest from their labors, for their deeds follow them."[16] (14:13)

3.  "See, I am coming like a thief! Blessed is the one who stays awake and is clothed, not going about naked and exposed to shame." (16:15)

4.  And the angel said to me, "Write this: Blessed are those who are invited to the marriage supper of the Lamb." And he said to me, "These are true words of God." (19:9)

5.  Blessed and holy are those who share in the first resurrection. Over these the second death has no power, but they will be priests of God and of Christ, and they will reign with him a thousand years. (20:6)

6.  "See, I am coming soon! Blessed is the one who keeps the words of the prophecy of this book." (22:7)

7.  Blessed are those who wash their robes, so that they will have the right to the tree of life and may enter the city by the gates. (22:14)

Once again in these texts we see the inseparability of liturgy and discipleship, as well as the merger of both with hope.

## Revelation and the Senses

One additional comment about this liturgical document we are reading: Revelation is a very sensory text. Attending to it involves an imaginative

16. The hymn "For All the Saints" (William How, 1864) is based on this text.

employment of all the senses, especially seeing, hearing, and smelling. It is famous for its visions, but it is "equally a book of auditions" (we hear thunder, angelic cries, harps, trumpets, voices like rushing water), and "[t]he absence of sound can be equally important" (see 8:1; 18:22–23).[17] The scent of incense (5:8; 8:3–4) is central to the book's focus on prayer and worship. Furthermore, tasting serves as an important metaphor several times (3:16; 8:11; 10:9–10), and even touching (e.g., 5:2–3, 7–8) figures in the book.[18]

## Theopolitical Text: A Critique of Empire and Manifesto against Civil Religion

If the Bible in general, and Revelation in particular, tells us the story, or stories, of God, Scripture also constantly reminds us that there are other stories competing for our attention—and our allegiance. One of those competing stories, perhaps the most insidious one, is the story of human power in the guise of deity. It is central to understanding and interpreting Revelation.

Nearly all interpreters of Revelation recognize that the entire book is a critique and parody of the Roman Empire and of the cult of the emperor that was rampant in the Roman province of Asia in the second half of the first century. Although the word "Rome" does not appear in the document, Rome is portrayed symbolically as Babylon, that great enemy-city of God's people.[19] Revelation parodies and criticizes both the oppressive nature of imperial power and the blasphemous claims made about it. This twofold critique is directed in a focused way at the imperial cult because that is where Roman power and its allegedly sacred character coalesced. Warren Carter describes it in the following way:

> The "imperial cult" refers to a vast array of temples, images, rituals, personnel, and theological claims that honored the emperor. Temples dedicated to specific emperors and images of emperors located in other temples were focal points for offering thanks-

17. Mangina, *Revelation*, 37.

18. On the role of the senses, see especially Peterson, *Reversed Thunder*, 15–17.

19. That "Babylon" refers, in the first place, to Rome seems clear from the mention of "seven mountains," alluding to Rome's topography, in Rev 17:9. "Babylon" is also used in 1 Pet 5:13 and in other post-70 Jewish and Christian literature of the period to refer to Rome.

giving and prayers to the gods for the safekeeping and blessing
of emperors and members of the imperial household. Incense,
sacrifices, and annual vows expressed and renewed civic loyalty.
The related street processions and feasting, often funded by the
elites, expressed honor, gratitude, and commemoration of significant events such as an emperor's birthday, accession to power,
or military victories. Acts of worship were also incorporated into
the gatherings of groups such as artisan or religious groups. . . .
[D]iverse [civic and group] celebrations presented the empire
presided over by the emperor as divinely ordained.[20]

Put simply, the imperial cult was an elaborate "God and country"
phenomenon, or type of "civic" or civil religion (see further below), that
in various ways attributed a sacred character to the Roman Empire and
to the emperor himself. This cult was the concrete manifestation of an
ideology, a political theology, which Carter describes as consisting of
three main convictions:

- The gods have chosen Rome.

- Rome and its emperor are agents of the gods' rule, will, salvation,
  and presence among human beings.

- Rome manifests the gods' blessings—security, peace, justice, faithfulness, fertility—among those who submit to Rome's rule.[21]

In other words, "Rome was chosen by the gods, notably Jupiter . . . to
manifest the gods' rule, presence, and favor throughout the world."[22] For
instance, the Roman poet Statius wrote about Domitian, the emperor
who likely ruled when Revelation was written, that "At Jupiter's com-
mand he rules for him the blessed world."[23] Statius also called Domitian
"ruler of the conquered world," "the world's sure salvation," and "blest
protector and savior."[24] This kind of theology required that prayers and
sacrifices be offered not only to the gods for the protection of the em-

20. Carter, *Roman Empire*, 7–8. For a longer overview, see Howard-Brook and
Gwyther, *Unveiling Empire*, 87–119 and 223–35. For a detailed study, see Friesen,
*Imperial Cults* and Price, *Rituals and Power*.

21. Carter, *Roman Empire*, 83. See also Carter's *Matthew and Empire*, 20–34, with
many quotations from Roman sources.

22. Carter, *Roman Empire*, 7.

23. Cited in ibid., 85.

24. Cited in Carter, *Matthew and Empire*, 25.

pire and the emperor—as the people's father-leader and Jupiter's vice-regent—but also to the emperor himself.

Three additional points about imperial theology will supplement Carter's three.[25]

- The rule of the gods through Rome was accomplished by and manifested in violence, domination, and "pacification" that was hardly peaceful. The famous *pax Romana* was a sovereignty dependent on military conquest, enslavement, and other forms of violence.

- The emperor himself was worthy of praise, devotion, and allegiance. He was also worthy of having divine and quasi-divine titles such as Lord, Lord of All, God, Son of God, and Savior. Examples of religious devotion to the emperor in the first century abound. Domitian, for example, was called, at least by some, "Lord of the earth," "that present deity," and "lord and god" (*dominus et deus*), the last of which he likely also applied to himself.[26] As a god the emperor nonetheless remained a human, so prayers and sacrifices could be offered both *for* him and *to* him.

- The imperial age is the long-awaited golden age, indeed the eschatological age, in which humanity's hopes have been fulfilled and will continue forever.

These six points of imperial theology were proclaimed in a variety of ways and in various venues. We can find imperial theology in the best writers of the day, such as Vergil and Epictetus, but it was particularly important for Rome to capture the hearts and minds of common folk, and that was done especially through the media: processions, games, spectacles, statues, the standards carried by soldiers, and coins. First-century coins depict the emperor as a god (actually, as various deities), as universal savior and ruler, as the one who made wars to cease and brought peace, as the subjugator of enemies, and so on.[27]

The imperial cult was especially widespread in Asia Minor and the cities where the churches of Revelation were located. Pergamum, site of

---

25. Helpful on the next two points is Rowe, *World Upside Down*, 107–11, and on the third, Howard-Brook and Gwyther, *Unveiling Revelation*, 114–15.

26. Carter, *Matthew and Empire*, 25–26; Witherington, *Revelation*, 5–6.

27. For photographs of numerous such coins, see Kraybill, *Apocalypse and Allegiance*.

"Satan's throne" (Rev 2:13)—possibly a reference to the temple of the imperial cult at the top of the city's imposing acropolis—was permitted in 29 B.C., by the very first emperor, Augustus, to erect a temple to him and to Rome. Cities like Ephesus and Smyrna also had significant temples of the imperial cult. Ephesus was frequently recognized as a proper guardian of the imperial cult, and the city blended its worship of Artemis with worship of the emperor. Smyrna had built a temple to the goddess Roma in 195 B.C. and then one to Emperor Tiberius in A.D. 26. There was some form of the imperial cult in all seven cities.

Revelation is therefore a *theopolitical* text. It makes claims about who is truly God and about right and wrong connections between God and the socio-political order; it challenges the political theology of empire and the religious ideology that underwrites it; and it reveals God and the Lamb alone as the true Sovereign One, source of all blessings, and proper object of worship. Moreover, Revelation tells us not only who is really sovereign but also what kind of sovereignty the true God exercises, namely what many have called nonviolent and non-coercive "Lamb power"—to which we will return in later chapters. (For now we must simply preview those chapters with this summary: the allegedly violent scenes in Revelation are understood properly as symbols or metaphors, not as examples of literal military violence carried out by God and the Lamb.)

Among many treatments of the book we could cite on this critical theopolitical dimension of Revelation, several especially stand out. Richard Bauckham rightly connects the apocalyptic and visionary character of Revelation to its critique of Rome, calling Revelation "a set of Christian prophetic counter-images to the images of imperial Rome."[28] Pablo Richard, a Chilean interpreter of Revelation, also correctly shows the link between the liturgical character of Revelation and its counter-imperial stance; Revelation, he says, is "a liturgical text that amounts to a theological and political manifesto."[29] In their book *Unveiling Empire: Reading Revelation Then and Now*, Wes Howard-Brook and Anthony Gwyther propose that Revelation answers five Roman myths with five counter-myths[30]:

28. Bauckham, *Theology*, 7.

29. Richard, *Apocalypse*, 40.

30. Howard-Brook and Gwyther, *Unveiling Revelation*, 223–35. See also Thompson, *The Book of Revelation*.

| *Rome's Myths* | *Revelation's Counter-Myths* |
|---|---|
| (i.e. false claims) | (i.e., subversive truths) |
| Empire | The Empire of our God |
| The Roman Pax | Babylon, the Shedder of Blood |
| *Victoria* | The Victory of the Lamb and His Followers[31] |
| Faith (= loyalty to Caesar/Rome) | Keeping the Faith of Jesus |
| Eternity | They [the saints] Will Reign Forever |

Furthermore, a recent thematic issue of the theological journal *Interpretation* was entitled "Revelation as a Critique of Empire." In the opening article in the issue, Craig Koester notes that the empire addressed in Revelation consists of three inseparable components, all of which are challenged by the book: political domination, religion in which the political order is identified with the divine, and economic networks that favored the elite and permitted human exploitation.[32] Revelation is therefore a "visionary critique" of "the beastly side of empire," the "deification of human power," and "the seamy side of commerce."[33]

Most of these interpreters also draw connections between aspects of the Roman empire and forms of empire today: the global capitalist economy and the powerful political, military, and economic reality that is the United States of America. These two are not unrelated, as many people outside the United States have observed. Pablo Richard, for instance, has written that

> [i]n the last twenty years we [in Central America] have experienced the cruel and terrible experience of Whole Market Empire, governed in a beastly way by the political and military bureaucracy of the United States of America. . . . Our countries live in oppression and exclusion by an economic, cultural, and military system of globalization led by the United States government operating as an imperial, arrogant, and cruel power.[34]

31. On Roman versus Christian victory, see also Rossing (*Rapture Exposed*, 115–22), who says that Revelation's message is "a reframing of the whole [Roman] concept of victory" by violence (121).

32. Koester, "Revelation's Visionary Challenge," 9–12.

33. Koester, "Revelation's Visionary Challenge," 12–18.

34. Richard, "Reading the *Apocalypse*," 146–47.

These are strong words, and not everyone will agree with them, though numerous significant North American interpreters of Revelation have drawn similar conclusions. Mainstream biblical scholars who have taught Revelation in places as varied as South America and India have found their students connecting the beast of Revelation 13 to the U.S.[35] More popularly, but no less insightfully, Jonathan Wilson-Hartgrove recounts his experience of America as Babylon while traveling in the actual land of Babylon (Iraq) with Christian Peacemaker Teams during and after the 2003 U.S. invasion of that country.[36] Howard-Brook and Gwyther draw sophisticated parallels between Roman and contemporary manifestations of empire in "global capital," in which the U.S. of course participates, but according to them neither the U.S. nor any other nation is the world's dominant empire any longer.[37]

Is the United States an empire? That depends on several factors, including one's definition of empire. I would offer the following definition for consideration:

> *An entity that has come to widespread (global or nearly global) dominance through deliberate expansion by means of the extreme exercise of some form(s) of power—economic, political, military, and/or religious—resulting in the creation of colony-like clients of the entity and of enemies who perceive the entity as oppressive.*

Howard-Brook and Gwyther cite the following as evidence that the United States has at least had "imperial earmarks": "slave labor; demonization, genocide, and displacement of indigenous people; colonization of distant lands . . . ; cultural arrogance; and global military power."[38] It is difficult for many—myself included—to resist the conclusion that the United States has had, and continues to have, an imperial character.

Nevertheless, while we may agree that Revelation is a critique of the Roman Empire, and of empire more generally (since "Babylon" is not identified as Rome per se), we will certainly differ about what constitutes empire, whether the U.S. ever was or is an empire, and even whether empire is inherently evil.[39] And of course many will argue that no U.S.

35. See Kraybill, "Apocalypse Now"; deSilva, *Seeing Things John's Way*, 337–38.

36. Wilson-Hartgrove, *To Baghdad*.

37. Howard-Brook and Gwyther, *Unveiling Revelation*, especially 236–37.

38. Ibid., 236.

39. To see at least part of what Revelation has in mind in identifying empire, we may consult chapter 18: an arrogant international economic power with clients around

president has ever been called a god,[40] even if his military successes have been seen as the fruit of divine calling and blessing, and even if the succession of military, political, and economic conquests accomplished by the U.S. is said to have produced an American superpower with various kinds of outposts and client states around the world.

It must, at the very least, be conceded the United States is *perceived* as an imperial power by many people in many parts of the world that have been affected by American military, political, and economic power. We should not, however, allow arguments about the precise nature of empire, or its embodiment in the American context, to keep us from hearing Revelation's sharp critique of the status quo. It is more important for us to see Revelation as a critique of secular power wherever and however it expresses itself oppressively, and especially as a critique of such power that is deemed *sacred* and granted devotion and allegiance. This manifestation and sacralization of power is undoubtedly part of the American situation (and also part of the experience of other nations). Thus J. Nelson Kraybill has recently written a study of Revelation entitled *Apocalypse and Allegiance: Worship, Politics, and Devotion in the Book of Revelation.* He writes perceptively that although "no Western nation has outright ruler worship today, we do have political, military, and economic powers to which millions give unquestioned allegiance.... The world he [John] inhabited—the Roman Empire—and the symbolic universe his vision created have uncanny parallels to our circumstances today."[41]

When secular power is deemed sacred and worthy of devotion and allegiance, the result is the phenomenon of civil religion, which may be defined as follows:

> *The attribution of sacred status to secular power (normally the state and/or its head) as the source of divine blessing, requiring devotion and allegiance of heart, mind, and body to the sacred-secular power and its values, all expressed in various narratives, other texts, rituals, and media that reinforce both the secular*

---

the world, all engaging in the uncontrolled pursuit of luxury, with commerce that even includes trading in human beings. This would seem to be an apt description of numerous political entities, both in the past and in the present.

40. Nevertheless, as New Testament scholar Andy Johnson has reminded me, the fresco in the U.S. Capitol rotunda is called "The Apotheosis [deification, exaltation] of George Washington," a depiction of him "ascending" to heaven.

41. Kraybill, *Apocalypse and Allegiance*, 15.

> *power's sacred status and the beneficiaries' sacred duty of devotion and allegiance, even to the point of death.*[42]

This definition of civil religion implies that it has three major dimensions:

1. *Ideology/theology*: the *sacralization of the state*, including: (a) its power, prosperity, and peace; (b) its activities and accomplishments, especially in expansion and war; (c) its guiding myths and values; and (d) its past heroes and current leader(s);

2. *Commitment/practices*: the corollary demand of *solemn devotion and allegiance* to the state as a sacred responsibility (including the willingness to kill and/or die for it) to be *expressed in public rituals*; and

3. *Syncretism*: the *reinterpretation of the culture's dominant religious tradition(s)* to incorporate this sacralization of the state and solemn allegiance to it; the mixing of religious faith and practice with political, nationalistic claims and practices.

More broadly, then, Revelation is a critique of civil religion (first of all, but not only, Roman civil religion), that is, the sacralization of secular political, economic, and military power through various mythologies and practices—creeds and liturgies, we might say—and the corollary demand for allegiance to that power.

Because civil religion is so closely connected with power, it often appears in extreme forms in empires and empire-like states (e.g., modern superpowers), grounded in the assumption that expansion and victory (in war or otherwise) are signs of divine blessing and protection, and in the common belief that God is on the side of the powerful. At the same time, however, civil religion is not exclusively the property of empires and superpowers; it is also to be found in former empires, would-be superpowers, ordinary states, and even poor, developing nations. Human beings seem to have a need to attribute a sacred, or at least quasi-sacred, character to their political bodies, their rulers, and the actions of those

---

42. One might ask whether a secular state, or one in which traditional expressions of religion are banned, can have a civil religion. If we understand religion to be about ultimate reality and value, then the answer is yes. We could therefore define civil religion as "the attribution of *ultimate* status to secular power," though usually this includes the borrowing of traditional religious language and symbols. We could call this, ironically, "secular civil religion."

entities. One tragic but frequent result is the sacralization of one's own people, whether nation, race, or tribe, and the demonization of the other. Out of such religion comes a culture of hatred and even violence. We know far too many examples of this in modern times.

Civil religion does not require an established (state) church, religion, or cult in order to exist, or even to thrive. It can therefore flourish even in places where there is technically a separation of "church" and "state." It can flourish whether or not the majority of the country's inhabitants perceive the country to be a Christian (or Jewish, Islamic, etc.) state. The United States (where I make my home), for example, has its own form of civil religion. We may speak both of its ideology—actually, its theology—and of its practices, which are of course related. Parallels to some of these features of civil religion exist elsewhere.

### *The Theology/Ideology of American Civil Religion in the Beginning of the 21st Century*[43]

There are several interconnected myths or theological themes that permeate American civil religion. Most if not all of these themes have been present for many years (even dating back to before the nation's founding), but of course they have evolved with the nation.

One foundational theopolitical conviction or sacred myth is *exceptionalism*, the idea that the United States has a unique place in God's plan,[44] that it is in some sense *chosen*. In American history this exceptionalism has manifested itself in such beliefs as the Puritan "city on a hill" (Matt 5:14), Manifest Destiny, and the identification of the U.S. as "the light of the world" (Matt 5:14; John 8:12; 9:5). Similar to and sometimes growing out of exceptionalism is American *messianism*, the notion that the U.S. has a special, central vocation in the salvation of the world, particularly through the spread of American practices of freedom and American-style democracy. This belief in an exceptional role and messianic destiny to spread freedom is the backbone of America's na-

---

43. Of the many fine discussions of this topic, see especially Hughes, *Myths*; Boyd, *Myth*; Jewett and Shelton, *Captain America*; and Jewett, *Mission and Menace*.

44. I use the word "God" because most Americans are monotheists, and many believe that their (rather vague) concept of God corresponds to the Bible's, though in fact the god of American civil religion has distinctly American traits.

tional religion.[45] Arising from it is a myth of *innocence*, of possessing "an element of messianic inerrancy."[46] This third myth holds that America always operates in the world according to the highest principles of ethics and justice, and that when criticized or attacked, America is the innocent, righteous victim.

Belief in an exceptional, messianic role naturally generates another sacred conviction (and associated practices), that of *extreme patriotism*, extreme love of country, and even *nationalism*, the belief that one's nation state, in this case the U.S., is superior to all other nation states. "Nationalism" (as I am using it here) is extreme devotion to one's country as "the greatest nation on earth" and therefore worthy of nearly unqualified—and sometimes thoroughly unqualified—allegiance. This devotion is often based on the conviction that the nation is chosen, blessed, and commissioned by God, its power and wealth being signs of God's approval. The U.S. is "one nation under God." Thus devotion to one's country and its mission in the world is ultimately a religious devotion. Greatness is defined especially as financial, political, and/or military strength, and this definition carries with it the conviction that both America and Americans should always enjoy and operate from a position of strength and security. Weakness is un-American; Americans want to be number one. For many, these kinds of secular strengths are seen as manifestations of power from God.

American civil religion values *human liberty and rights* as a divine gift and considers it, perhaps on par with strength, as one of the highest national values. The protection and furtherance of freedom is therefore a divine mandate and mission. The operative notion of both political (corporate) and personal (individual) freedom is that of God-given (inalienable) rights to life, liberty, and the pursuit of happiness, an idea derived both from the Enlightenment and from one of the most important sacred texts of this civil religion, the Declaration of Independence. A corollary myth is a form of *secularized Calvinism*, the notion that hard work mixed with a degree of generosity toward others will inevitably result in greater and greater freedom and prosperity, often understood as a sign of God's blessing. (The so-called "prosperity gospel" is an offshoot of this myth.)

---

45. Müller-Fahrenholz, *America's Battle*, 8.
46. The term is from Müller-Fahrenholz, *America's Battle*, 8.

Yet another key sacred myth in American civil religion is that of *militarism and sacred violence*.[47] This is the conviction that part of America's exceptional and messianic place in history is its divinely granted permission, indeed its divine mandate, to use violence (killing of native peoples, invasions, wars, etc.) when peaceful means are undesirable or unsuccessful. Such allegedly sacred violence has justified various forms of expansion and, more recently, of the messianic mission of protecting and promoting freedom and justice. This myth can foster a crusade mentality ("ridding the world of evil") rooted in an apocalyptic dualism, but without the corollary commitment to nonviolence we will find in Revelation.

The "myth of redemptive violence undergirds American popular culture, civil religion, nationalism, and foreign policy," argues Walter Wink.[48] It underwrites the belief that killing and/or dying for the national interest is a sacred duty and even privilege. Service to the nation—especially military service, and particularly dying for one's country—is the highest form of both civic and religious devotion. After all, the civil-religion argument goes, quoting but misinterpreting Jesus, "greater love has no man than this, that a man lay down his life for his friends" (John 15:13; RSV).[49]

These are some of the basic sacred myths and convictions of American civil religion. This ideology, or theology, has remarkable parallels with the Roman imperial theology discussed above.

### Some of the Symbols and Practices of American Civil Religion

The sacred myths of civil religion are expressed, reinforced, honored, and propagated in sacred symbols, spaces, rituals, and holy-days. These occasions use sacred language, music, texts, and stories. Space does not

47. This is of course hardly unique to the US. For example, while I was editing this chapter, North Korea promised to launch a "retaliatory sacred [nuclear] war."

48. Wink, *Engaging the Powers*, 13.

49. The use of this text is one of the few aspects of American civil religion that has any christological connection because in general a non-specific god is much easier to manipulate to nationalistic ends. But even here the christological focus is only superficially Christian, and indeed misguidedly so. It has taken a maxim that Jesus applied to himself, his own saving death, and his disciples and re-generalized it, apart from Jesus' own example and teaching, as an allegedly Christian principle used to underwrite dying in the context of military combat (i.e., killing), which is precisely not the kind of death Jesus modeled or advocated.

permit a full discussion, but some of these American symbols and practices—often with close parallels elsewhere—are listed here.

- *Sacred symbols and spaces*
  - » National flags as sacred objects
  - » National flags (sometimes juxtaposed with "Christian flags") in churches[50]
  - » Crosses in military or other non-church contexts (e.g., military medals in the form of a cross)
  - » Blending of Christian and national images (e.g., cross and flag, Jesus and flag)

- *Sacred rituals and holy-days*
  - » Civil rituals made religious
    - Official days of prayer
    - National feasts/holy-days
      - ▷ Martin Luther King Day (recognizing a rare prophetic component of American life and civil religion)
      - ▷ Presidents Day
      - ▷ Memorial Day (arguably, in principle if not practice, the chief feast because of its connections to freedom and sacrifice in sacred violence[51])
      - ▷ Independence Day/Fourth of July
      - ▷ Veterans Day
      - ▷ Thanksgiving
    - State funerals
    - Moments of silence
    - Congressional chaplain
    - Prayer at political and civic events
    - Prayer around the flag pole
    - National days of prayer, prayer breakfasts
    - The pledge of allegiance, at school or other civic gatherings, to the flag as icon of a nation "under God"

50. See Boyd, *Myth*, 12: "In our minds—as so often in our sanctuaries—the cross and the American flag stand side by side."

51. Implied, for example, by Müller-Fahrenholz, *America's Battle*, 13.

- The national anthem at sporting events
- Swearing on the Bible
- Chaplains' prayers before military combat missions

&raquo; Religious rituals made civil

- Pledge of allegiance in church
- Recognition of active military or veterans in church at national holidays
- Prayers for "those serving our country" or "the/our troops" in church[52]
- Sermons and children's sermons on patriotic themes
- Use of patriotic music in worship
- Religious events on national holidays
- Religious gatherings in times of national crisis

- *Sacred language*

  &raquo; War as "mission"

  &raquo; "Sacred" duty/honor

  &raquo; Divine passive voice: "we are called" (e.g., at a certain moment in history, usually before war)

  &raquo; "God bless America"/"God bless our troops"

  &raquo; Echoes of/allusions to the Bible in civic and political discourse

  &raquo; Attribution of biblical language for God or God's people to the U.S. (e.g., "the light of the world"; "city on a hill")

  &raquo; Lack of theological specificity (e.g., omission of Jesus' name from public prayer and Scripture reading)

- *Sacred music/national hymns*

  &raquo; Patriotic songs of sacred devotion with much ("God Bless America"), some ("America/My Country, 'Tis of Thee"), or even no explicit religious language (the national anthem)

---

52. Christian references to "our troops," in prayer or any other forms of discourse, are theologically inappropriate because "we" (the church, Christians) do not have troops. Such talk confuses our being Christian with being American (or British, or whatever) and manifests a profound forgetfulness about two important aspects of the church stressed in Revelation: its international character as a worldwide assembly of people from every tribe and nation (Revelation 7) and its peaceful, nonviolent character as a community of the Lamb.

» Hymns with explicitly nationalistic and militaristic language (e.g., "Battle Hymn of the Republic," "Navy Hymn")

» Hymns with allegorical militaristic language interpreted literally and nationalistically (e.g., "Onward Christian Soldiers")

- *Sacred texts*

    » The Declaration of Independence, the Constitution, and the Bill of Rights

    » Famous speeches by sacred leaders and heroes (e.g., Patrick Henry, Abraham Lincoln, Douglas MacArthur, John Kennedy, Martin Luther King)

    » Biblical texts that seem to underwrite national values such as freedom and redemptive violence

- *Sacred stories of sacred leaders and heroes* ("saints"/"martyrs"/"prophets")

    » Founding Fathers

    » Leaders in crisis (e.g., Kennedy's *Profiles in Courage*)

    » Great warriors (e.g., Patton)

    » Veterans in general

These various aspects of American civil religion come to expression in two kinds of venues: the civil and political (speeches, parades, school events, sporting events, military ceremonies, etc.), on the one hand, and the religious (church worship services), on the other.

From this listing we can recognize another aspect of the similarity between Roman and contemporary American civil religion. The former involved the politicization (specifically, the imperialization) of the sacred, and the sacralization of the political (specifically, the imperial). This is parallel to what has happened in the U.S.: many civic and political events have a religious dimension, and religious events sometimes take on a civic and political—specifically nationalistic, and even militaristic—dimension. This process continues to this day, despite the formal constraints of law and consequent changes in practice (such as the abolition of school prayer).

One major difference, however, is extremely important to recognize: the syncretism of Rome's civil religion involved the blending of

Roman ideology and *pagan* religiosity, but the syncretism of American civil religion involves the blending of American ideology and *Christian*, or at least theistic and quasi-Christian, religiosity. The early church had a natural suspicion of Roman civil religion because it was so blatantly pagan and idolatrous—though even it could be appealing. Contemporary Christians can much more easily assume that Christian, or quasi-Christian, ideas, language, and practices are benign and even divinely sanctioned. This makes American civil religion all the more attractive— that is, all the more seductive and dangerous. Its fundamentally pagan character is masked by its Christian veneer.

No matter what the churches proclaim, Christianity in the United States seems to have two liturgical seasons, the Holy Season, which runs from Advent to Easter (or perhaps Pentecost), and the Civil Season— Civil Religion time—which runs from Memorial Day to Thanksgiving. Civil religion in the U.S. never goes away, but its major feasts are in that six-month period. God-and-country language and rituals are more prevalent, and syncretism in the churches ("when you see the red in the flag, think of the blood of those who died to make us free, and also think of Jesus' blood that was shed to make us *really* free") runs rampant but is hardly ever questioned.

But when we consider carefully the nature and scope of American civil religion, it is difficult to avoid the question, "Is this, too, a form of idolatry, 'the deification of nationalism.'"[53] What makes American civil religion particularly seductive is that it borrows so heavily from Christianity; its reinterpretation of the dominant religious tradition(s) does not produce the syncretism of polytheistic paganism but the syncretism of Christianized Americanism or Americanized Christianism. This form of religiosity is so pervasive that we would not be wrong to contend that if America's original sin vis-à-vis others is racism, as Martin Luther King claimed, then its original sin vis-à-vis God is civil religion. This of course does not mean that either racism or civil religion is unique to the United States, only that American history—and thus also Christianity in America—has been plagued by these two fundamental failings, the one horizontal (people to people), the other vertical (people to God).

---

53. Reddish, *Revelation*, 105.

### Revelation as Manifesto and Summons to "Uncivil" Religion

*Revelation is a manifesto against civil religion and a summons to uncivil worship and witness.*

Revelation is a sustained stripping of the sacred from secular power—military, political, economic—and a parallel sustained recognition of God and the Lamb as the rightful bearers of sacred claims, the only worthy recipients of divine accolades. It proclaims that there exists a non-civil religion, that there can be a community of "uncivil" people. Thus one of the main purposes of Revelation is to challenge sacralized imperial power—and its seductive allure—with an alternative vision of power that will give believers comfort, assurance, hope, and especially courage to resist in accord with the paradigm of Jesus. This alternative vision of power is the power of the one true God and the slain Lamb, Christ "the faithful witness, the firstborn of the dead, and the ruler of the kings of the earth" (1:5). It provides for the church a "set of Christian prophetic counter-images," a "counter-imperial script."[54] Revelation is therefore a prophetic, pastoral, visionary guide to worshiping and following the Lamb, a template for faithful witness against civil religion and for true worship of the true God. It calls us to unlearn and abandon the false but often seductive gospel of empire and civil religion as it calls us to learn and practice, in worship and witness, the truth of the Lamb's eternal gospel.

This is why a liturgical reading of Revelation leads inevitably to a theopolitical reading. The god(s) we imagine and worship, especially in the public square, may be something other than God. John Calvin famously contended that the human heart incessantly manufactures idols (see Isa 44:9–11). What are the idols that we are tempted to accommodate? The pantheon of the first century included, among many others, Aphrodite, Asclepius, Dionysius, Mars, and Caesar. Today we have different names for their counterparts: Sex, Health/Fitness, Pleasure, War, and Power/Security, among others. Like the ancients, who had temples, statues, and inscriptions to represent their deities, we find our idols represented in the media as well: in magazines and books, in our movies and our music, on TV and online. Each and all of these can be inappropriately valued as something to live, die, and kill for. When they

54. The first phrase is from Bauckham (*Theology*, 17), the second phrase from Carey ("The Book of Revelation as Counter-Imperial Script").

are understood as components of the *summum bonum*, as essential elements of the culture's highest good, they become part of the noble cause that ultimately justifies killing and dying. "Every version of the kingdom of the world defends itself and advances its cause by rallying the self-interest of its citizens into a collective tribal force that makes each citizen willing to kill and be killed for what it believes to be the good of the society."[55]

It has often been said that the most common idols in the West are Power, Sex, and Money; with this I am not in any profound disagreement. However, inasmuch as these idols are connected to a larger vision of life, such as the American dream, or the inalienable rights of free people, they become part of a nation's civil religion. I would contend, in fact, that the most alluring and dangerous deity in the United States is the omnipresent, syncretistic god of nationalism mixed with Christianity lite: religious beliefs, language, and practices that are superficially Christian but infused with national myths and habits. Sadly, most of this civil religion's practitioners belong to Christian churches, which is precisely why Revelation is addressed to the seven *churches* (not to Babylon), to all Christians tempted by the civil cult.

To summarize: Is Revelation a critique of empire? Yes—but that is not its ultimate theopolitical function. The fate of empire is certain; what is *un*certain is the fate of those who currently participate in the cult of empire. The more significant critique is the critique of the church, and specifically of its participation in the idolatry of the imperial cult, the civil or national religion. Will the churches repent? For the churches, one main question emerges: "Beast or Lamb?"

### The Structure of Revelation

Many interpreters of Revelation have noted the many groups and sequences of seven in the book. The following outline, in fact, does not look terribly different from the ones proposed by Primasius and especially Bede in the sixth and eighth centuries, respectively[56]:

---

55. Boyd, *Myth*, 56.

56. Cited in Murphy, "Revelation," 683. The pattern of seven in the set of final visions (19:11—22:5) is noted by Talbert, *Apocalypse*, 88–103.

| Chapters | Main Content |
|---|---|
| 1:1–8 | Prologue: Apocalyptic/Prophetic/Epistolary/Liturgical/Theopolitical Introduction |
| 1:9–20 | Opening Vision: Christ Present Among the Churches |
| 2–3 | 7 Pastoral-Prophetic Messages from Christ to the Churches |
| 4–5 | Central and Centering Vision: God and the Lamb (Christ) in the Heavenly Throne Room |
| 6:1—8:1 | 7 Seals (7:1–17 = interlude between 6 and 7) |
| 8:2—11:19 | 7 Trumpets (10:1—11:13 = interlude between 6 and 7) |
| 12:1—13:18 | The Foe in the Conflict: Visions of the Unholy Trinity |
| 14:1–20 | Interlude: Visions of Salvation and Judgment |
| 15:1—16:21 | 7 Bowls of Judgment |
| 17:1—19:10 | 7th Bowl Expanded: The Fall of Babylon and The Heavenly Celebration |
| 19:11—22:5 | 7 Scenes of the End Culminating in the Final Vision: New Heaven, New Earth, New Jerusalem (21:1—22:5) |
| 22:6–21 | Epilogue: Apocalyptic/Prophetic/Epistolary/Liturgical/Theopolitical Conclusion |

The book's structure may be simplified as follows:

I. Revelation 1–3 / Opening Vision of the Risen Lord and His Seven Pastoral-Prophetic Messages

II. Revelation 4–5 / Central and Centering Vision of God and the Lamb

III. Revelation 6–20 / Visions of the Judgment of God, with Interludes

IV. Revelation 21–22 / Final Vision of the New Creation

This abbreviated structure provides the framework for four of the main chapters of this book (chs. 5, 6, 8, and 9).

The bulk of Revelation's content is an otherworldly journey, somewhat typical for apocalyptic literature, consisting of a series of "discrete visions and revelatory narratives"[57] (4:1—22:5). The main visions and narratives are about divine judgment, with interludes (providing breath-

---

57. Aune, *Revelation 1–5*, lxxxiii.

ing room for the hearers/readers) of various heavenly scenes, hymns, and foreshadowings of the eschatological conclusion. These various visions and episodes reveal both the invisible present and the future that is still to come. Rather than being one extended linear narrative, the sequence of short visions and narratives is somewhat repetitious, though also always intensifying, with the seven seals and trumpets of judgment (6:1—11:19) paralleled by the seven angels and seven bowls (14:6—19:10). These two groups of judgment visions grouped in sevens are interrupted by visions of the unholy trinity (12:1—13:18) and additional brief visions of salvation and judgment (14:1–20). The visions of final renewal and salvation constitute the conclusion (19:11—22:5), "a tour through an eschatological art gallery."[58]

This long, main section is preceded by an opening vision of Christ (1:9–20), who is both the source and the main subject of the visions, as he is of the seven messages (chaps. 2–3) that follow the opening vision and precede the central, centering heavenly throne-room vision of God and the Lamb (chs. 4–5). All of this introduces the long series of visions of judgment (and salvation) that famously comprise the bulk of the book. The work as a whole opens and closes with bookends (1:1–8; 22:6–21) that envelop the substance of the book, indicating its hybrid character and its liturgical and theopolitical concerns.

The narrative of the main section of Revelation is not strictly chronological. As Mitchell Reddish says,

> A progression is certainly intended in the events described, as evidenced by the opening of the seventh seal, which introduces the seven trumpets. Yet the progression is not strictly linear. Rather, later events sometimes retell earlier events . . . Instead of a straight linear progression, the structure of Revelation presents a movement that is spiral. Earlier events are presented in different forms and use different images.[59]

This narrative movement is called recapitulation. This is not to negate the claim that Revelation has a plot. Rather, we must recognize that the

58. Boring, *Revelation*, 195. The words "I saw" mark each of the seven visions in this section.

59. Reddish, *Revelation*, 21. Schnelle (*New Testament Theology*, 754) suggests that Revelation is more like a "series of concentric circles, with the already inaugurated kingdom of God and of Jesus serving as both the foundation and the center of the seer's thought."

plot unfolds like a symphony, with variations on the main theme as the piece moves toward its goal. This non-linear movement means that an outline of the book is more like a spiral, a series of connected circles that moves forward.[60]

One aspect of the content of Revelation that needs to be stressed once again is that, although the rapture is the theological starting point for the "Left Behind" series and many other popular interpretations of Revelation, *there is no rapture in the book of Revelation.*[61] (It is supposedly narrated at 4:1, the introduction to the book's central vision). When I pointed this out in one of my classes, a student nearly accused me of heresy for denying the second coming of Christ. I said to her, and I repeat now, that the book of Revelation clearly teaches, and calls on its readers to pray for, the return of Christ. It is not the second coming of Christ that is absent from Revelation but the alleged rapture of the Church by Christ in a kind of secret prequel to the real second coming. The former—Christ's second (and final!) coming—is part of the book of Revelation, the rest of the New Testament, the creeds, and the historic teachings of the Christian faith. The present book affirms that future coming without hesitation.[62]

## Conclusion: A Theopoetic, Theopolitical, Pastoral-Prophetic Text

Revelation speaks both to the accommodating segments of the churches and to the persecuted segments of the churches, as a truly pastoral-prophetic word always does, challenging the former and comforting the latter. It is a theopoetic, theopolitical text that provides us with an inspiring vision of the present and future reign of God and the slaughtered Lamb (Christ); a powerful critique of empire and civil religion; and a challenging summons to follow the Lamb in a community of faithful resistance, liturgical living, and missional hope. Revelation was written to "enable [its hearers] to control their fear, to renew their commitment,

60. See the graphic in Koester, *Revelation and the End of All Things*, 39.

61. See especially the article "Farewell to the Rapture" by N.T. Wright, at http://www.ntwrightpage.com/Wright_BR_Farewell_Rapture.htm.

62. The technical theological term for the second coming is *parousia*, meaning "presence" or "advent." See Matt 24:3, 27; 1 Cor 15:23; 1 Thess 2:19; 3:13; 4:15; 5:23; and elsewhere. It was often used of the arrival of the emperor or other powerful officials. In the New Testament, the association of *parousia* with Jesus retains this theopolitical accent.

and to sustain their vision."[63] It does this through a series of images and symbols that should not be over-interpreted (some would say they should not be interpreted all, just experienced). Arguments about the meaning or cultural referent of this or that detail are inevitable, but such arguments should not inhibit the experience of the text's theopoetic vision. Indeed, as one critic said about the details of the images in "Ode on a Grecian Urn," the famous poem by John Keats, such disputes "testify to the enigmatic richness of meaning" in the text.[64] Above all, however, the details of the symbolism should not be handled as if Revelation were a script about the details of the end of history. Rather, the details serve a greater liturgical and theopolitical agenda.

### Questions for Reflection and Discussion

1. In what sense is Revelation a liturgical text? How might identifying it as such affect our interpretation of it? In what sense is Revelation a political, or theopolitical, text? How might identifying it as such affect our interpretation of it?

2. What do you think of the claim that civil religion, as an aberration of Christianity, is prevalent in the West, especially the U.S.? What do you think of the claim that Revelation is a manifesto against civil religion, whether in the first century or the twenty-first? How might identifying it as such affect our interpretation of it?

3. How might identifying Revelation as a pastoral-prophetic text affect our interpretation of it?

4. Is it possible to read Revelation in the ways suggested in this chapter and still believe that it forecasts the future?

---

63. Metzger, *Breaking the Code*, 106.

64. Abrams, *Norton Anthology*, 2:663n1.

# 4

## How Do We Read It? Interpreting Revelation

How are we to read and interpret Revelation? This has been a problem basically since the day it left the island of Patmos. Some of the results have been imaginative—and strange—indeed. G. K. Chesterton's comment is apt: "though St. John the Evangelist saw many strange monsters in his vision, he saw no creature so wild as one of his own commentators."[1] So also Luther's: "Some have even brewed it [Revelation] into many stupid things out of their own heads."[2]

One response has been to excommunicate it from the church, by taking it out of the Bible, either literally or functionally—by neglecting it. So before we consider the interpretation of Revelation, we need to look briefly at is presence in the Bible, or canon—its canonicity.

### In or Out? The Question of Canon

Despite having some strong supporters in the early church, Revelation made it into the Christian Bible by the skin of its teeth.[3]

Although no one compiled a list of criteria for books to be included in the developing Christian canon—specifically, what was to become the New Testament—it is clear that certain concerns were operative. The leaders of the early churches wanted to know with certainty that the writings they would consider authoritative for faith and life were

1. Chesterton, *Orthodoxy*, 13.
2. Luther, "Preface to the Revelation of St. John [II]," 400.
3. For a brief discussion, see Wall, *Revelation*, 25–32.

ancient, apostolic, acknowledged throughout the Christian churches, and theologically orthodox.

At first leaders in the early church generally identified Revelation as ancient and apostolic, quoting it in their own work. But soon the book's fantastic visions and images became the playground of theologians with idiosyncratic beliefs that many others deemed dangerous. As we noted in chapter 1, the Montanists derived much of their theology from Revelation (especially 20:1–6, concerning the so-called millennium), and orthodox leaders responded by questioning the book's apostolic authorship—and its orthodoxy. By the time of the church historian Eusebius (early fourth century), Revelation was accepted by some and rejected by others. Eusebius, therefore, included it in his list of books he called "disputed" or even "spurious" in the church's debate about the developing canon. Churches in the West did incorporate Revelation into the canon when it was finalized in the fourth century, but the Eastern churches remained suspicious. Cyril of Jerusalem (315–86) omitted it from the canon and even banned it from all public and private reading. In general, many in the East said that the millennium (20:1–6) "distorted the spiritual nature of Christianity."[4] (Revelation remains absent from the Orthodox lectionary to this day.)

At issue in these debates was not merely the authorship of Revelation but the hermeneutical question: How do we read it? Should the text be taken literally or symbolically, allegorically? (The more things change, the more they stay the same, as the saying goes!) Once the churches decided that Revelation should be in, or remain in, the canon, the problem of how to interpret it did not disappear. In fact, its canonization actually exacerbated the interpretive problem because now Christians *had* to interpret it and *had* to integrate it with the rest of Scripture. The debate began in earnest, and the main currents of the history of interpretation were already set out in the first few centuries of serious theological work on the book.[5] Are the visions about specific figures and events, or do they transcend historical references and recur throughout history? Is the millennium literal or symbolic, earthly or heavenly? Is the main subject matter the predictions of judgment or the nature of Christ and the church? And so on.

4. Boring, *Revelation*, 3.

5. For bibliography on the history of interpretation, see note 6 in this book's Prelude.

There is an alternative to taking the canonization of Revelation seriously. We may follow the path of the early Luther and of Calvin, who thought Revelation's symbolism veiled Christ and thus was not good for the average Christian. Yet we should probably see this alternative as a mistake, for the Reformers' theology on the whole was heavily indebted to the church fathers, and many of those fathers depended theologically on Revelation despite its difficulties. Avoiding Revelation, therefore, is not really theologically responsible; another interpretive strategy is needed.

## Approaches to Revelation

Judith Kovacs and Christopher Rowland are scholars of the history of Revelation's interpretation and impact. They suggest that there are two ends of a wide interpretive spectrum for the book of Revelation: the "decoding" pole and the "actualizing" pole. Decoding interpreters focus on details, looking for correlations between the text and specific events and people (later events and people in church history and/or in their own time), while actualizing interpreters seek to "convey the spirit of the text" and to "perform" it in new circumstances. Every interpretation of Revelation, Kovacs and Rowland contend, falls somewhere between these two poles of the spectrum.[6] We may also refer to these two poles as a hermeneutic (interpretive strategy) of *correspondence* and a hermeneutic of *analogy*.

Kovacs and Rowland also suggest something that others have noted as well: interpreters of Revelation tend to focus on the past, the present, or the future in their reading of Revelation. Some, in other words, think that it should be read primarily or exclusively as an ancient document for the ancient church, some see it as a text that speaks above all to us today (that is, to any age, because its message is timeless), and some see it fundamentally as a set of predictions about the future. Few interpreters, however, would rule out the relevance of the time period that is not their own focus; even popular interpreters like Hal Lindsey and Tim LaHaye see Revelation as a text relevant both to the first century and to our time (indeed for all time), even if it primarily tells us about the future tribulation and associated events.

---

6. Kovacs and Rowland, *Revelation*, 8.

If we put these two simple systems of classifying approaches to Revelation together we can construct a graphic with an x-axis and a y-axis on which we can plot interpreters' interests between decoding and actualizing strategies and among past, present, and future foci[7]:

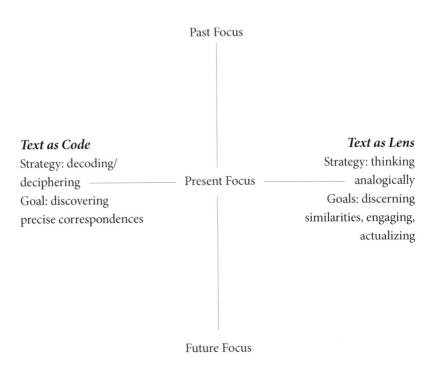

Past Focus

*Text as Code*
Strategy: decoding/ deciphering
Goal: discovering precise correspondences

Present Focus

*Text as Lens*
Strategy: thinking analogically
Goals: discerning similarities, engaging, actualizing

Future Focus

### Five Interpretive Strategies

It is possible to expand still further the combination of these two helpful systems of classification—the decoding/actualizing axis and the past/ present/future axis—by suggesting that there are at least five primary interpretive strategies for Revelation being practiced today. (Most, if not all, of these are actually quite ancient in the history of interpretation.) These approaches are not, however, mutually exclusive.[8]

---

7. I have adapted this graphic from several similar graphics presented by Rowland in various lectures and publications, including Kovacs and Rowland, *Revelation*, 8.

8. The terms for various approaches to Revelation, and especially the definitions of those terms used here, are my own and may differ from the usage of other scholars.

**1.** The first approach is the *predictive* approach, which is the most common approach to Revelation, focusing on the future. This approach is not, however, a recent invention; it goes back to some of the earliest interpreters of Revelation, such as Justin Martyr and Irenaeus in the second century and Victorinus in the third, who produced the first surviving commentary on Revelation. Throughout the centuries, many Christian interpreters have seen the fulfillment of the tribulations, the millennium, and/or the figures in Revelation in their own time or the very near future. "History is littered with failed attempts to use Revelation to predict history."[9] Interest in decoding and correlating has been heightened before epochal moments (such as the years 1000 and 2000) and during turbulent political events, whether in the world or in the church.

We find this approach in two basic forms. Some interpreters are focused on history, seeing Revelation as a prediction of world or church history (at least Western history), usually culminating in or near the time of the interpreter. This is sometimes called the historicist or church-historical approach. In the Middle Ages, Joachim of Fiore (12th century) and Nicholas of Lyra (14th century) read Revelation as a sequential chart of church history. Their reading strategy influenced many later interpreters.

Most recent predictive interpreters are focused on eschatology, seeing Revelation as primarily concerned about the "end times." Sometimes called the futurist approach, it is obviously what is found in the many popular books, web sites, and other media that view Revelation as an advance DVD or blueprint of the end. The most common form of this approach today is dispensationalism, popularized especially by the Plymouth Brethren teacher J. N. D. Darby (1808–82), then by the Scofield Bible, then by Hal Lindsey (*The Late Great Planet Earth*), and most recently by Tim LaHaye and Jerry Jenkins (the "Left Behind" series). Dispensationalists, as we have noted, divide history into various ages, or dispensations, in the divine story; connect the tribulation of Revelation 6–19 with the 70th week in Daniel 9:25–27; and believe in a two-stage or double return of Jesus beginning with the "rapture" of the church, supposedly found in Rev 4:1 and elsewhere. This is a decoding approach to Revelation, with the interest being in connecting symbols in Revelation with later figures and events, especially ones contemporary

---

9. Barr, "John's Ironic Empire," 20.

with the interpreter. For example, Hal Lindsey suggested that the locusts in Revelation 9 might be attack helicopters.

It should be noted that this approach can be very political. Not only have people sought to correlate Revelation's characters and events with political figures and situations, but at times the approach has directly influenced political strategy, as in the case of U.S. relations with countries in the Middle East.[10]

**2.** The second approach is what we will call the *preterist* approach, which focuses exclusively on the past ("preterite" being a linguistic term for the past tense). Sometimes called the contemporary-historical approach, it is a non-theological academic approach that might use the historical-critical method of biblical studies, or perhaps socio-rhetorical methodology. In either case, it views Revelation strictly as a document from and for its own time, a specimen of ancient religious literature. It developed in part as a reaction to futuristic readings. The interpreter may have no explicit interest in the alleged predictions, or even the ongoing relevance, of the text. Decoding is done to ascertain the meaning of symbols exclusively in the first century. Certain academic commentaries, such as the highly acclaimed three-volume work of David Aune, fall into this category.[11]

The other three approaches focus on the present message of Revelation, or on its timeless character. By timeless, I do not mean that Revelation is full of vague generalities without theological teeth, but that it is timeless in the sense of always timely, a living and active word, always able to speak as powerfully and pointedly in a later context as in its original one. Each of these three timeless-but-always-timely approaches plays a significant role in this book.

**3.** The third approach we will call *poetic*, or *theopoetic*. Proponents of this approach contend that Revelation uses mythical and poetic language to express great truths about God, evil, history, and so on. It is sometimes called the idealist, spiritual, non-historical, timeless, or transtemporal

---

10. See, for example, Boyer, *When Time Shall Be No More*; Tuveson, *Redeemer Nation*; Jewett and Shelton, *Captain America*.

11. This is not to say that Aune has no theological interests; he does, and he reveals them in other places. But his commentary is an example of the preterist historical-critical approach. Ben Witherington, on the other hand, in his commentary explicitly merges socio-rhetorical interpretation, which by itself could be a preterist approach, with contemporary theological reflection.

approach. This approach has always been somewhat reactionary as well, responding to perceived interpretive abuses in a predictive approach but also to deficiencies in a purely historical reading. Church fathers such as Origen, the great third-century allegorical interpreter, and, to a lesser extent, Augustine (354–430), building on the work of an interpreter named Tyconius, reacted against futuristic interpretations.

More recently, Paul Minear called Revelation an "animated and impassioned dance of ideas," and J. P. M. Sweet said it was "more like music than rational discourse."[12] Eugene Peterson labels it a "theological poem" that "does not . . . call for decipherment" but "evokes wonder," and Richard Hays writes of its "theopoetic" language.[13] Although these interpreters do not rule out historical study, they reject decoding approaches, whether preterist or futurist, as violations of the genre and language of Revelation. Thus this approach is not merely reactionary; it argues that the importance and truth of Revelation are not limited to its original connection with Rome and the particular historical context in which it was written, or to its alleged correlation with specific future realities.

4. The fourth approach can be called *political*, or *theopolitical*. This approach, for our purposes, does not refer to the political implications of predictive, dispensationalist interpretations but to a basic view of Revelation as a document of comfort and (especially) protest, to borrow words from the title of South African theologian Allan Boesak's interpretation of Revelation during the apartheid era: *Comfort and Protest* (1986). Similar book-length treatments have come from American activist Daniel Berrigan and South American liberation theologian Pablo Richard, while others have blended more historical approaches with interpretations that focus on justice (Elisabeth Schüssler Fiorenza) or anti-imperialism (e.g., Wes Howard-Brook and Anthony Gwyther). Martin Luther King Jr. also turned to Revelation in his "Letter from a Birmingham Jail" and in sermons. The theopolitical approach may focus on criticizing injustice, promoting transformation and justice, or both.[14]

12. Minear, cited in Peterson, *Reversed Thunder*, xii; Sweet, *Revelation*, 13.

13. Peterson, *Reversed Thunder*, 7 and xiii; Hays, *Moral Vision*, 170, 173, 184.

14. One should also include the work of William Stringfellow and of Jacques Ellul here, though the latter's approach is also quite theopoetic.

5. The fifth approach can be termed the *pastoral-prophetic* approach. This approach views Revelation primarily as a document of Christian formation designed to call the church to faithfulness in the face of inevitable conflict with hostile powers. One commentator who combines this approach with careful historical work is Charles Talbert. He writes that Revelation "functions in the interests of spiritual purity, single-minded devotion to God," or "first-commandment faithfulness."[15] The commentaries of Gerhard Krodel and Robert Wall, among others, have a similar tone.

This pastoral-prophetic approach is bound to be closely related to the previous two. If we read Revelation poetically, concluding that Babylon is not merely Rome, as the preterists might, and is definitely not some future reconfiguration of the Roman Empire in modern Europe, as some futurists would say, then its seductive and oppressive power can be felt—and must be both named and resisted—in the political realities of our own day. These last three approaches are similar to one another in that they both go beyond mere correspondence to more timeless concerns about God, evil, empire, civil religion, and the like, responding to new situations.

Without ignoring the past or the future (in a general sense), the focus of this book is on Revelation as a word to the church in the present. We will therefore combine the (theo-)poetic, the (theo-)political, and the pastoral-prophetic approaches. We will do so by grounding our contemporary interpretation of Revelation in its message for the first-century church, looking for contemporary analogies to first-century realities (as we did with the issue of civil religion in the last chapter), while always keeping an eye on the promises for the future of God's creation contained especially in Revelation 21–22. Unlike many traditional commentaries on Revelation, the focus of this book is on the big picture, not the details. For the details—the symbolic value of the many elements in the text, especially in their first-century context—consulting a good commentary is advisable. Although the meaning of Revelation should not be limited to its significance in its original context, understanding and building on that first, or most literal, sense is critical to responsible interpretation.

---

15. Talbert, *Apocalypse*. He claims that "our own times . . . mirror the prophet's circumstances almost exactly" (12).

## Common Mistakes and Corollary General Principles of Responsible Interpretation

Many people who read Revelation have no idea what to do with it, so they tend to read it woodenly, or literally, as they have seen or heard it interpreted by popular preachers and writers. The preceding discussion, together with the previous two chapters, has suggested that we would do well to read Revelation with a certain set of lenses. We may now briefly note several common mistakes in reading Revelation and some brief antidotes based on our discussion thus far. This general discussion will be followed by a more specific critical overview of the "Left Behind" approach to Revelation (because of its widespread influence) and then by some additional details about the alternative approach taken in this book.

Some of the most common mistakes in interpreting Revelation, and their corollary antidotes, follow. They are all closely connected to one another:

Common Mistakes and Antidotes in the Interpretation of Revelation

| Mistake | Antidote |
|---------|----------|
| 1. Failing to recognize Revelation's apocalyptic character, and the character and function of apocalyptic literature. | 1. Understanding the features of apocalyptic literature (symbolism, poetry, appeal to imagination) and its function of providing comfort and challenge, hope and warning. |
| 2. Failing to take Revelation seriously as a product of, and message to, its own time. | 2. Looking first of all for clues to its meaning for late-first-century believers in Asia Minor. |
| 3. Postulating arbitrary contemporary fulfillment of apocalyptic symbols and visions, based on the dubious assumption that prophecy and history must be culminating in the present. | 3. Interpreting Revelation's symbolism first of all within a first-century rather than a twenty-first-century framework, and looking for its symbolically rich message that suggests contemporary analogous realities rather than literal, specific future ones. |

| Mistake | Antidote |
|---|---|
| 4. Treating the Bible like a puzzle with pieces to be fitted together—a text from this book here, another from that book there, etc.—in order to figure out alleged events to come. | 4. Reading each biblical book, including Revelation, holistically and contextually for its unique message. |
| 5. Becoming preoccupied with (sometimes misguided) questions about the meaning of certain unknowable or less significant aspects of the book, such as the identity of the beast, Armageddon, the length and date of the millennium, etc. This includes allowing a particular view of the millennium to control one's reading of the entire book. | 5. Staying focused on bigger, thematic issues rather than on disputed details, letting Revelation appeal to the disciplined, informed imagination about theological/spiritual matters, and not treating it like an advance video of the future. |
| 6. Failing to hear Revelation in light of the larger Christian tradition and contemporary scholarship. | 6. Remembering that people like Hal Lindsey, Tim LaHaye, Jerry Jenkins, and David Jeremiah are not the first, only, or best interpreters of Revelation. |

## Problems with the "Left Behind" Series (and similar interpretations of Revelation)

This last point leads us to a brief discussion of the "Left Behind" series of books, films, and related media by Tim LaHaye and Jerry Jenkins. Estimates on the sales of these products vary, but 75 million is probably a fair estimate. Although not original, this approach, whether manifested in the "Left Behind" series itself or in countless other, similar publications, is undoubtedly the most popular and influential approach to interpreting Revelation in the U.S., and probably in the world. As a way of interpreting Revelation, however, it is riddled with problems, including hermeneutical (general interpretive), theological, and political deficiencies. Space does not permit even a complete listing, much less a full discussion, of these concerns, but the following brief lists indicate their breadth and gravity.[16]

## Hermeneutical (Interpretive) Problems with the "Left Behind" Approach

1.  The series is not really fiction but a combination of theology and proleptic documentary, like an advance DVD, because it views biblical prophecy as "history written in advance" (*Left Behind*, 214). The correspondence between the books and the commentary by LaHaye (*Revelation Unveiled*) is revealing, but not surprising.

2.  It treats the Bible as a puzzle to be pieced together into a script about the future, with various texts from various books taken out of context and linked to current or expected events. The method has sometimes been called biblical "hopscotch," and the result is a patchwork quilt with scenes from Revelation as the most prominent and thematic aspect of the quilt.

3.  It claims to be literal, but it is not or is only selectively so. A better description would be correlative, meaning in search of precise correspondences, as opposed to either literal or analogical.

4.  It misunderstands the nature and function of both prophetic and apocalyptic literature, and it grossly misinterprets just about every biblical text it utilizes. Prophetic does not merely mean predictive, and apocalyptic is heavily symbolic.

5.  It finds aspects of the second coming that are not in the Bible, such as two comings of Jesus, and a rapture in Revelation. Rather, "Jesus will return—once."[17]

6.  It imposes a foreign, 19th-century theological, interpretive construct onto the ancient biblical texts: dispensationalism.

7.  It assumes that we are on the brink of the rapture and tribulation, and that is really all that matters.

---

16. There are numerous books critical of the "Left Behind" series, including Rossing, *The Rapture Exposed*; Tuck, *The Left Behind Fantasy*; Olson, *Will Catholics Be "Left Behind"?*; and Standaert, *Skipping Towards Armageddon*.

17. Rossing, *Rapture Exposed*, 186.

8. It misses the most important movement in the book, which is not temporal but theological; the focus on God as Alpha and Omega (1:8; 21:6; 22:13) means that Revelation "*does not move from rapture to millennium but from God to God.*"[18]

## Theological and Spiritual Problems with the "Left Behind" Approach

1. The series misunderstands the NT references to the "end times." For the NT, the "end times" is the period between the first and second coming of Jesus.

2. It reduces the gospel to "God and Jesus and the Rapture and the Glorious Appearing," amounting to an unhealthy preoccupation with the details about events surrounding Christ's second coming.

3. It reduces the primary reason for conversion to fear.

4. It reduces discipleship to (a) faith in Jesus' death in order to avoid being left behind or destroyed; (b) evangelizing others so they won't be left behind or destroyed; (c) correlating "Bible prophecy" with current events; and (d) preparing to die or kill for the gospel/kingdom.[19]

5. It is escapist and therefore has no ongoing ethic of life between the times, between the first and second comings. There is no compulsion to love one's neighbor, practice deeds of mercy, work for peace and justice, etc. Contrast the hope of imminent return and the ethic in 1 Thessalonians, which actually has an ethic for life in the hope of the second coming.

6. It is inherently militaristic. Anything resembling pacifism, international cooperation, or disarmament is satanic, and believers are called to participate in a literal war that is guaranteed victory by the return of a conquering Jesus. Christian heroes join this Jesus, carrying and using Uzis and the like.

18. Koester, "On the Verge of the Millennium," 135.

19. My student Caroline Lawson Dean, in a paper on the popular 1972 evangelistic movie *A Thief in the Night* and its sequels, pointed out that such rapture movies tend to have a variety of "didactic" scenes, or "teaching moments," in which two basic things are explained: how to become a Christian after the rapture and what the sequence of end-times events will be.

7.  It is inherently anti-Catholic. The only good, saved Catholics are those who are basically Protestant.

8.  It fails to see the church as a peaceful alternative to empire rather than its chaplain or its warmaking opponent.

## *Political Problems with the "Left Behind" Approach*

1.  It is uncritically pro-American.

2.  It privileges the modern state of Israel in an uncritical way.

3.  It is suspicious of anything to do with the work of the United Nations or international organizations.

4.  It sees wars in the Middle East as part of God's plan, in effect, therefore, as *desiderata*, or a good.

5.  It inculcates a survivalist and crusader mentality into the minds of its readers.[20]

Overall assessment: This is a thoroughly misguided approach to the Bible, theology, and the Christian life. It could be passable fiction, at some amateur level, except that it really is theology—and *dangerous* theology. The misguided character of the series becomes thoroughly warped especially in the last two books, with the portrayal of ultimate faithful discipleship as killing for Jesus' sake and the corollary depiction of Jesus as warrior. This makes the overall series dangerous spiritually, theologically, and politically. Craig Hill notes that "proponents of the Rapture have mangled the biblical witness almost beyond recognition."[21]

The only adequate starting point for a cure for this kind of misreading is grasping the fundamental theological outlook, themes, and purpose of Revelation. Thus a brief consideration of Revelation's theology follows, before we return to our discussion of an alternative interpretive strategy to that of the "Left Behind" series and similar approaches to Revelation.

20. One well-known former evangelist who read Revelation in a similar way sold freeze-dried food to his followers in anticipation of the pale-green horse (famine) of Revelation 6.

21. Hill, *In God's Time*, 207.

## The Theology of Revelation: An Overview

It is tempting to postpone the discussion of the theology, or "teaching," of Revelation until the end of this book, after we have examined all of the aspects of the Apocalypse that we intend to cover. But that would probably be a mistake, for one of the problems in reading Revelation responsibly is having an overall interpretive, or hermeneutical, framework within which to read the book. Therefore, before we explore some of the details, we consider the big picture. Naturally, this big-picture overview is the result of careful study of all those details, as perplexing as they can sometimes be. But readers are invited, nonetheless, to test the claims made in this discussion as they work through the details of the ensuing chapters.[22]

### Discerning the Purpose of Revelation

As we have already noted, most people interpret the book of Revelation as a kind of advance DVD of the end of the world. The focus of the book, they think, is eschatology, the last things. In a sense, of course, eschatology is indeed a focus of the last book of the Bible, but in a profound sense eschatology is not the *ultimate* focus of Revelation. Rather, as in the rest of Scripture, the eschatology we find in Revelation is a means to an end. Its intention is to give hope to people in trying and/or tempting times so that they will remain faithful to their covenant commitment to God.

In other words, the purpose of the book of Revelation is to persuade its hearers and readers, both ancient and contemporary, to remain faithful to God in spite of past, present, or possible future suffering— whatever form that suffering might take, and whatever source it may have—simply for being faithful. In spite of memory, experience, or fear, Revelation tells us, covenant faithfulness is *possible* because of Jesus and *worthwhile* because of the glorious future God has in store for us and for the entire created order.

Revelation, we might say, provides us with a vivid, imaginative, and prophetic call to an "anti-assimilationist" and life-giving Christian

---

22. For other brief summaries of the theology of Revelation, see Reddish, *Revelation*, 22–26 and Beale, *Revelation*, 171–77. For an excellent, thorough treatment, see Bauckham, *Theology*.

witness to, against, and within an immoral and idolatrous imperial culture of death.[23] It does so, not only by offering the hope of God's future
salvation, but also by showing us that God is sovereign even now. The
combination of that future assurance and the present reality of God's
sovereignty means that life now should and can be lived as a life of worship and faithfulness to God and the Lamb.

We may tease out this general overview by suggesting that there are
seven theological themes in the book of Revelation that, taken together,
constitute its message. I have chosen not to provide specific texts from
Revelation at this point, since the visionary character of the book means
that a verse here and there seldom captures either the power of the visions or the full significance of their theological claims, much less the
effect of their integration into one book.

### Seven Theological Themes in Revelation

1.  *The Throne: The Reign of God and the Lamb.* God the creator reigns!
    Jesus the redeemer, the slaughtered Lamb, is Lord! The reign of the
    eternal God, the beginning and the end, is not merely future or past
    but *present*, and it is manifested in—of all things—the slaughtered
    Lamb. God is inseparable from the Lamb, and vice versa. Each can
    be called the Alpha and Omega, and they rule together on one
    throne. This is a cruciform (cross-centered and cross-shaped) un-
    derstanding of divine power.

2.  *The Reality of Evil and of Empire.* Evil is real. Empire is now—not
    merely future or past but *present*. Empire, by nature, makes seduc-
    tive blasphemous and immoral claims and engages in corollary
    practices that bring disorder to both vertical (people-God) and hor-
    izontal (people-people) human relations, promising life but deliver-
    ing death—both physical and spiritual.

3.  *The Temptation to Idolatry and Immorality.* The Christian church
    is easily seduced by empire's idolatry and immorality because these
    claims and practices are often invested with religious meaning and
    authority; they become a civil religion. For that reason, immoral-
    ity is ultimately idolatry: the idolatry of violence, oppression, greed,
    lust, and the like. Humanity's ultimate inhumanity—treating fellow

23. The term "anti-assimilationist" comes from Talbert, *Apocalypse.*

humans as disposable commodities—is therefore at root an attack on God as creator and redeemer.

4. *The Call to Covenant Faithfulness and Resistance.* In the midst of empire and civil religion, whatever its forms, the church is called to resistance as the inevitable corollary of covenant faithfulness to God, a call that requires prophetic spiritual discernment and may result in various kinds of suffering.

5. *Worship and an Alternative Vision.* The spiritual discernment required of the church, in turn, requires an alternative vision of God and of reality that unveils and challenges empire, a vision in need of the Spirit's wisdom to see and apply. Revelation provides this vision of "uncivil" worship and vision, centered on the throne of the eternal holy God and the faithful slaughtered Lamb, and on the coming new creation.

6. *Faithful Witness: The Pattern of Christ.* Christian resistance to empire and idolatry conforms to the pattern of Jesus Christ and of his apostles, saints, prophets (like John), and martyrs: faithful, true, courageous, just, and nonviolent. It is not passive but active, consisting of the formation of communities and individuals who pledge allegiance to God alone, who live in nonviolent love toward friends and enemies alike, who leave vengeance to God, and who, by God's Spirit, create mini-cultures of life as alternatives to empire's culture of death. This is a Lamb-shaped or cross-shaped (cruciform) understanding of discipleship and mission.

7. *The Imminent Judgment and Salvation/New Creation of God.* God the creator and Christ the redeemer take evil and injustice seriously and are about to come both to judge humanity and to save the faithful and renew the cosmos. The will of God is for all to follow the Lamb and participate in the saving life of God-with-us forever.

We will see these themes unfold in the rest of the book as we consider Revelation section by section in subsequent chapters. We will also return to these themes in the final chapter as we reflect on living the message of Revelation today.

## A Single Message?

Can, or should, all of these themes be reduced to a single theme or message? According to Udo Schnelle, Revelation "conveys a single idea: it communicates to the threatened earthly community the assurance of heavenly victory."[24] Somewhat similarly, Frances Aran Murphy says that the message of Revelation is "resurrection," "or resurrection to eternal life," meaning "the transposition of temporal-created life into eternal-created life."[25] But Murphy rightly adds that the "leitmotif of the Apocalypse is worship combined with judgment," which focuses on the slaughtered Lamb, whose sacrifice is the judgment of the world and whose disciples bear witness by sharing in his fate.[26]

Revelation itself seems to give us a synopsis of its own message in several places that contain many of the seven themes noted above: the seven beatitudes scattered throughout the book (see discussion on p. 39); ch. 14, especially vv. 1–13; the text of 21:5–8, which we might call the "seven last words of God"; and the epilogue (22:6–21). I would suggest, therefore, that a slightly expanded version of the subtitle of this book reflects these texts and is a good summary of Revelation's message: *uncivil worship and witness: following the Lamb out of fallen Babylon into the new creation.*[27] We will need to unpack this rather carefully, of course.

## An Alternative, Cruciform Interpretive Strategy

After deconstruction there must be reconstruction. We have begun this process with a summary of Revelation's theology. What follows is an alternative set of principles—a Lamb-centered, cruciform interpretive strategy, or hermeneutic—for reading Revelation. It is an alternative to the popular way of reading Revelation as seen in the "Left Behind" series and in similar approaches. But this interpretation is not idiosyncratic; rather it incorporates and synthesizes some of the major trends in the interpretation of Revelation noted above and required by the previous

24. Schnelle, *Theology of the New Testament*, 772.

25. Murphy, "Revelation," 686.

26. Murphy, "Revelation," 686.

27. This is unintentionally but not inappropriately reminiscent of the subtitle of John Howard Yoder's classic *The Politics of Jesus*, which is *Vicit Agnus Noster*. These three words are the first half of an old Moravian creed: *Vicit Agnus Noster, Eum Sequamur*, or "Our Lamb has conquered; let us follow him."

chapter as well as the preceding theological summary. As noted earlier, we may refer to this approach generally as theopolitical (*uncivil*), theo-poetic (*worship*), and pastoral-prophetic (*witness*). Such an interpretive approach will incorporate the following concrete strategies:

1. *Recognize that the central and centering image of Revelation is the Lamb that was slaughtered.* In Revelation, Christ dies for our sins, but he dies also, even primarily, as the incarnation and paradigm of faithfulness to God in the face of anti-God powers. Christ is Lord, Christ is victorious, and Christ conquers by cruciform faithful resistance: not by inflicting but by absorbing violence; not by actually killing but by speaking his powerful word.[28] Revelation is counter-imperial, challenging Rome's theology of Victory and Power with what many have called "Lamb power."[29] We are victorious by following the Lamb, not Babylon, Rome, or analogous imperial powers.

2. *Remember that Revelation was first of all written by a first-century Christian for first-century Christians using first-century literary devices and images.* These images reflect certain first-century realities; they do not specifically predict 21st-century realities. However, like other powerful images, these images in Revelation evoke connections to similar realities at other times, including our own—which leads to the next principle.

3. *Abandon so-called literal, linear approaches to the book as if it were history written in advance, and use an interpretive strategy of analogy rather than correlation.* Revelation is image, metaphor, poetry, political cartooning. Revelation imaginatively reveals the nature of any and all systems that oppose the ways of God in the world, especially as revealed in Christ the Lamb who was slaughtered. Those systems are not limited to particular future powers but are found in all places and times. We should therefore be examining our ideologies and -isms for manifestations of idolatry and immorality as expressed in imperialism, militarism, nationalism, racism, classism (the worship of the corporate self and the degradation of the corporate other), consumerism, and hedonism (the worship of things and pleasure). This means we must especially examine our own Western, Northern, American, and even Christian systems and values, not some

28. We will discuss this at length in chapter 8.

29. See, e.g., Rossing, *Rapture Exposed*, 103–22; Ewing, *Power of the Lamb*.

putative one-world government, for evidences of that which is antichrist.

4. *Focus on the book's call to public worship and discipleship.* Revelation calls Christians to a difficult discipleship of discernment—a nonconformist cruciform faithfulness—that may lead to marginalization or even persecution now, but ultimately to a place in God's new heaven and new earth. Revelation calls believers to nonretaliation and nonviolence, and not to a literal war of any sort, present or future. By its very nature as resistance, faithful nonconformity is not absolute withdrawal but rather critical engagement on very different terms from those of the status quo. This is all birthed and nurtured in worship. But we need to be diligent, because, as Harry Maier contends, we in the West are now largely like the Laodiceans, and many of us need to read Revelation as such.[30] If he is correct, we are in very bad shape but do not know it, so conversion to true worship and discipleship will be a difficult journey.

5. *Place the images of death and destruction in Revelation within the larger framework of hope.* The death and destruction in Revelation are symbolic of the judgment and cleansing of God that is necessary for the realization of the hope offered in Christ for a new heaven and new earth in which God and the Lamb alone reign forever among a redeemed, reconciled humanity from all tribes, peoples, and nations. The church bears witness in word and deed to this future reality, but it knows that only God can bring that final, future reality to earth, so it constantly prays, "Come, Lord Jesus."

This fivefold strategy, even developed in book form, may not be sufficient to convince dispensationalists (or others) that that kind of approach to Revelation is misguided and irresponsible. After all, Revelation, like beauty, is in the eye of the beholder, right? At that moment, we may draw on the wisdom of Christopher Rowland:

> The nature of Revelation's polyvalent imagery means that there is at the end of the day no refuting of readings like this [escapist dispensationalism]. One can only appeal to consistency with the wider demand of the gospel and its application by generations of men and women in lives of service and involvement with the suffering and the marginalized to counter such world-denying

30. In his *Apocalypse Recalled*, especially 130–39.

and dehumanizing appropriations of Revelation and other biblical books.[31]


## Questions for Reflection and Discussion

1.  Which approach(es) to Revelation discussed in this chapter is (are)
    most attractive to you? Why?

2.  Why do you think the predictive approach to Revelation, seen in
    the "Left Behind" series and elsewhere, is so popular and persistent?

3.  What is your reaction to the list of weaknesses in the "Left Behind"
    series and to the alternative approach advocated in this chapter and
    throughout the book thus far?

4.  How does the summary of Revelation's theology presented in this
    chapter compare to the understanding(s) of its message you have
    heard and/or held?


31. Rowland, "The Book of Revelation," 544.

# 5

## Seven Pastoral-Prophetic Messages from the Risen Lord

## (Revelation 1–3)

The first chapter of Revelation tells us about John, the author. We have already said something about him and his situation as a faithful witness and Christian prophet in exile (1:1–2, 9–11). But what John really wants us to know is not who he is or what he has done, but who the God he has encountered is, and what this God has revealed to him to convey to the churches.

### Opening Words

As we have already seen, John begins the Revelation by telling us what it is: apocalypse, prophecy, and letter. All three elements appear early in the book.

It is important to begin reading Revelation at the beginning—the very beginning. Some people read Revelation as if the first and most important words about the book were in 1:19. That verse tells us that John will write down, and thus Revelation will tell us, "what you [John] have seen, what is, and what is to take place after this." Some interpreters have found in this text not only the contents and the structure of Revelation, but also the purpose for reading it: to gain information, especially about what will take place—the events of the end times. But this is the wrong starting place.

Revelation 1:3 contains the first of the seven benedictions, or blessings, in the book of Revelation (see the list on p. 39 above). It is pronounced both on the one who reads it aloud (in the assemblies) and on the hearers/keepers of the prophecy. The emphasis on keeping the words of the prophecy reminds us that this book is not primarily a depiction of events to come as a means of satisfying our curiosity but is rather a call to "first-commandment faithfulness" (Talbert's apt phrase[1]), a call to conversion and discipleship *in light of* past, present, and future realities. The prophet is a visionary, not merely of present crises or future events, but of an alternative way of being grounded in the vision of God.

This is consistent with the biblical sense of prophecy, and this sense is both reinforced and strengthened throughout the last book of the Bible, beginning with the first chapter. To miss this fundamental point is to miss the point of Revelation and to guarantee irresponsible interpretation of its contents. Revelation 1:3 is thus the interpretive (or hermeneutical) key to the book with respect to our motivation for reading it and our basic strategy in doing so. We read Revelation as words from a prophet-pastor (and ultimately from God), in order to be formed and transformed, not merely informed. Everything that follows 1:3, even the words of 1:19, functions to further the book's pastoral-prophetic promise and challenge.

## The Opening Vision

Revelation also opens with some amazing claims about God and Christ. These assertions challenge the blasphemous claims made by and about the emperor, remind the audience of who and whose they are, and give them and us hope for ultimate triumph. This is theology in poetic mode for a pastoral-prophetic purpose.

It was important for the early churches—and it is crucial for us—to understand that Jesus is not merely a heroic human being but shares in the divine identity.[2] Revelation 4 and 5 will make that point in a powerful way, but already it unfolds here in the first chapter. Grace and peace come from one almighty but triune source: God the Father, the Spirit ("seven spirits" signifying the fullness of the one divine Spirit), and Jesus Christ (1:4–6). While there is a special focus on Jesus' unique role in

1. Talbert, *Revelation*, 11.
2. See especially Bauckham, *Jesus and the God of Israel*.

God's plan, there are also parallels drawn between Jesus and God the Father:

| God | Jesus |
|---|---|
| who is (1:4, 8) | firstborn of the dead (1:5) |
| who was (1:4, 8); I am the Alpha (1:8) | I am the first (1:17) |
| who is to come (1:4, 8); [I am] the Omega (1:8) | he is coming with the clouds (1:7); [I am] the last (1:17) |
| his throne (1:4) | ruler of the kings of the earth (1:5); to him be glory and dominion forever and ever (1:6); cf. Dan 7:13–14 |
| the Almighty (1:8); cf. Dan 7:9 "an Ancient One took his throne, his clothing was white as snow, and the hair of his head like pure wool. . . ." | "His head and his hair were white as white wool, white as snow; his eyes were like a flame of fire" (1:14); cf. Dan 7:9 |

The opening vision (1:9–20) draws on Daniel 7:9–14 to depict Christ as a powerful, priestly, and present (to the churches) figure. But by attributing to Jesus the features of *both* the human one ("one like a human being" or "son of man"; Rev 1:13; Dan 7:9) and the Ancient One (Rev 1:14; Dan 7:9) in Daniel 7, John tells us that Jesus partakes of God's identity and reign. Thus both the prologue of Revelation (1:1–8) and its opening vision tell us that Jesus really is Lord.

The presence of this Lord Jesus among the churches (signified by "lampstands"; 1:12–13, 20) serves the pastoral-prophetic function announced in 1:3. First, it is a sign of *security*. The all-powerful One will protect the church. "Do not be afraid" (1:17) is a word not just to John but to all who read or hear these words. They will be kept safe no matter what comes; they will share in Jesus' conquest, his victory. Second, the vision is a sign of *hope*. The one who was killed is now living, and will live forever in glory. He permits the church to participate in his victory over empire and over death—after they have also shared his faithful witness (1:5) that led him to the cross. Third, the vision is a call to *discipleship*. The one who speaks the word of God summons the church to obedience.

These three aspects of the vision all emerge in the seven messages to the churches (Revelation 2–3): ultimate security, cruciform hope, faithful discipleship.

## Seven Pastoral-Prophetic Messages to the Churches

Among the perennially most understandable and preachable texts in Revelation are the messages to the seven churches. Best known for the unforgettable image of Jesus spitting the lukewarm church at Laodicea out of his mouth (3:16) and the equally memorable image of Jesus standing at the door and knocking (3:20), these messages provide both a window into the life of seven first-century churches, with their strengths and weaknesses, and an ongoing challenge to contemporary readers.

### Debunking a Misunderstanding

Before we begin a serous consideration of these two chapters, we must dismiss a common popular misunderstanding of them. Prevalent in certain circles is the view that the seven churches depict seven eras of church history from the apostolic period to the present, together known as "the present age" or "the church age." Although this approach does not deny that the seven messages had any immediate relevance for the first-century churches or for individual believers and churches since that time, it views their primary purpose as predictive. As the influential Scofield Reference Bible puts it in the study notes introducing Revelation 2–3, "Most conclusively of all, these messages do present an exact foreview of the *spiritual* history of the church, and in this precise order."[3] This approach—a "bird's-eye view of church history"[4]—has been especially popular for approximately the last one hundred years in conservative Protestant circles, but it actually goes back in essence to at least the Middle Ages.

The best known of its various incarnations has been popular among dispensationalists for the last century. This interpretation, with only a modest amount of variation and with a consistent anti-Catholic bias, can be found in the notes of the Scofield Bible (1909, 1917), in the graphic representations of Revelation by Baptist minister Clarence Larkin (ca.

---

3. *Scofield Reference Bible*, 1917, 1331–32.
4. Lindsey, *There's a New World Coming*, 28.

1919),[5] and in the commentaries on Revelation by Hal Lindsey (*There's a New World Coming*, 1973, 1984) and Tim LaHaye (*Revelation Unveiled*, 1999). It looks like this:

Dispensationalist Interpretation of the Churches in Revelation 2–3

| 2:1–7 | Ephesus | Apostolic church | to ca. 100 or 150 |
|---|---|---|---|
| 2:8–11 | Smyrna | Persecuted church | ca. 100–312 (Constantine) |
| 2:12–17 | Pergamum | Compromised church favored by empire but judged by Christ | ca. 312–606 (election of Pope Boniface X) |
| 2:18–29 | Thyatira | Worldly, lax medieval church dominated by papacy and characterized by superstition and paganism | ca. 606–1500/1517 (Protestant reformation), but also continuing until the tribulation |
| 3:1–6 | Sardis | Reformation churches, still too much like the medieval church, more dead than alive | ca. 1517–1750, but also continuing today |
| 3:7–13 | Philadelphia | True church, loved by Christ, characterized by revival and missionary activity | ca. 1750–early 20th century, but also continuing until rapture |
| 3:14–22 | Laodicea | Lukewarm, apostate, anti-supernatural church | Ca. 1900–tribulation |

5. Some of Larkin's work may be viewed at http://www.sacred-texts.com/chr/tbr/img/01900.jpg. Lindsey (*There's a New World Coming*, 27) notes his dependence on the *New Scofield Reference Bible*.

As creative and appealing as this approach may be, it has several major problems. First, Revelation gives no hint of interest in or knowledge of specific "eras" of the church. On the contrary, the context of chapters 2 and 3, not to mention the actual content of those chapters, does not suggest concern with future churches but with real, first-century churches facing first-century problems. This does not rule out any symbolic or ongoing significance to the churches, but this must be a matter of careful theological reflection, not wild speculation. Second, and perhaps more importantly, this kind of schema uncritically reflects the perspective of very conservative (largely fundamentalist) and very American Protestantism, which (at least in this instance) finds its heroes in the earliest church and the Protestant missionary movement, and its enemies in both the Catholic church and the magisterial Reformation and its heirs ("mainline Protestantism"). These biases appear in both the descriptions and the dates offered above (e.g. 1900 referring to the approximate date of various fundamentalist-modernist splits). This kind of interpretation of church history has no basis in the text but simply reflects the bias of the interpreter, and a very Eurocentric and Americentric reader at that. Revelation 2–3 is too theologically rich to deserve such irresponsible misreadings.

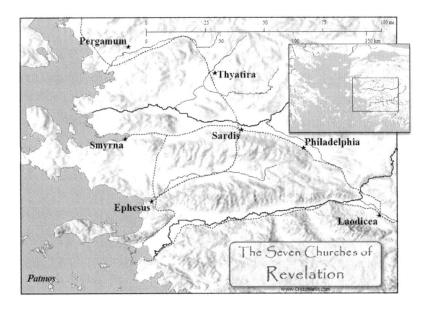

## The Form of the Messages

Frequently referred to as letters, the texts addressed to seven churches in Western Asia are probably better characterized as prophetic oracles, or perhaps pastoral-prophetic messages. Some scholars, most notably David Aune, have even suggested that they are similar to imperial edicts.[6] Jesus speaks as a royal, even imperial, figure through John to the churches. His words are to be taken with the utmost seriousness. But Jesus also speaks as a pastor, one who walks among the churches (2:1; cf. 1:13). The messages to the various "angels" of the churches constitute a series of pastoral visits.[7] Because Jesus is both awe-inspiring and present, he can speak strong words of comfort and of challenge, appealing to the churches' hearts (emotions) as well as their minds (reason).[8]

Almost any reader of these seven messages will notice a structural pattern. Some interpreters of Revelation have tried to correlate their form with the components of ancient imperial edicts and also with the parts of ancient rhetorical discourse, and these analyses may be right. At the very least, however, we may identify a fairly consistent literary structure with the following parts:

- Address to the church's "angel" (= messenger? leader? prophet? guardian angel?)
- Description of Christ, drawn largely from the opening vision
- Commendation (in all but Laodicea)
- Condemnation (in all but Smyrna and Philadelphia)
- Challenge: exhortation/warning
- Eschatological promise to those who conquer (are faithful)
- Invitation to heed the Spirit

Eugene Peterson reduces these parts to three substantive elements of "spiritual direction": affirmation, correction, and motivating promise.[9] While these three dimensions may be the heart of each message, the other elements are also significant (particularly the warnings), especially

6. See Aune, *Revelation 1–5*, 126–29.
7. Richard, *Apocalypse*, 52.
8. See deSilva, *Seeing Things John's Way*, 175–92; 229–55.
9. Peterson, *Reversed Thunder*, 50–52.

as they relate to Revelation as a whole. The following table summarizes, for each of the seven messages, these seven elements (except the invitation to heed the Spirit, which does not vary in content):

The Seven Pastoral-Prophetic Messages to the Churches in Revelation

| Text and Church | Christ | Commendation | Condemnation | Challenge: Exhortation/ Warning | Eschatological Promise to Conquerors/ Faithful |
|---|---|---|---|---|---|
| 2:1–7 Ephesus | Holds 7 stars, walks among 7 lamp-stands[10] (see 1:13, 16) | Works, toil, endurance; intolerance of evildoers, testing false apostles, suffering without growing weary; hatred of Nicolaitans' work | Abandoned initial love | Remember from where fallen; repent; do works as previously. Otherwise: removal of lampstand | Eat from tree of life (see 22:2, 14, 19; Gen 2:9; 3:22) |
| 2:8–11 Smyrna | First and last; was dead and came to life (see 1:8, 17) | Affliction, poverty, slander from those who claim to be Jews | NONE | Don't fear impending suffering; some to be jailed; 10 days of affliction. Be faithful unto death. | Crown of life, escape from second death (see 20:6, 14; 21:8) |
| 2:12–17 Pergamum | Has sharp two-edged sword (see 1:16) | Holding fast to Name in city of Satan's throne, even with martyrdom of Antipas | Some follow Balaam in the way of idolatry/sexual immorality (= Nicolaitans) | Repent. Otherwise: Christ will come to make war against followers of Balaam/Nicolaitans | Hidden manna, white stone with a new name (see 22:4) |

10. Or menorahs.

| Text and Church | Christ | Commenda-tion | Condemna-tion | Challenge: Exhortation/ Warning | Eschatological Promise to Conquerors/ Faithful |
|---|---|---|---|---|---|
| 2:18–29 Thyatira | Son of God (see 1:6) with eyes like flame of fire and feet like burnished bronze (see 1:14–15); searches mind and hearts, rewards according to works | Works: love, faith, service, endurance; recent works greater than earlier ones | Tolerance of Jezebel, false prophet of idolatry/sexu-al immorality (teachings = "deep things of Satan"); refusal to re-pent | Distress to adulterers, unless they repent; death to children of Jezebel; oth-ers: hold fast | Authority over nations to rule them (see Ps 2:8–9), morn-ing star (see 22:16) |
| 3:1–6 Sardis | Has 7 spir-its of God and 7 stars (see 1:4, 16) | [Follows censure:] a few have not soiled clothes but walk with Jesus in white and are worthy | Name/reputa-tion of being alive, but real-ly dead; works imperfect or incomplete | Wake up, strengthen what remains at point of death; re-member, obey, repent; otherwise: Christ to come like thief | Clothed like faithful in white robes; Christ will not blot out name from book of life (21:27) but will confess it before Father and angels (cf. 21:7) |
| 3:7–13 Philadel-phia | Holy one, true one, who has keys of David, who opens and shuts, and whose ac-tion no one can reverse | Works; kept Christ's word about endur-ance and have not denied his name despite having little power | NONE | Synagogue of Satan (= false Jews) will bow before them and learn Christ loves them; protection from coming universal trial; hold fast | Christ will make them a permanent pil-lar in temple of God (cf. 21:22), will write God's name on them, the name of the new Je-rusalem (see 21:2, 10) and Christ's own new name |

89

| Text and Church | Christ | Commenda-tion | Condemna-tion | Challenge: Exhortation/ Warning | Eschatological Promise to Conquerors/ Faithful |
|---|---|---|---|---|---|
| 3:14–22 Laodicea | The "Amen," the faithful and true witness (see 1:5); origin/ beginning of God's creation | NONE | Neither cold nor hot in works, but lukewarm; not rich but wretched, poor, blind, naked, piti-able | Wishes them to be cold or hot; since they are not: about to be spit from mouth; buy from Christ gold, white robes, eye salve; reproof and discipline of beloved; be earnest, repent; Christ knocks at door, will enter and eat with anyone who opens | A place with Christ on his throne (see chap. 5) |

## The Content of the Messages

When we read these seven messages, we are struck by two major problems that the churches are confronting: the reality of various kinds of persecution, and the strong temptation to accommodate, with accommodation perhaps being seen by some as the way to avoid or stop persecution. The seven messages tell us that there is a wide spectrum within the churches, from the highly accommodating to those who are persecuted—undoubtedly for not accommodating.

The most prominent form of accommodation at issue is eating food sacrificed to the gods (idols, in Christian perspective), which was the cultural norm and expectation, demonstrating support of the political and social status quo. It is practiced and advocated within the churches by various individuals and groups to whom John gives symbolic names: the followers of Balaam and the Nicolaitans at Pergamum (2:14–15), the Nicolaitans (by implication) at Ephesus (2:6), and Jezebel and her followers at Thyatira (2:20–25).[11] Those in leadership of this movement he calls pseudo-apostles and pseudo-prophets (2:2, 20), and like other prophets before him, he refers to the idolatry as spiritual fornication and adultery (2:14, 20–22).

As for the persecution, it seems to have come in several forms: harassment for being identified as a Christian (bearing the name) at Ephesus and Philadelphia; economic and/or social deprivation, as well as slander from certain Jews, at Smyrna and Philadelphia; fear of impending arrests, suggesting investigations by provincial officials (perhaps officials of the imperial cult, and possibly based on reports from Jewish leaders) at Smyrna; and harassment, even including a violent death, at Pergamum. John attributes this persecution ultimately to Satan (2:9, 13, 24; 3:9), which corresponds to his description of Satan and the Satanic beasts of Revelation 12 and 13 (discussed in chapters 7 and 8 below).

The cities in which these early Christian assemblies met were important urban centers, some with populations of 100,000 or more: Ephesus (200,000–250,000), Smyrna (75,000–100,000), Pergamum (120,000–180,000), and Sardis (100,000).[12] The Christians in their little house churches were a tiny minority. How would they survive the pressure to "toe the line" culturally, politically, and religiously? We learn something of their struggles, and of Christ's words to them, in the seven messages.

### The Churches Individually

Space permits only a brief survey of each of the messages to the churches.

2:1–7. The church in Ephesus existed in a major port city that was home to the provincial proconsul (appointed governor) and to major temples devoted to the goddess Artemis and the emperor. Ephesian Artemis was worshiped throughout the Empire, and her temple was known as one of the seven wonders of the ancient world. The problem at Ephesus is often read as a story of the dangers of rigid orthodoxy

---

11. Balaam was a prophet associated with Israel's turn to idolatry and immorality with the Midianites; he was then killed by the Israelites in judgment (Num 31:8). Jezebel was the Phoenician wife of Israel's King Ahab (1 Kings 16:31) who opposed and killed YHWH's prophets while supporting Baal's (1 Kings 18–21). The Nicolaitans are otherwise unknown, though the name means "conquerors of the people."

12. Estimates are from various sources. See, e.g., Stark, *Rise of Christianity*, 131–32.

(emphasis on right belief), which will inevitably lead to a failure of either spirituality (love of God) or of orthopraxy (right practice, especially love of neighbor). But this propagates two unbiblical ideas: (1) a division between belief/assent, on the one hand, and love, on the other; and (2) love of God as an inner attitude rather than active loyalty. The Ephesians are praised for their steadfast, publicly verifiable, non-accommodating stance, so the situation is better read as a case of *incomplete orthopraxy* requiring repentance and supplementation, rather than *inappropriate orthodoxy* requiring the rejection of allegedly rigid beliefs. The Ephesians' loyalty to and love for God is evident; in the midst of bouts with accommodating false teachers and harassing neighbors, the love they need to regain is for one another (see John 13–17).[13]

*Temple to Artemis and the Emperor in Ephesus*

2:8–11. The church in Smyrna was also located in a port city famous for its beauty and its longstanding loyalty to Rome, expressed in a thriving imperial cult. (It was also the city of the famous martyred bishop Polycarp, killed here in about 156 for his loyalty to Jesus.) It is likely that some Jews have betrayed their own identity as God's people (from John's perspective) by colluding with those possessing economic power (perhaps officials in the trade guilds, the networks of tradespeople

13. Other interpreters think the lost love is love for God, or for both God and others.

similar to modern unions, or in the temples that served also as banks) and/or Roman political officials in persecuting the Smyrnaean church. The economic impact and the potential for legal action have apparently not led any in the church to accommodate. The challenge is to remain fearless and faithful—to trust and obey.

2:12–17. The church in Pergamum lived in the shadow of the provincial capital's imposing acropolis, on which many official buildings and religious sites were located, including a tremendous altar to Zeus and a towering temple of the imperial cult. This could well have prompted the famous image of the throne of Satan (2:13). The majority of the church has remained faithful in spite of the death of a martyr (Antipas; 2:13), the only casualty actually named in the seven messages. Some, however, have returned to eating food sacrificed to idols, perhaps to avoid the fate of Antipas. The challenge for the accommodationists is to cease and repent, and for the faithful to hold fast.

*The acropolis of Pergamum, where the "throne of Satan" was. The ruins of the temple of the imperial cult are in the center, and the altar of Zeus on the right, surrounded by trees.*

*Ruins of the altar of Zeus, Pergamum*

2:18–29. Thyatira's church found itself in a city known for its many trade guilds. Although the church had made progress in its life and witness (2:19), it may have been the desire to avoid the kind of economic and social disempowerment occurring in Smyrna and nearby Philadelphia that led many, perhaps the majority (see 2:20, 24) of the church, to follow "Jezebel," whether she is a literal false prophet or a symbol for accommodation. The message to this woman and her children/followers is both the longest and the most severe of the seven, indicating the seriousness of the situation. Once again, the challenge (implicitly) for the accommodationists is to cease, and for the faithful to hold fast.

3:1–6. Sardis, like Pergamum, had an imposing, though more rugged, acropolis that was interwoven into the city's identity in a historically humiliating way. Twice Sardis had been taken by sneak attack, with forces coming over the supposedly impregnable acropolis. This could be why John is given to use the words of Jesus, "I will come like a thief" (3:3),[14] indicating that he will return even when some in the church least expect it. The majority of the church at Sardis is so comatose that it is near death, and in true apocalyptic form John urges the church to wake

14. See also Matt 24:4; Luke 12:39; 1 Thess 5:2.

up and rise from the dead. Since a minority is said to have not soiled its clothing (3:4), we should understand this state of slumber not as apathy, but as actively getting soiled through certain "works" (3:2) while clinging to a good reputation (3:1) and assuming nothing is wrong. Thus the main problem is not indifference but presumption, and the need of those at Sardis is to identify and end the inappropriate activity.

*Ruins of Sardis, with the acropolis in the background*

3:7–13. As in Smyrna, the church in Philadelphia, a city of great Greek culture but also deep devotion to Rome, found itself in conflict with some of the Jews in the city. Is it coincidental that these two churches receive no reprimand? Or is it perhaps the case that when pursued not merely by idolatrous Gentile neighbors and/or officials, but by their close siblings in monotheistic faith, these early Christians more fully understood the meaning of their commitment and the necessity of publicly maintaining it, no matter the consequences? Once again the challenge is to resist and remain faithful. Jesus' promise to "keep you from the hour of trial" (3:10, NRSV) is better translated "keep you safe in the time of trial" (NAB).[15]

15. See Aune, *Revelation 1–5*; 240; Boxall, *The Revelation*, 73; Reddish, *Revelation*, 76; Witherington, *Revelation*, 106–7. There is no hope of rapture to escape the tribulation here.

3:14–22. Christians in Laodicea lived in the wealthiest city in the area, and apparently they shared in that wealth. It was a commercial center and crossroad, and there were temples to numerous deities. Scholars have found cultural allusions in this message not only to Laodicea's wealth but also to the local production of eye salve, the use of black wool, and especially the city's lack of a good water supply. It has often been suggested that John is aware of the nearby hot springs in Hierapolis and the good cold water brought into Laodicea from outside the city. The lukewarm water may be a reference to that of the springs as they cascade over the cliff at Hierapolis, or to Laodicea's own water.

The problem with the Laodicean church is that it is neither hot nor cold but lukewarm, which is so disgusting that Jesus is about to spit or even vomit (3:15–16). Lukewarmness is not an ancient metaphor for indifference. The text, therefore, does not present a spectrum with two extremes—hot (for Jesus) and cold (against Jesus)—and a wishy-washy middle. Rather, it presents two antithetical points, the first of which is illustrated with two images, hot water and cold water. Both of these are pleasing and beneficial, while lukewarm water is precisely the opposite, disgusting to taste and not salutary. "Lukewarm" here means so prosperous and supposedly self-sufficient (3:17) as to be completely out of fellowship with Jesus. This is not a middle-of-the-road church but the most accommodating, not only participating with the status quo when necessary as a means of survival, but fully embracing the lifestyle and values of the elite and powerful.

The only solution for this church is to re-invite Jesus into its corporate life (3:20), which will necessitate a rejection of the idolatries that have impoverished, denuded, and blinded the church (3:18). The challenge is to accept a complete makeover.

### The Seven Messages Together

While each church receives a message reflecting its own situation, there is one overarching issue: whether or not to compromise. Specifically, will these churches be faithful witnesses both *to* Jesus and *like* Jesus (and John!) by refraining from participation in the cultural norm of pagan religion, including the imperial cult, even if it entails serious consequences: social, economic, and political? Will they join the Nicolaitans, Balaamites, followers of Jezebel, and Laodiceans who are participating in various forms of compromise and accommodation, which John labels idolatry, or will they abstain—"come out" (18:4)—and be willing to suffer like John, like Antipas of Pergamum (2:13), and like Jesus himself?

These assemblies of believers are participating in a struggle, even in a war—the war of the Lamb. The Lamb is there with them, as their shepherd and example, calling them to renewed devotion. They will be victorious in this war, not by wielding swords, but by following Jesus in "uncivil" worship and faithful witness. But some of them, at least, are at risk of losing the cosmic battle, and of course John wants them to win. They all need to be faithful witnesses, which *may* mean actual martyrdom for some.

These messages, and other parts of Revelation, are sometimes said to exalt martyrdom, perhaps even in a way that is irresponsible. But to say that Revelation extols martyrdom is true only if we realize that the first-century meaning of "martyr" was "witness" (Greek *martys*); only later in church history did "martyr" refer to witnesses who had died for their faith. Revelation calls its hearers, not to death as a good or an end in itself, but to faithful discipleship and witness even if that might lead to death. This difference is not a matter of semantics but of substance. The message of these seven addresses from the risen Christ is not a call to death but to discipleship, including abstention from all that defiles. This costly discipleship, as Dietrich Bonhoeffer described it,[16] is much more demanding than many Christians in the first century (or any century) realized or desired. It is the task of Revelation, in part, to convince its hearers and readers that faithful discipleship has both costs and rewards. That is why the seven messages contain both words of challenge and promises drawn from the visions of chapters 21 and 22.

## The Contemporary Message of the Messages

That Revelation 2–3 contains an outline of church history seems rather forced and quite far-fetched. But the idea that these seven churches somehow symbolize the range of possible Christian churches—particularly the range of common dangers the churches face—is much more plausible.

Pastor-theologian T. Scott Daniels, the late New Testament scholar Bruce Metzger, and spiritual theologian Eugene Peterson are among the

---

16. In his book *Discipleship* (= *The Cost of Discipleship*).

many who have correlated the seven churches (or at least five of the seven) with typical dangers facing all churches at any time.[17] Most recently, Daniels contends that each of the churches manifests, or could manifest (in the case of Smyrna and Philadelphia), a specific deadly sin because it has developed an ethos, a kind of corporate personality. Daniels believes that every church in every age has such a distinctive collective spirit.

The observations of these three interpreters are as follows:

Dangers Facing the Churches in Revelation

| Text and Church | Metzger | Peterson | Daniels |
|---|---|---|---|
| 2:1–7 Ephesus | losing the love one had at first | "abandoning their first zestful love of Christ" | boundary keeping, ungenerous orthodoxy |
| 2:8–11 Smyrna | fear of suffering | [none] | [consumerism] |
| 2:12–17 Pergamum | doctrinal compromise | indifference to heresy | accommodation, failed witness |
| 2:18–29 Thyatira | moral compromise | tolerance of immorality | privatized faith, dividing body and soul |
| 3:1–6 Sardis | spiritual deadness | apathy | apathetic faith |
| 3:7–13 Philadelphia | failure to hold fast | [none] | [fear] |
| 3:14–22 Laodicea | lukewarmness | substitution of material riches for life in the Spirit | self-sufficiency |

Even dispensationalist interpreters would basically agree with these writers in their assessment of the enduring spiritual messages to be

17. Daniels, *Seven Deadly Spirits*; Metzger, *Breaking the Code*, 46; Peterson, *Reversed Thunder*, 52. Daniels suggests that Smyrna and Philadelphia could have developed a spirit opposite from that for which they are praised.

taken from each of the seven churches apart from their correspondence to periods of church history.[18]

To these we might now add from the discussion in this chapter (apart from Smyrna and Philadelphia, which receive no criticism):

- Ephesus: incomplete orthopraxy (lack of mutual love)

- Pergamum: accommodation, especially to civil religion

- Thyatira: accommodation to avoid economic and social disempowerment

- Sardis: presumption

- Laodicea: the misguided prosperity, self-sufficiency, and idolatry of the elite and powerful status quo

Peterson contends that "[a] random selection of seven churches in any century, including our own, would turn up something very much like the seven churches" addressed in Revelation.[19] The main point of Revelation 2–3, when heard faithfully today, is to listen for the Spirit of God identifying our own church's peculiar unholy spirit and offering us the presence and grace of Christ to transform us into a more faithful people of God.

Particular messages may be especially appropriate to particular churches in their unique historical situations. A persecuted church might need to hear the message to Smyrna or Philadelphia, while a church that has accommodated to the norms of its host culture, especially to its lust for power and its civil religion, needs to hear the message to Pergamum or Laodicea. In fact, Harry Maier proposes that privileged Christians in the West need to read Revelation "as a Laodicean."[20] Somewhat ironically, Maier's view of the Western churches is not that different from that of dispensationalists, who also see the contemporary church as Laodicean. (But unlike dispensationalists, Maier would no doubt include dispensationalist churches within this description.) Reflecting on the message

18. See, for instance, Lindsey, *There's a New World Coming*, 57–58, agreeing with the spiritual interpretation offered by dispensationalist scholar John Walvoord in his book *The Revelation of Jesus Christ*.

19. Peterson, *Reversed Thunder*, 56.

20. *Apocalypse Recalled*, especially 30–39.

to Laodicea, one may also be prompted to echo the prayer in the third stanza of the hymn "God of Grace and God of Glory"[21]:

> Cure Thy children's warring madness, Bend our pride to Thy control.
> Shame our wanton selfish gladness, Rich in things and poor in soul.
> Grant us wisdom, grant us courage,
> Lest we miss Thy kingdom's goal. (*twice*)

## A Summary of the Seven Messages

Having looked at all seven prophetic texts in both their similarities and differences, we may now be in a position to summarize their combined message. Perhaps we should look at the seven messages as one message, calling the church to be the aggregate of all the explicit and implicit marks of a holy church found in these two chapters of Revelation. Pastor-theologian John Stott, for instance, finds the marks of the church to be love (Ephesus), suffering (Smyrna), truth (Pergamum), holiness (Thyatira), authenticity (Sardis), mission (Philadelphia), and wholeheartedness (Laodicea).[22]

Based on our analysis, we might say that Christ desires a church characterized by the fullness of orthodoxy and orthopraxy, faithfulness and fearlessness, devotion to Jesus but not to the state, and a preference for the poor rather than the rich. Or, perhaps more in line with Jesus' language, we could summarize the message as follows:

> Because I love you and want you to share in the new creation that is about to appear, I am calling you to hold on to your faithful public witness to me, or else to repent and renew it. As I said previously, "Beware of false prophets" and "Not everyone who says to me, 'Lord, Lord,' will enter the kingdom of heaven, but only the one who does the will of my Father in heaven" (Matt 7:15, 21). Or as I will say later, "Come out!" (Rev 18:4)—and stay out, for as I promised before I left you, "I—the risen and victorious one—am with you always, to the end of the age" (Matt 28:20).

21. Text by Harry Emerson Fosdick, 1930.
22. See Stott, *What Christ Thinks of the Church*.

## Questions for Reflection and Discussion

1.  In your view, does the dispensational approach to Revelation 2–3 have any merit? Why or why not?

2.  In your experience, what are the most prominent forms of cultural accommodation in the Christian churches today?

3.  With which of the seven churches do you, or might your Christian community, most identify? What might be the concrete message of the risen Christ to your community?

4.  Where in the world do you see contemporary manifestations of the strengths and weaknesses of these seven churches?

# 6

## The Central and Centering Vision: God and the Lamb

## (Revelation 4–5)

The prophetic messages to the churches, and to the church as a whole, are complete: seven words, each directed toward a specific context yet applicable to the Christian church as one body and to specific congregations in various times and places. The book of Revelation now undergoes a dramatic shift from the kind of text we understand fairly easily, the relatively straightforward record of pastoral-prophetic oracles, to the kind of text that may confuse, scare, or distress us. In Revelation 4 and 5 we return to the visionary texts we first encountered in Revelation 1, and we will remain with this genre until almost the very end of the book. Most contemporary readers would feel more at home with another fifteen chapters like the two we now leave behind, but that is not the way of apocalyptic.

### A Unified Vision

Chapters 4 and 5 of Revelation belong inseparably together. They are like "two panels of a visionary diptych," says one commentator,[1] referring to the two-panel paintings, tapestries, and altarpieces especially common in the Middle Ages. The subject of this two-panel painting is the heavenly throne-room of God, which John was privileged to visit in a vi-

1. Boxall, *The Revelation of Saint John*, 93.

sionary experience. It is depicted as a blend of temple and throne-room scenes from the Ancient Near East, as reflected in Isaiah 6 and Daniel 7, and from the Roman Empire, where the emperor was honored and worshiped as sovereign of the universe.

John's peek into heaven—which appears to be a "beehive of activity"[2]—is a *vision* of worship that then becomes a *call* to worship. Worship, as Eugene Peterson writes, is

> a meeting at the center so that our lives are centered in God and not lived eccentrically. We worship so that we live in response to and from this center, the living God. Failure to worship consigns us to a life of spasms and jerks, at the mercy of every advertisement, every seduction, every siren . . . . If there is no center, there is no circumference. People who do not worship are swept into a vast restlessness, epidemic in the world, with no steady direction and no sustained purpose.[3]

Of course, as Peterson implies and Bob Dylan famously sang, "you gotta serve somebody." The alternative to worship focused on the true center, the true authority for life (symbolized here in the throne), is worship focused on false centers: idols. Babylon is "the place of antiworship."[4]

The record of John's experience introduces two images that dominate the rest of the book: the throne of God and the Lamb of God. The word "throne" appears 43 times from chapter 4 until the end of the book (19 times in chapters 4 and 5 alone), and the word "Lamb" (referring to Christ) 28—7 x 4—times. Together these images constitute the hermeneutical, or interpretive, key to the entire book. They reveal in pictures the essential theology of the book of Revelation: God the creator reigns and is worthy of our complete devotion, and Jesus the faithful, slaughtered Lamb of God reigns with God, equally worthy of our complete devotion.

This combination of images creates two mind-boggling paradoxes. The first is that God shares sovereignty and honor, expressed in the receiving of worship, with the Messiah Jesus. The second is that this Jesus who is worthy of worship has exercised his messianic office and power by being slaughtered. His power is power in weakness, as Paul would put it (2 Cor 12:9). We will return to this theme later. First, however, we need

2. Aune, "The Influence of Roman Imperial Court Ceremonial," 8.

3. Peterson, *Reversed Thunder*, 60.

4. Peterson, *Reversed Thunder*, 66.

## The Structure and Theology of Revelation 4–5: Theophany, Christophany, and The Christological Reconfiguration of God

As noted above, the images of "throne" and "lamb" run throughout the book of Revelation. Many interpreters claim that one or both of these images provide the theological key to the book, one normally symbolizing sovereignty and power, the other sacrifice and vulnerability. It is, we will see, the conjunction of these two images that is the key to Revelation, and that symbiosis begins in chapters 4 and 5, printed here from the NRSV. **Boldfaced text** shows parallels between chapter 4 and chapter 5; underlined text shows parallels within one chapter. For Old Testament precedents, see Exodus 3 and 19, Ezekiel 1 and 10, Daniel 7, and Isaiah 6.

4 After this I looked, and there in heaven a door stood open! And the first voice, which I had heard speaking to me like a trumpet, said, "Come up here, and I will show you what must take place after this."

*The Majesty of God*

²At once I was in the spirit, and there in heaven stood **a throne, with one seated on the throne**! ³And the one seated there looks like jasper and carnelian, and around the throne is a rainbow that looks like an emerald. ⁴Around the throne are twenty-four thrones, and seated on the thrones are **twenty-four elders**, dressed in white robes, with golden **crowns** on their heads. ⁵Coming from the throne are flashes of lightning, and rumblings and peals of thunder, and in front of the throne burn seven flaming torches, which are the **seven spirits of God**; ⁶and in front of the throne there is something like a sea of glass, like crystal.

*The Majesty of God Christologically Reconfigured*

5 Then I saw in the right hand of **the one seated on the throne** a scroll written on the inside and on the back, sealed with seven seals; ²and I saw a mighty angel proclaiming with a loud voice, "Who is worthy to open the scroll and break its seals?" ³And <u>no one in heaven or on earth or under the earth</u> was able to open the scroll or to look into it. ⁴And I began to weep bitterly because no one was found worthy to open the scroll or to look into it.

⁵Then one of the elders said to me, "Do not weep. See, the Lion of the tribe of Judah, the Root of David, has conquered, so that he can open the scroll and its seven seals." ⁶Then I saw between the throne and the **four living creatures** and among the **elders** a Lamb standing as if it had been slaughtered, having seven horns and

seven eyes, which are the **seven spirits of God** sent out into all the earth. 7He went and took the scroll from the right hand of the one who was seated on the throne.

## The Worship of God

Around the throne, and on each side of the throne, are **four living creatures**, full of eyes in front and behind: 7the first living creature like a lion, the second living creature like an ox, the third living creature with a face like a human face, and the fourth living creature like a flying eagle. 8And the four living creatures, each of them with six wings, are full of eyes all around and inside. Day and night without ceasing they **sing**, "Holy, holy, holy, the Lord God the Almighty [cf. Isa 6:1–4], who was and is and is to come." 9And whenever the **living creatures give glory and honor and thanks to the one who is seated on the throne**, who lives forever and ever, 10**the twenty-four elders fall before the one who is seated on the throne** and worship the one who lives forever and ever; they cast their crowns before the throne, **singing**, 11**"You are worthy**, our Lord and God, **to receive glory and honor and power**, for you created all things, and by your will they existed and were created."

## The Worship of God *Christologically Reconfigured*

8When he had taken the scroll, **the four living creatures and the twenty-four elders fell before the Lamb**, each holding a harp and golden bowls full of incense, which are the prayers of the saints. 9They **sing** a new song: "**You are worthy** to take the scroll and to open its seals, for you were slaughtered and by your blood you ransomed for God saints from every tribe and language and people and nation; 10you have made them to be a **kingdom** and priests serving our God, and they will **reign** on earth." 11Then I looked, and I heard the voice of many angels surrounding the throne and the living creatures and the elders; they numbered myriads of myriads and thousands of thousands [cf. Dan 7:10], 12singing with full voice, "Worthy is the Lamb that was slaughtered **to receive power** and wealth and wisdom and might and **honor and glory** and blessing!"

## Summary: The Christological Reconfiguration of God

13Then I heard every creature in heaven and on earth and under the earth and in the sea [cf. Phil 2:9–11], and all that is in them, singing, "To the one seated on the throne and to the Lamb be blessing and honor and glory and might forever and ever!" 14And the four living creatures said, "Amen!" And the **elders fell down and worshiped.**

to look more carefully at this two-panel visionary painting. It consists of a theophany (revelation of God) and a Christophany (revelation of Christ) and, through both together, a christologically reconfigured vision of God. (See shaded box on 104–5.)

## The Theophany (Revelation 4)

Images and descriptions of throne-rooms were common in the ancient world. David Aune refers to this one as a "pastiche" of throne-room scenes from Israelite-Jewish, other Ancient Near-Eastern, Hellenistic, and Roman-imperial sources.[5] Readers of Scripture will especially hear echoes of the prophetic visions of God's throne.[6] "The throne represents the power and rule of God. By emphasizing the throne, John is pulling back the curtain and showing his reader the true locus of the world's power"[7]—and who is really "Lord and God" (4:11).

In addition, there are numerous similarities to the rituals associated with the Roman imperial court, such as the presence of attendants around the imperial throne, the offering of hymns and acclamations to the emperor, and the practice of attendants and lesser kings giving golden crowns to him. (A traveling imperial throne with attendants carried the emperor into the cities and provinces for the people's adulation.) In this vision, John encounters the God of Israel, who is perceived afresh in light of Christ and who implicitly displaces any so-called lord, god, or universal ruler.

One interpreter rightly notes that chapter 4 is also "a symphony of OT theophanies."[8] There are echoes of the stories of Moses and the burning bush (Exodus 3) and the giving of the Law to Moses at Sinai (Exodus 19–24), in addition to the visions noted above. Some of these parallel features include God being depicted on a throne (1 Kings 22:19; Isa 6:1; Ezek 1:26), having a white appearance (Dan 7:9), and being surrounded by beauty (Ezek 1:18, 26–28), as well as the presence of a sea (Ezek 1:22; Dan 7:2–3), fire/smoke/lightning (Exod 3:2–3; 19:16, 18; Isa 6:4; Ezek

---

5. Aune, "The Influence of Roman Imperial Court Ceremonial," 6.

6. In addition to the prophetic visions listed above, see also 1 Kings 22:19–33 and the nonbiblical text *1 Enoch* 14:8—16:4, 39:1—40:10, and 71:1–17.

7. Reddish, *Revelation*, 92.

8. Prévost, *How to Read the Apocalypse*, 83.

1:4, 13–14; Dan 7:9–10), angels (1 Kings 22:19; Exod 3:2; Dan 7:10), and various other living creatures (Ezek 1:5–25; 10:15–22; Dan 7:3–7).

What precisely does John experience, especially with his ears and eyes? The voice of Christ (4:1; see 1:10–11) summons him into heaven to see the future (4:1). But before he can see the future, he must see who holds the future, and who is worthy to bring about that future. John sees a throne and one seated on the throne (4:2), but relatively little is said about the identity of the one on the throne. Rather, this one is described as resembling precious stones, radiant and beautiful, and surrounded by a rainbow that is similarly precious, bright, and stunning. This is obviously "the Lord God the Almighty" (4:8), the eternal and holy one of Israel who is enthroned at the center of the cosmos, surrounded in concentric circles by seven flaming torches and by four living creatures and 24 elders. The creatures and elders together worship the one on the throne with songs of praise ("Holy, Holy, Holy"—known as the trisagion[9]) and bodily gestures of adoration.

We of course would like to identify these figures. It may be best to see the living creatures as heavenly beings, perhaps representing all of creation, and the 24 elders as the people of God, the number being taken either from the 24 priestly orders instituted by David (1 Chron 24:1–19) or, more likely, from the 12 tribes of Israel and the 12 apostles (see Rev 21:12, 14). The 24 elders wear white robes—symbolizing purity, victory, and worship—and golden crowns— symbolizing their share, by divine grace, in God's reign.

More important than the identity and appearance of the creatures and elders, however, is their activity: ceaseless praise and worship, hymning the worthy-ness of God as the eternal one (4:8) and creator (4:11). The worship of God is the heartbeat of the cosmos, even when we humans on earth do not see it, participate in it, or value it. Only God is worthy to receive what others, especially powerful political figures, may want or demand: our total devotion, our praise, our crowns.

## The Christophany (Revelation 5)

In chapter 5, the second panel of this visionary diptych of the heavenly throne-room, there is a two-step dramatic shift in focus, indicated by the words "Then I saw," first in 5:1 and then in 5:6. The first part of the

---

9. From the Greek words for "three" and "holy."

chapter focuses on a mysterious scroll, held in the right hand of God, the hand of power and authority. It contains writing on both sides of the papyrus or parchment (highly unusual in antiquity), and is sealed with seven seals. This scroll has been variously identified as the Scriptures, the Book of Life (e.g., 20:12), and a legal document, but most often as the eschatological plan of God to judge and save the world—a plan that is, rather literally, about to unfold. This last interpretation makes the most sense in light of parallels from other apocalyptic literature as well as the narrative flow of the book of Revelation, as the seals, beginning in chapter 6, are identified with divine judgment.

The problem that distresses John is that no one in all creation is worthy to open this scroll, to set in motion the eschatological judgment and salvation of God. But one of the elders says that there is in fact one who is worthy, named as "the Lion of the tribe of Judah, the Root of David," both images of messianic power and rule. This is also the one who "has conquered" (5:6).

Both John and we, as readers, await the unveiling and identification of this powerful, conquering messianic Lion; perhaps both John and we suspect that the elder is directing our attention to Jesus, Lion of Judah and Son of David—and he is. But in "perhaps the most mind-wrenching 'rebirth of images' in literature,"[10] the vision John receives and describes for us is not what anyone would expect. It is the vision of a slaughtered Lamb, not a ferocious Lion. "The shock of this reversal," writes Richard Hays, "discloses the central mystery of the Apocalypse: God overcomes the world not through a show of force but through the suffering and death of Jesus, 'the faithful witness [*martys*] (1:5).'"[11]

As a narrative whole, Revelation first builds to this astonishing image, and then everything afterwards flows from it. The image likely draws on both the Passover lamb (Exodus 12) and the suffering servant of God, who is led like a lamb to the slaughter (Isa 53:7; cf. Jer 11:19).[12] It is the central and centering image, the governing metaphor, the focal point of Revelation: a slaughtered Lamb, a crucified Lord.[13] As Richard Bauckham puts it, it is crucial that we

10. Boring, *Revelation*, 108.

11. Hays, *Moral Vision*, 174.

12. Bauckham, *Theology*, 70–76 and many commentators especially stress the Passover background.

13. The NRSV "as if it had been slaughtered" (5:6) is potentially misleading; the

recognize the contrast between what he [John] hears (5:5) and what he sees (5:6). He hears that 'the Lion of the tribe of Judah, the Root of David, had conquered'. The two messianic titles evoke a strong militaristic and nationalistic image of the Messiah of David as conqueror of the nations, destroying the enemies of God's people . . . . But this image is reinterpreted by what John sees: the Lamb whose sacrificial death (5:6) has redeemed people from all nations (5:9–10). By juxtaposing the two contrasting images, John has forged a new symbol of conquest by sacrificial death.[14]

The image of a slaughtered, (self-) sacrificial Lamb, does not, however, mean that this Lamb is powerless. In fact, the contrary is the case; the Lamb is indeed the messianic Lion who has seven eyes of perfect perception, or wisdom, and seven horns of perfect power (5:6). Like the figure in Daniel 7:13–14, he shares in the royal dominion of God. But in Revelation the nature of power is being redefined. The power of the Lamb in Revelation takes two forms: the power of his death, the symbol of which is the slaughtered lamb, and the power of his spoken word, the symbol of which is the sword of his mouth (1:16).[15]

Here in chapter 5 the focus is on the power of his death. The Lamb's power, his "conquering," has been manifested, not in the raw power associated with a lion, but in the power of faithfulness to death, a violent death that resulted in "ransoming," or redeeming, a royal and priestly people for God. The imagery of the Lamb and of "a kingdom and priests serving our God" (5:10; cf. 1:6; Exod 19:6) is reminiscent of the Passover and Exodus stories,[16] only this time the redeemed people come, not from

---

death was real, and the NAB (New American Bible) is better: "that seemed to have been slain." Beale (*Revelation*, 621) calls Revelation 12 the "center and the key to the entire book." While chapter 12 may be the physical center of the book—and certainly outlines in symbols its plot, conflict, and central characters—it does not function as the hermeneutical (interpretive) key through which everything else must be interpreted. That role is assigned to the slaughtered Lamb by virtue of its pervasive and paradoxical role in the book.

14. Bauckham, Theology, 74.

15. The two images of powerful witness in death and powerful word are combined in Rev 19:11–21, where Christ, the Word of God (10:13), comes in judgment with the sword in his mouth (his word; 19:15, 21) and blood on his clothing (his death; 19:13). These two aspects of Lamb power cohere very well with Paul's convictions that the crucified Christ is the power of God (1 Cor 1:23–24) and that the gospel is the power of God (Rom 1:16).

16. The Lamb image may also refer to the lamb sacrificed twice daily (Exod 29:38–

one nation, but "from every tribe and language and people and nation" (5:9; cf. 7:9; 21:24; 22:2).[17]

It is this one—that is, the faithful, crucified Savior who is now the resurrected, ascended ("standing"; 5:6), and victorious Lord—who is worthy to take the seal (and thus later to open it, unleashing final judgment and salvation). This he does. The amalgam of heavenly images and activities that ensues vividly expresses the early Christian conviction that the crucified Jesus has ascended to the right hand of God and is worthy of the same praise and honor due to God. That is why first the elders (and perhaps also the living creatures; 5:8–10) and then also myriads of angels (5:11–12) sing praises to the Lamb that was slaughtered, the redeemer, echoing the hymns sung to God the creator in chapter 4. Finally, every creature from every part of the cosmos (5:13) sings together to the one on the throne, and to the Lamb. The entire scenario is a vivid enactment of the poetic text in Phil 2:6–11, where the one who was obedient to death is acknowledged as Lord, worthy of the acclamation due God alone, by all who are "in heaven and on earth and under the earth" (Phil 2:10).[18]

Thus the Lamb of God is clearly Jesus, even though his name does not appear in this chapter, and as redeemer he is both worthy of the kind of praise due to God and worthy to inaugurate God's powerful eschatological judgment and salvation. Why? Because in his death he has already manifested the true meaning of power, judgment, and salvation. The work of Christ is the work of God, and vice versa, for Christ, Revelation proclaims, shares in the very identity of God. In fact, already in Revelation we have seen that Jesus shares the Father's (symbolically) white hair (indicating antiquity; 1:14), name (1:17), and dominion (1:5–6), and that he has joined his Father on the divine throne (3:21). Later in Revelation John refers to the throne as "the throne of God and of the Lamb" (22:1, 3), to the source of salvation as both God and the Lamb (7:10), and to the divine wrath as the wrath of God and the Lamb (6:16–17). In addition, God and the Lamb together constitute the New Jerusalem's temple and light (21:22–23).

---

42; Numbers 28), but the primary reference seems to be the Passover lamb.

17. This global reality of salvation is the basis for the corresponding vision of the present and future people of God in chapters 7 and 21–22.

18. Some scholars believe Phil 2:6–11 is an early Christian hymn.

Richard Bauckham rightly comments, "When the slaughtered Lamb is seen 'in the midst of' the divine throne in heaven (5:6; 7:17), the meaning is that Christ's sacrificial death *belongs to the way God rules the world*. The symbol of the Lamb is no less a divine symbol than the symbol of 'the One who sits on the throne.'"[19] It is critical that we not miss the paradoxical significance of this Lamb of God sharing in the identity and sovereignty of God. In his exaltation Jesus remains the Lamb, the crucified one. He participates in God's identity and reign, making him worthy of worship, as the slaughtered Lamb, *and only as such*. This is the consistent witness of the New Testament: that the exalted Lord remains the crucified Jesus.[20] And this one is "the true face of God."[21]

When this witness is neglected or forgotten, trouble follows swiftly. Any reading of Revelation—and any practice of theology more generally—that forgets this central New Testament truth is theologically problematic, even dangerous, from its very inception. It is doomed, not to failure, but to success—and that is its inherent defect. Human beings, even apparently faithful Christians, too often want an almighty deity who will rule the universe with power, preferably on their terms, and with force when necessary. Such a concept of God and of sovereignty induces its adherents to side with this kind of God in the execution of (allegedly) divine might in the quest for (allegedly) divine justice. Understanding the reality of the Lamb as Lord—and thus of Lamb power—terminates, or should terminate, all such misperceptions of divine power and justice, and of their erroneous human corollaries. Of course, both historically and today, the misperceptions persist.

Revelation is often misread as a demonstration of precisely this kind of coercive divine power in human history, especially in interpreting the visions of judgment. We will need to return to this issue in a later chapter. For now, however, we must stress that only when chapters 4 and 5 are read as Revelation's hermeneutical key to reality, divinity, history, and ethics will we be able to place the visions of judgment in proper perspective.

On the subject of ethics, or the practices of daily life (to which we will also return in more detail), one brief point must now be made. We

19. Bauckham, *Theology*, 64. "In the midst of" is a better translation than the NRSV "between."

20. See, e.g., John 20:26–29; Gal 2:19–20.

21. Prévost, *How to Read the Apocalypse*, 83.

have just seen that Lamb Christology in Revelation is inseparable from theology proper (the doctrine of God) and soteriology (the doctrine of salvation). It is also true that Lamb Christology is inseparable from ethics. Paradoxically, the slaughtered Lamb reveals God and also reveals what it means to be faithful to God. It reveals how God saves humanity and how humanity in turn can serve God. Here John the seer again echoes Paul, for whom the cross symbolizes both the divine means of salvation and the human expression of that salvation in daily life. As for Paul, so also for Revelation: the cross—meaning the faithful death of the slaughtered Lamb—is both the *source* and the *shape* of our salvation.[22]

## Worship of God and the Lamb

Not surprisingly, some of the best interpretations of Revelation 4 and 5 take the form of sacred music, since these chapters are full of hymn texts. Some of these musical interpretations draw on other images and visions from Revelation as well.

Few hymns evoke the spirit of worship as powerfully as Reginald Heber's 1826 hymn for Trinity Sunday, "Holy, Holy, Holy":

> Holy, holy, holy! All the saints adore Thee,
> Casting down their golden crowns around the glassy sea;
> Cherubim and seraphim falling down before Thee,
> Which wert, and art, and evermore shalt be.

Also inspired by Revelation 4 is the 18th-century German Catholic hymn "Holy God, We Praise Your Name." It names "angel choirs" of "cherubim and seraphim" as well as "saints on earth," "the apostolic train," "prophets," and "white-robed martyrs" (see 7:9–17), who "in unceasing chorus praising, fill the heavens with sweet accord: 'Holy, holy, holy Lord!'"

Many pieces of sacred music have been inspired by the images of Jesus as the worshiped Lamb. Perhaps the best-known of these is the penultimate chorus of Handel's "Messiah" (noted in chapter 1), which is drawn from Rev 5:9, 12–13 and is followed by just one last chorus, "Amen," taken from the response of the four living creatures in Rev 5:14:

> Worthy is the Lamb that was slain, and hath redeemed us to
> God by his blood, to receive power, and riches, and wisdom, and

22. See my *Reading Paul*, 78–90.

strength, and honor, and glory, and blessing. Blessing and honor, glory and power, be unto Him that sitteth upon the throne, and unto the Lamb, for ever and ever.

Amen.

The well-known 18th-century hymn "All Hail the Power of Jesus' Name" (Edward Perronet, 1779) explicitly invites us to join the prostrate angels and "yonder sacred throng" of Revelation 5 (as well as chapters 7, 14, etc.) to "hail Him [Jesus] who saves you by His grace" and "crown Him Lord of all." The triumphant 19th-century hymn "Crown Him with Many Crowns" (Matthew Bridges, 1852) combines images from chapters 5, 7, and 19 (see especially 19:12), inviting us to add our voices to the heavenly chorus:

> Crown him with many crowns, the Lamb upon his throne.
> Hark, how the heavenly anthem drowns all music but its own!
> Awake, my soul, and sing of Him who died for thee.
> And hail Him as thy matchless King through all eternity.

The jubilant 20th-century Lutheran hymn "This is the Feast" by John Arthur draws directly from chapter 5, with hints from passages elsewhere, to issue the same invitation:

> Worthy is Christ, the Lamb who was slain, whose blood set us free to be people of God / . . . Sing with all the people of God and join in the hymn of all creation / Blessing and honor and glory and might be to God and the Lamb forever / Amen / This is the feast of victory for our God, for the Lamb who was slain has begun his reign / Alleluia.

Both Handel's famous chorus and these hymns remind us that the worship of God and the Lamb is grounded in the great act of redemption, which Rev 1:5 appropriately connects to the great love that the Lamb had and has for those he died to redeem. The beautiful American folk hymn "What Wondrous Love," probably written by 19th-century Methodist minister Alexander Means, celebrates this love and calls us to join the great chorus of praise to God and the Lamb:

> What wondrous love is this, O my soul, O my soul!
> What wondrous love is this, O my soul!
> What wondrous love is this
> That caused the Lord of bliss

To bear the dreadful curse for my soul, for my soul,
To bear the dreadful curse for my soul!

To God and to the Lamb, I will sing, I will sing,
To God and to the Lamb, I will sing.
To God and to the Lamb who is the great I AM,
While millions join the theme, I will sing, I will sing,
While millions join the theme, I will sing.

More recently, Chris Tomlin has captured a similar sentiment in his song "We Fall Down":

We fall down, We lay our crowns
At the feet of Jesus
The greatness of Your Mercy and love
At the feet of Jesus
And we cry holy, holy, holy (*three times*)
Is the lamb.

It would be difficult to find a more appropriate conclusion for, or response to, the central and centering vision of Revelation than these songs of Christian worship.

## Summary

What do we mean when we say that Revelation is revelation? With special reference to chapters 4–5, it means:

1. Revelation provides us with a complete deconstruction and reconstruction of our symbolic and narrative universe, our understanding of God, our understanding of power, our understanding of victory. Why? Not Caesar, but the slaughtered Lamb, is Lord of all!

2. The Lamb shares in the divine identity and reign.[23] In fact, the vision of the slaughtered Lamb is now the definitive divine self-revelation of God's being and rule. As with Paul's statement about the crucified

---

23. The Christology of Revelation "can be appropriately described as *total participation of Jesus in God's rulership*: the deity of Jesus Christ and the primacy of the Father are both equally valid statements of the divine reality, without the distinction in persons being dissolved" (Schnelle, *Theology of the New Testament*, 756).

Christ as the power and wisdom of God (1 Cor 1:18–25), so also for Revelation: the slaughtered Lamb is the revelation of God's power and wisdom (horns and eyes).

3. The slaughtered Lamb is now not only our central and centering vision, but also the interpretive lens through which we read the remainder of the book. Divine judgment and salvation must be understood in light of—indeed defined by—the reality of the slaughtered Lamb who is worthy of divine worship.

It is these truths—together with the endless liturgy of praise that is always the background music of the book of Revelation—that we must keep in mind as we proceed to read the rest of Revelation.

## Questions for Reflection and Discussion

1. In what ways does Christ as the Lamb of God "reconfigure" the identity of God?

2. In what ways are Christ and/or God associated with secular power in our culture?

3. How might seeing the vision in chapters 4 and 5 as the interpretive key to Revelation affect our reading and actualization (embodiment) of it?

4. How might the liturgical and musical character of the vision in chapters 4 and 5 shape us theologically, spiritually, and pastorally, as well as liturgically?

# 7

## Conflict and Characters: The Drama of Revelation

In chapter 3 we noted the dramatic character of Revelation. In the opening of the book, in the visions of chapters 1, 4, and 5, and in the seven pastoral-prophetic messages, we have met the protagonists of this drama: God on the heavenly throne; the faithful, slaughtered Lamb; and the prophetic Spirit. We have also been introduced to those who are linked to this holy Trinity, both those in heaven (twenty-four elders and thousands more) and those on earth (members of the seven churches). Finally, we have been introduced, in cursory form, to the antagonists in the story: Satan, who has his own (non-heavenly) throne, and those who represent him or side with him in opposition to God and the people of God. These opposing forces are engaged in a cosmic, apocalyptic conflict—right in the midst of places like Ephesus and Pergamum, not to mention New York or Nairobi. Because of this, some have even called Revelation a war scroll.

We know the end of the story: God wins. This war scroll is more like a hymn of victory.[1] There will be judgment on evil and on evildoers, and salvation for God's faithful people. But before we examine in detail the book's visions of judgment (chapter 8) and final victory and salvation (chapter 9), we must pause to consider more fully the nature of the conflict itself and especially the characters involved in the conflict. We will proceed more topically than chapter by chapter.

---

1. Prévost, *How to Read the Apocalypse*, 23.

## The Plot of Revelation

We may think of Revelation as a plot that unfolds as follows:

### *The Prologue: The Cosmic Stage is Set*

God created humankind to live in a state of worship of God, communion with others, and harmony with creation. We might call this the culture of life, the reign of God, or even the city of God. God gave the people of Israel faithful prophets to remind them of this purpose. God also sent Jesus as the Messiah. Though pursued by Satan (ch. 12), Jesus was faithful even to death, which God vindicated in his resurrection and ascension, making him equally worthy of worship and allegiance (ch. 5). The good news of Jesus' liberating and loving death, and of his resurrection and ascension to the position of Lord, has been preached throughout the world. Many have received that message in the cities of the Roman province of Asia, forming small communities of faithful allegiance to God and the Lamb, inspired by the prophetic Spirit. But Satan, having been cast down from heaven, remains opposed to God and God's purpose, and has continued to pursue God's people (ch. 12). He has seduced key human beings to be complicit in creating an anti-culture of idolatry, evil, and chaos, a culture of death—"Babylon." One or more of God's faithful have been killed, and at least one, John, has been exiled for his faithful witness.

### *Act One: Satan is on the Move*

Satan is directing the powerful, idolatrous culture of death, which has seduced both nations and individuals, including some in the churches of Asia. In his employ are two key figures, the beast from the land and the beast from the sea (ch. 13). The former claims godlike power and prerogatives over all the earth, while the latter urges people to worship it. This unholy trinity constantly pursues the faithful people of God, seeking to win their allegiance and worship. The faithful are being seduced, and some are caving in.

## *Act Two: The Prophet Speaks*

In the midst of increasing pressure and the threat of an imminent out-
break of serious persecution, John calls the churches back to faithfulness to God (chs. 1–3). He reminds them that God has already acted
for their salvation in the prophetic ministry and faithful death of Jesus
the Lamb. Jesus' death was an act of faithful obedience to God and of
love for oppressed humanity. Together with his resurrection/ascension,
it was also a divine act of cosmic warfare, the decisive victory over the
unholy triumvirate and its power of oppression and death. John reminds
the churches that all who believe this good news, faithfully worshiping
God and the Lamb in liturgy and life, are liberated from their sins and
from both the power and the fate of Babylon.

Despite the seductive power of Babylon, the churches who heed
the voice of the prophetic Spirit bear faithful witness to God and the
Lamb, becoming a partial and proleptic (anticipatory) embodiment of
the coming city of God.

## *Act Three: God Judges*

The powerful, idolatrous culture of death, Babylon, is under divine
judgment and doomed to fall (chs. 17–18). God and the Lamb begin
that judgment now (much of chs. 6–20), resulting in the swift and certain demise of the unholy trinity. This is the longest act in Revelation,
consisting of multiple scenes and comprising the bulk of the narrative,
but it can be summarized in just a few words: "Fallen, fallen is Babylon
the great" (18:2).[2] Not only does God defeat the unholy trinity, but God
defeats death itself (20:14), the ultimate instrument of idolatrous power
and the ultimate enemy of the human race.

## *Act Four: God Renews*

Babylon, the city of oppression and death, is replaced by the new
Jerusalem, the new heaven and earth, the new culture of wholeness and
life (chs. 21–22). It is a place where pain and sorrow are absent, a time
when oppression and death are gone. The healing of the nations begins,
and humanity is restored to God's original intentions for worship, com-

2. Cf. Isa 21:9; Jeremiah 51.

munion, and harmony. God and the Lamb come to dwell permanently with a renewed humanity.

Having looked briefly at these four acts, plus their prologue, we turn now to the chief characters in the drama. Since the previous chapter examined the characters of God and the Lamb (the chief protagonists) in some depth, we will begin with God but spend more time on Satan, the beasts (the antagonists), and those caught in the middle of the cosmic battle.

## God, the Lamb, and the Spirit

Richard Bauckham has made a brief but compelling case that the portrait of God in Revelation is Trinitarian, beginning with its unique Trinitarian salutation:[3]

> Grace to you and peace from him who is and who was and who is to come, and from the seven spirits who are before his throne, and from Jesus Christ, the faithful witness . . . (Rev 1:4b–5)

We will briefly consider each of these three as characters in the drama of Revelation.

### The Alpha and Omega, the One on the Throne

God the Father, the almighty creator, is a quite fully developed character in Revelation.[4] The many characterizations include the two we have already explored—God as the Alpha and Omega and as the One who sits on the throne—plus God as the holy and righteous judge of all peoples, the coming one, and the re-creator. Each aspect plays a significant role in the drama.

As Alpha and Omega, first and last, beginning and end (1:8; 21:6), God is not only the eternal one—and the only true God (see Isa 44:6)—but also the coming one: "who is and who was and who is to come" (1:4; cf. 4:8). The prophetic "day of the Lord" is imminent. This God is at work, ready to bring both judgment and salvation. The God of Revelation is

3. Bauckham, *Theology*, 23–25. Bauckham then structures most of his book around the three persons of the Trinity.

4. See Bauckham, *Theology*, 23–53.

also the sovereign one, expressed especially in the all-pervasive theme of the throne (beginning at 1:4 and ending at 22:3) and the ascription "Almighty" (used a total of nine times). The image of the throne is an implicit challenge to any and all imperial thrones with occupants who may think they govern the world and deserve worship or other forms of ultimate allegiance.

As judge, God justly (16:7) puts into action the divine holiness and justice that cannot ultimately tolerate the evil and injustice that cover the earth, nor the idolatry from which they spring. At the same time, however, God the judge in Revelation acts—even in judgment—in a way that does not disallow repentance, though humans repeatedly refuse that mercy (9:20–21; 16:9, 11). Moreover, God's judgment is an expression of faithfulness to the creation, the final act needed before the renewal of creation. God as re-creator of creation is intimately linked to the divine roles of sovereign and judge, but also to the divine traits of faithfulness and mercy. It is the same one who sits on the throne and who ultimately defeats evil who will come in judgment and salvation, saying, "I am making all things new" (21:5).

David deSilva carefully demonstrates that the God of Revelation stands in continuity with the God of Israel's Scriptures. This is the God who indicts domination systems, delivers his people (as in the exodus), vindicates the faithful, rules the cosmos, promises final shalom, and exhibits extraordinary patience with rebellious humanity—though not forever. This God alone is worthy of worship and ultimate allegiance.[5]

All of this theology proper (doctrine of God), however, must be understood in connection to and in light of Christ the Lamb, as we saw in the previous chapter. The God of Revelation is not a violent and capricious deity on the warpath, but the Holy One of Israel who has, above all, brought salvation in Christ.[6]

### Christ The Lamb, the Faithful Witness

There is also a full Christology in Revelation.[7] The array of Christ's titles alone is impressive: faithful (and true) witness, firstborn of the dead, rul-

---

5. deSilva, *Seeing Things John's Way*, 158–74.

6. The nonviolence of the apparently violent God in Revelation is discussed in the next chapter.

7. See Witherington, *Revelation*, 27–32 and especially Bauckham, *Theology*, 54–108.

er of the kings of the earth, Son of Man, first and last, Alpha and Omega, living one, Son of God, holy one, true one, Amen, Lion of the tribe of Judah, Root of David, Lamb, Lord, Word of God, King of kings and Lord of lords, bright morning star. In this treatment of Revelation's theology, Richard Bauckham nicely summarizes Revelation's Christology. Regarding Christ's person ("The Lamb on the throne"), Bauckham treats Christ as the First and the Last, the worship of Jesus, and Jesus' divine identity. Regarding Christ's work ("The victory of the Lamb and his followers"), he treats the titles of Christ; the work of Christ as messianic warfare, eschatological exodus, and witness; the death of Christ as the Lamb of God; believers' sharing in Christ's victory; unsealing the scroll; defeating the beast; the conversion of the nations; the Parousia; and related topics.

Of several important images of Jesus in Revelation, we should especially note the two that are most prominent early in Revelation: Lamb and faithful witness. The image of the slaughtered Lamb centers our attention on Christ's death. It is a sacrifice, but it is also much more. The Lamb imagery highlights Christ's vulnerability in faithful witness.[8] Those liberated by the death of the Faithful Witness (1:5) are shaped into his image as faithful witnesses as well.

No less important than these images, however, is the fact that Jesus is so fully identified with the One on the throne, as we noted in the previous chapter. He too is the Alpha and Omega (1:17; 22:13), he also is worthy of worship (chapter 4), he too is the coming one (1:7; 22:12, 20), and more. "What Christ does, God does"[9] and vice versa. But also—and this is critical— *how* Christ does is how God does. We see in the slaughtered Lamb of God both *that* God is ultimately victorious over sin and death and *how* God is victorious over sin and death. The divine status of Christ does not make him aloof from the churches, however. He is present among them in their trials (1:13), and the Lamb is destined, ironically, to be his people's shepherd (7:17), a pastoral role he exercises even now.

As we move into the rest of Revelation, the image of Christ as divine warrior will emerge. This image must not, however, be allowed to stand on its own, separated from Christ the Lamb and Faithful Witness. "His [John's] Messiah Jesus does not win his victory by military conquest. . . .

8. Johns, *Lamb Christology*, 204.

9. Bauckham, *Theology*, 63.

But still it is a victory over evil, won not only in the spiritual but also in the political sphere . . ."[10]

## The Prophetic-Missional Spirit

The Spirit is less developed than God and the Lamb in Revelation, but the Spirit's role is nonetheless crucial. The Spirit functions primarily as the prophetic voice of God and the Lamb, speaking to the churches, but also bringing them into the presence of God for worship and enlarging their vision, forming them into faithful witnesses to the Faithful Witness (Jesus), and comforting them in times of tribulation and grief. John may be *on* Patmos, but he is *in* the Spirit (1:10; 4:2; 17:3; 21:10).

The nomenclature for the Spirit in Revelation is unusual but appropriate: "the seven spirits of God" (1:4; 3:1; 4:5; 5:6), the fullness of God's Spirit. As such, the Spirit is closely connected to both God and the Lamb. The seven spirits are before God's throne (1:4; 4:5), signifying their relationship to God. When Jesus speaks to the churches, at the end of each address he instructs them to "listen to what the Spirit is saying to the churches" (2:7, 11, 17, 29; 3:6, 13, 22). The voice of the Spirit, that is, is the voice of Jesus. The Spirit prophetically calls the churches to play their appropriate role in the unfolding drama: to abandon idolatry and be faithful to God, especially during tribulation. Together the Spirit and the Bride (Jesus) call people to experience the life that only God gives (22:17); thus the Spirit is not only prophetic, but also missional, sent out into the world (5:6).

The prophetic-missional Spirit calls the church to bear witness in the world (19:10). This suggests that the Spirit's association with worship and visions (1:10; 4:2; 17:3; 21:10) means that the Spirit equips the church for faithful witness in the world by keeping the church centered in worship and guided by visions of God (4:2), evil (17:3), and the eschatological promise (21:10)—all of which are necessary for faithful witness. Finally, acting as the Comforter, the Spirit reassures the church that faithful witness will result in ultimate rest and reward, not defeat (14:13).[11]

10. Bauckham, *Theology*, 68.

11. On the Spirit in Revelation, see also Bauckham, *Theology*, 109–25.

## Evil Personified: The Unholy Trinity and the Harlot

The cosmic, apocalyptic drama portrayed in Revelation has as its pro-
tagonist the triune God and as its antagonist a somewhat parallel unholy trinity of Satan and two beasts, a parody of God-Christ-Spirit.[12]
These characters are developed in some detail in Revelation 12 and 13.
Chapter 12 presents the central conflict narrative in *cosmic* perspective,
chapter 13 in *political* perspective. Chapter 13 "reveals Rome's political-
economic-religious system to represent the devil's rule, to be antithetical
to God's purposes, and to be an enslaving system,"[13] one that deceptively
demands inappropriate allegiance. In chapters 17–18 the system is further depicted as a harlot, or whore, doomed for destruction. It is crucial,
however, that we not limit these figures either to past figures and realities
or to future figures allegedly prophesied by Revelation. The beasts and
Babylon can be, and have been, present in multiple times, places, and
modes.

### One Dragon, Two Beasts

The dragon and his two minions are two of the most vivid characters
in the apocalyptic drama. The dragon is explicitly identified as "that
ancient serpent, who is called the Devil and Satan, the deceiver of the
whole world" (12:9). He is red, symbolizing his dealing in death, and has
seven heads with diadems and ten horns, symbols of power (12:3). He
is not only the deceiver but also the ultimate persecutor of God's people,
including the Messiah (12:3–4, 13–17), though his persecution can also
be executed by humans who think they are doing God's will (2:9; 3:9).
Satan is the source of the deified, idol-ized human political power depicted in chapter 13; this has already been vividly foreshadowed in the
description of Pergamum as the site of Satan's throne (2:13).

The beast from the sea is a kind of incarnation of this Satanic power
of persecution, deception, and idolatry, also having seven heads and ten
horns (13:1), which are later identified as hills, rulers, and client kings

---

12. The parallels are rather stunning. In each trinity, the first member (God the
Father; Satan) is the source of the power and rule of the second (the Lamb/Son; the
beast from the sea); both the first and the second are worshiped; both the first and the
second resemble figures in Daniel 7; and the third (the Spirit; the beast from the land)
promotes and speaks for the second.

13. Carter, *Roman Empire*, 18.

(17:9, 12).[14] It makes blasphemous public claims ("names" and "words," like lord, god, son of God, savior, etc.) about its royal power (13:1, 5; cf. 17:3), but the actual source of its power is the dragon (13:2, 4). In response to the beast's resurrection-like recovery from a mortal wound (probably an allusion to stories about the return of Nero), people worshipped both it and the dragon (13:3–4)—an obvious parody of the resurrection of Jesus and the resulting worship of God and the Lamb. Though the beast's reign is short (13:5), it commands international worship and engages in persecution of the church (13:7–9), as one would expect of the offspring of Satan. Its special number is 666 (see discussion below), and it has been called the "antichrist," though the term itself, as we have noted, is absent from Revelation.

The second beast, from the land, functions primarily to promote the worship of the first beast (13:12). It operates with borrowed power and by means of deception. Its lamb-like appearance is a mask for Satanic speech (13:11), and its public display of signs is really smoke and mirrors to deceive people into worshiping the first beast (13:13–15). It requires elites and non-elites alike to receive the mark of the beast to participate in the economy (13:16–17).

Most interpreters of Revelation would identify the first beast, from the sea (that is, coming from the west by way of the Aegean Sea to reach the cities of western Asia Minor), as the Roman Empire, the emperor (perhaps one specifically, such as Domitian), or imperial power. The second beast, from the earth (that is, of local origin), is then seen as those who promote the imperial cult, perhaps local government and/or religious officials in and around cities like Ephesus and Pergamum. The mark of the beast might be an imperial slogan, seal, or image.

The history of the interpretation of the antichrist is long and fascinating.[15] Cosmic and historical figures from Jewish literature were taken up in various ways by the writers of the New Testament. Persecution and/or deception are the two functions of the various antichrist figures, and these themes continue into church history as various religious and political figures are seen either as analogous to, or the fulfillment of, the incarnation of evil depicted in Revelation and elsewhere. Various

---

14. The dragon and the beasts resemble various mythological creatures. "The primeval chaos monster has reared its ugly head again, this time in Roman dress" (Reddish, *Revelation*, 230).

15. See McGinn, *Antichrist*.

popes—even well before Luther's famous Protestant denunciations of the papacy—and political figures have been seen as the antichrist: such world figures as Napoleon, Hitler, Stalin, Mussolini, Khrushchev and Saddam Hussein, but also John F. Kennedy and Pope John Paul II, who both suffered wounds to the head. Much Protestant discussion of the antichrist has tended towards anti-Catholicism, and many of the alleged identifications are ludicrous proposals emerging from a misguided interpretive process.

The identifications from the first century, however, make perfect sense within the context of Revelation. But these historical symbols also need to be plumbed for their ongoing significance. Together they speak of theopolitical megalomania and of any collaboration of political power and religious sanction—civil religion—that falsely claims to represent the true God and God's will. As Eugene Boring writes:

> [T]he beast is not merely "Rome" . . . It is the inhuman, anti-human arrogance of empire which has come to expression in Rome—but not only there . . . All who support the cultural religion, in or out of church, however Lamb-like they may appear, are agents of the beast. All propaganda that entices humanity to idolize human empire is an expression of this beastly power that wants to appear Lamb-like.[16]

The role of deception in such theopolitics is particularly important, and its ability to impact the masses is perhaps most famously chronicled in the films of Hitler speaking to myriads of average citizens in Nazi Germany (a kind of anti-image of Revelation 7). A recent U.S. Holocaust Museum exhibit on Nazi propaganda was appropriately called "State of Deception." But the example of Nazi Germany may strike many as an abnormal extreme. Eugene Peterson notes, however, how "normal" the politics of Revelation 12–13 is. He rightly claims that God's politics is the antithesis of the normal politics on display in these chapters, where politics is seen to be about the "exercise of power, either through the manipulation of force (militarism) or the manipulation of words (propaganda)."[17] These kinds of power are not limited to the easy targets of criticism such as totalitarian regimes.

The function of propaganda is to make evil look good, the demonic divine, violence like peacemaking, tyranny and oppression like

16. Boring, *Revelation*, 156–57.

17. Peterson, *Reversed Thunder*, 118. See also p. 123

liberation. It makes blind, unquestioning allegiance appear to be freely chosen, religiously appropriate devotion. The grand lie does not appear to start as deception, but only as rhetorical exaggeration. The exaggeration deepens, lengthens, and broadens in an almost organic act of self-distortion. Eventually the rhetoric becomes a blatant falsehood, but now people have not only come to believe the lie, they also live the lie; over time they have been narrated into it. At that point, the exaggeration-turned-falsehood becomes uncontested *and uncontestable* truth, and its effects highly dangerous. Evil in the name of good and of God is now nearly inevitable, as the lie functions as an apocalypse, a religious revelation that only a true Apocalypse can unveil.

### 666 in Revelation 13

The first beast is famously identified as a person whose number is 666 (13:18), one of the most well-known symbolic and even superstitious numbers of all time. While I was writing this book, my wife and I had to buy a new car. After consulting with his manager, our salesperson brought back a written price that ended with 666, but it had been scratched out and rewritten as 665. "My manager does not like that number," the salesman explained. He is not alone. I recently heard a similar comment at the grocery store when my bill was $6.66. As a teenager, I had an aversion to phoning a friend who had the prefix 666; recently, residents of a town in Louisiana were given the option of changing telephone prefixes from 666 to 749. There is even a technical term for the fear of the number: hexakosioihexekontahexaphobia.

Symbolically, 666 is probably to be understood as a parody of perfection, which would be 777. The person who bears the number pretends in vain to be divine, embodying instead "utter imperfection."[18] But the number should also be interpreted as an example of gematria, the ancient practice of assigning significance to the mathematical sum of the letters in a word in systems where letters are used to represent numerals, whether Hebrew, Greek, or Latin. More on this momentarily.

Candidates for being the fulfillment of 666 and thus being the antichrist have been numerous over the centuries. Modern adaptations of the principles of gematria have led people to propose Adolf Hitler (if a = 100, b = 101, c = 102, etc., Hitler = 666); Henry Kissinger (whose name

18. Richard, *Apocalypse*, 112–13.

in Hebrew allegedly has a value of 111 [x 6 = 666]); former President Ronald Wilson Reagan (six letters in each name[19]); Bill Clinton (whose name could supposedly add up to 666 in Hebrew and Greek); and Barack Obama. Other associations with 666 have also been seen as evidence of the antichrist: John F. Kennedy receiving 666 votes at the 1956 Democratic Convention (and later being wounded in the head; see Rev 13:3); Ronald and Nancy Reagan moving into a house with the number 666; and so on.

Many, perhaps the majority of scholars today, believe that 666 is a reference to the emperor Nero, for the following reasons[20]:

1. The Greek for Nero Caesar, *nerōn kaisar*, transliterates into Hebrew as NRWN QSR (reading right to left) and, using Hebrew gematria, with the conventional number values as shown below, adds up to 666:

| SUM | Resh (ר) | Samech (ס) | Qof (ק) | Nun (נ/ן) | Waw (ו) | Resh (ר) | Nun (נ/ן) |
|-----|----------|------------|---------|-----------|---------|----------|-----------|
|     | R | S | Q | N | W | R | N |
| 666 | 200 | 60 | 100 | 50 | 6 | 200 | 50 |

2. The same two words can also be transliterated without the final "n" in *nerōn* into Hebrew as NRW QSR:

| SUM | Resh (ר) | Samech (ס) | Qof (ק) | Waw (ו) | Resh (ר) | Nun (נ/ן) |
|-----|----------|------------|---------|---------|----------|-----------|
|     | R | S | Q | W | R | N |
| 616 | 200 | 60 | 100 | 6 | 200 | 50 |

This gives the sum of 616, which is the number that actually appears in some manuscripts of Revelation.[21] Richard Bauckham and others believe that the existence of these two manuscript variants, each of which "matches" the values for Nero, conclusively demonstrates that Nero was intended.[22]

19. Or 616 if one uses "W" instead of Wilson. (See the discussion of 616 below.)

20. The format and some of the content of these small tables is adapted from Prévost, *How to Read the Apocalypse*, 38–39.

21. For one example, see Oxyrnchus Papyrus LVI 4499 (late 3d/early 4th c.): http://www.csad.ox.ac.uk/POxy/beast616.htm.

22. See Bauckham, *Climax*, 384–452.

3. Gematria with Hebrew and Greek can also, however, yield other emperors' names. For example, 616 may represent Caligula (with Greek transliterated into Hebrew) or Gaius, Caligula's given name (with Greek alone). And 666 may represent Domitian. In the middle of the last century, German scholar Ethelbert Stauffer took Domitian's abbreviated titles on coins and inscriptions, *Imperator Caesar Domitianus Augustus Germanicus* in Latin, or *Autokrator Kaisar Dometianos Sebastos Germanikos* in Greek, abbreviated *A KAI ΔΟΜΕΤ ΣΕΒ ΓΕ* (A KAI DOMET SEB GE), and derived 666 from this common abbreviation:

| A | K | A | I | Δ | O | M | E | T | Σ | E | B | Γ | E | SUM |
|---|---|---|---|---|---|---|---|---|---|---|---|---|---|-----|
| A | K | A | I | D | O | M | E | T | S | E | B | G | E | |
| 1 | 20 | 1 | 10 | 4 | 70 | 40 | 5 | 300 | 200 | 5 | 2 | 3 | 5 | 666 |

All of these calculations point to the likelihood that 666 indicates, at the literal level, an imperial figure who in a very ungodly way pretends to be God. Like other forms of symbolism in Revelation, this identification does not end the discussion of the meaning of 666. Although we should not be looking for a specific individual who is the "prophesied" antichrist and is somehow associated with the number 666, we should always be ready to identify and disassociate from political powers that claim divine or quasi-divine status, or even "simply" divine blessing, and demand total, or even "simply" unquestioning, allegiance. At times this disassociation may become costly—very costly; disassociation may need to become disobedience. The symbolic significance of the second beast, however, is that because of the seductive power of pro-beast propaganda, identifying and then avoiding or disobeying such idolatrous powerful claims is extraordinarily difficult. Only prayer and fasting, as Jesus once said, can cast this demon out.

### Revelation 17–18: Babylon the Harlot

The "great whore" (17:1 NRSV) or harlot of chapter 17 is called Babylon (17:5), a Jezebel-like figure and a parody of the feminine images of *Roma Aeterna* and *Dea Roma* (Eternal Rome and Goddess Rome). She is "seated" on many waters (peoples; 17:15) and on the blasphemous beast with seven heads (17:2–3). These heads are identified (17:9–10) as both seven mountains (as in Rome's seven hills) and seven kings (the fullness of emperors). Clad in luxury, the whore has fornicated with the inhabitants of the earth and become drunk with the blood of the saints (17:2–6), and as the all-powerful city who rules all others (17:18), she has ten client kings in her grip who will make war on the Lamb but also eventually turn on her (17:12–17).

*"The Whore of Babylon," by Albrecht Dürer, ca. 1496–98*

Babylon, the great whore, the seductive and self-glorifying city, is the antithesis of the people/the city of God: the woman in chapter 12, the Lamb's bride of chapters 19–22, the new Jerusalem of chapters 21–22. And the harlot remains with us. It does not take a political activist or liberation theologian to recognize the ongoing power of "Babylon." New Testament scholar Bruce Metzger, writing in 1993, said the following:

> Babylon is allegorical of the idolatry that any nation commits when it elevates material abundance, military prowess, technological sophistication, imperial grandeur, racial pride, and any other glorification of the creature over the Creator . . . . The message of the book of Revelation concerns . . . God's judgments not only of persons, but also of nations and, in fact, of all principalities and powers—which is to say, all authorities, corporations, institutions, structures, bureaucracies, and the like.[23]

Even, Metzger adds, the Christian churches.

## The Church/the People of God

We have already seen, by looking at Revelation 2–3, that the church in Revelation is an imperfect entity, and that both churches and individual Christians live somewhere on a spectrum ranging from faithfulness to faithlessness. In spite of this existential reality, John insists that the church is a people that has been liberated and forgiven by the blood (death) of the Lamb (1:5; 5:9); that it produces faithful and "victorious" servants who have affirmed their identification with the Lamb's blood by shedding their own blood (6:10; 7:14); and that it is destined for ultimate victory and glory, symbolized especially by white robes (3:4–5; 4:4; 6:11; 7:9, 13–14; 19:14; 22:14). Like Jesus himself, the church is symbolized by the colors red and white, slaughtered yet victorious.

Revelation contains several visions that tell us still more about the author's understanding of the church, part of the people of God, within the cosmic drama. It should be noted at the outset that although John does not use the phrase "the people of God," he seems to work with an understanding of such an entity. This people is most vividly represented by the woman of chapter 12, who is described as "clothed with the sun, with the moon under her feet, and on her head a crown of twelve stars" and "about to bear a child" (12:1–4). The dragon (identified as the devil/

23. Metzger, *Breaking the Code*, 88.

Satan/the serpent) wishes to devour the child, a son "who is to rule all the nations with a rod of iron" (12:5; cf. Psalm 2), but the child is taken to God's throne. The woman flees into the wilderness, where she is protected and nourished by God, but also pursued by the serpent, who now wishes "to make war on the rest of her children," identified as "those who keep the commandments of God and hold the testimony of Jesus" (12:17; cf. "our comrades," or brothers; 12:10).

This vision suggests that the woman is not primarily an individual (such as Mary, the mother of Jesus) but a symbol of the entire people of God, from whom come first the Messiah Jesus and then other children. What they have in common as God's people is that they are targets in the cosmic attack of Satan. The persecuted but faithful Christians of John's day are part of a greater body of faithful witnesses that comprise the people of God throughout time. This body would include the twelve patriarchs of Israel (plus, implicitly, all the faithful of Israel) and the apostles (plus, implicitly, all the faithful Christians before John's time), for these seem together to constitute the 24 elders who worship God (e.g., 4:4, 10) and whose names adorn the gates of the New Jerusalem (21:12–14). It includes other faithful "saints and prophets" whose blood was shed (16:6; 18:24). It would also include, of course, the faithful witnesses of John's own day, whether still on earth or already in heaven because of their fearless witness to Jesus (12:11; 17:6). And it includes the Messiah himself, the forerunner of the faithful.

## Faithful Witness(es)

The most significant characteristic of the church as the people of God in Revelation is its calling to be a faithful witness (e.g., 2:10; 17:14). This call must be heeded even despite the interrelated pressures of opposition and temptation. It is rooted in Jesus the faithful witness (1:5; 3:14; 19:11), and it is exemplified in John the faithful witness now on Patmos (1:9), the martyred Antipas of Pergamum (2:13), and all the faithful witnesses/martyrs now in heaven (6:9–11; 7:13–17; 12:11; 17:6). The call is also highlighted by the parabolic vision of the two witnesses (11:1–13).[24] John's commission to be a Christlike, prophetic, faithful witness is reaffirmed in his vision of eating the bittersweet scroll (10:8–11; cf. Ezek 3:3), but the exiled John then recognizes that God has called others as

24. See the succinct but insightful discussion in Bauckham, *Theology*, 80–88.

witnesses, too. Their faithful, prophetic testimony to and among the nations (symbolized by the court of the Gentiles at the temple in 11:2) caused them to share the fate of their faithful Lord—both death and resurrection. As Peterson says,

> The place of worship is protected, but the place of witness is not. The court of the gentiles, where witness takes place, is not measured [protected] . . . . Witness takes place in the face of hostility. . . . The witness may be a hero to Christians, but in the world the witness is solitary, suspect, ignored, and occasionally abused.[25]

The task of a witness is to speak courageously in word and deed, testifying to the truth of God and prophesying against all falsehood that distorts and parodies divine truth. Witnesses offer testimony to the vision of God given them in the hope that others will repent from error and turn to the truth, but their success is measured, not by the quantity of their converts, but by the steadfastness of their testimony. This suggests that the church should be missional and prophetic, a martyrological community, a gathering of witnesses.

Such a calling is difficult and dangerous, but it carries with it the promise of God's protection in the present and God's reward in the future. The protection, symbolized in Revelation by the ancient practice of sealing (7:3–8; 9:4; contrast the antithetical marks/seals of the beast in 13:16–17; 14:9, 11; 16:2; 19:20; 20:4), does *not* mean that the church avoids temptation and tribulation, but that it is protected from defeat by these inevitable realities. That is, it is and will be victorious.

It is difficult to tell whether the witnesses in Revelation have much success in calling others to worship God and follow the Lamb as they bear witness. But three pieces of evidence do suggest success. First, the aftermath of the death and resurrection of the two witnesses is an earthquake that only kills one-tenth of the population, while the others glorify God (11:13). Second, the martyrs are the first fruits of salvation (14:4), implying that a greater harvest of believers will take place (14:14–16). And third, the New Jerusalem is populated with a multitude of peoples and nations (chaps. 21–22, anticipated in 15:2–4).[26]

---

25. Peterson, *Reversed Thunder*, 112.

26. Similar in emphasis is Bauckham, *Theology*, 94–104.

### A Multinational Martyrological Community

These two states of the church—as a persecuted pilgrim people now and as a vast triumphant heavenly people later—are on graphic display in Revelation 7, one of the most important texts about the church in the entire New Testament. Its dramatic and rhetorical function as an interlude between the sixth and seventh seals does not diminish, but rather enhances, its theological prominence.

In the first part of the chapter (7:1–8), we see the church on earth, situated in the midst of the tribulation associated with the seven seals of judgment. It is depicted as 144,000 sealed people from the tribes of Israel (7:4), establishing continuity between the church and the original chosen people. These 144,000 have had their foreheads sealed, a mark of their identity as God's people and of God's protection of them during tribulation (7:3 versus 13:16–17; see OT precedents in Exod 12:23; Ezek 9:4). Here, as later in chapter 12, "[f]aithful Christians are preserved through (not from!) the great persecution that is about to be unleashed upon them."[27]

In the second part of the chapter (7:9–17), we are given a vision of the church in heaven, where there is an innumerable multinational multitude, robed in white (symbolizing victory and resurrection), who acclaim the victorious salvation of God and the Lamb. These are those who have "come out of the great ordeal" (7:14) and already experience some of the blessings of the eschatological reality later portrayed in Revelation 21–22 (7:15–17).

Some interpreters understand the 144,000 and/or the multitude to be only the martyrs who have died in the tribulation, but it is more likely that each group represents the whole church. In any case, however, the images convey two crucial dimensions of the church: (1) its international, multicultural character, and (2) the reward it receives for faithful witness. The latter is reinforced in chapter 11.

The beautiful vision of "a great multitude that no one could count, from every nation, from all tribes and peoples and languages, standing before the throne and before the Lamb, robed in white, with palm branches in their hands" (Rev 7:9) is—or should be—at the heart of the church's self-understanding. *This is what God is up to in the world.* While completing this book, I made my sixth pilgrimage to Taizé, the ecumeni-

---

27. Boring, *Revelation*, 128.

cal community of prayer and reconciliation in central France. Singing and praying in different languages with thousands of people, young and old alike, from around the world is always for me a foretaste of the vision of the multicultural heavenly people of God we find in Revelation.

The vision of a heavenly, and ultimately eschatological (see "the healing of the nations" in 22:2), reality is foundational to the church's mission of global evangelization, its work for peace and justice among the nations, and its rejection of all forms of nationalism. Unfortunately, Christians have often been attracted to one or another of these essential marks of the church rather than all of them together. Contemporary Christian faith, if inspired by the vision in Revelation 7, would no longer be split between those who want to convert the lost and those who work for peace. Participating in the *missio Dei* did not, and does not, accord well with cafeteria-style Christianity.

If Christians around the globe truly understood themselves as part of this international community, and fully embraced that membership as their primary source of identity, mission, and allegiance, it is doubtful that so many Christians could maintain their deep-seated national allegiances, or their suspicions of foreigners. This would require a radical transformation within much of the Christian church, a recapturing of the wisdom of the earliest church. The second-century writing called the *Epistle to Diognetus* captures the spirit of Revelation 7 (and probably the entire New Testament), offering what is arguably the most appropriate attitude for Christians to have toward the country in which they happen to live:

> [Christians] live in their own countries, but only as aliens. They have a share in everything as citizens, and endure everything as foreigners. Every foreign land is their fatherland, and yet for them every fatherland is a foreign land." (5:5–6)

Some forms of love for home and country may be appropriate and benign, especially when balanced by appreciation of other cultures. But it is difficult to understand how a church that takes Revelation 7 (and 21–22) seriously could tolerate, much less promote or practice, any form of nationalism as we have defined it. Even patriotism, in light of the vision of Revelation 7, must be more critical than enthusiastic or even cautious[28]: at some point, most if not all forms of patriotism will,

28. See Sittser, *A Cautious Patriotism.*

or should, clash with the ethos of Revelation 7, at which point a choice must be made. Unfortunately, for many Christians the choice is virtually predetermined by virtue of their socialization not only in the society but also, and sometimes most especially, in the church.

What may be lacking is not only an adequate global ecclesiology (theology of the church) but also a knowledge of and devotion to the church's heroes, especially its martyrs. The current dearth of martyrs in the Western church may be welcome, but its accompanying amnesia of past martyrs and our ignorance of contemporary martyrs elsewhere in the world are tragic. In addition to failing at practicing the communion of the saints, this lack also feeds the desire for national heroes and martyrs. In church history, there has often been a strong correspondence between the absence of truly Christian heroes and martyrs and the presence of religious-like commitment to the nation state and *its* heroes and martyrs—i.e., civil religion.

This is not only because the absence of martyrdom means that the state is not persecuting the church (and may even seem to protect it), but also because Christians know instinctively that they collectively need to have something ultimate for which to live and die. Without a close connection to the church's saints and martyrs, Christians will often follow the cultural norm and make their nation state (or tribe or race), rather than the Gospel, that ultimate. Although the presence of this connection to saints and martyrs certainly does not guarantee the defeat of nationalism and civil religion, its absence contributes greatly to their triumph.

### Messianic Warriors

With all this in mind, we may now turn very briefly to Revelation's image of the church as participant in the messianic war (a subject that will reappear in the next chapter). Unlike the scenes in certain books and movies about "the end times," the warfare in Revelation is not literal, and the best proof of this is its paradoxical character: Jesus' followers share in Jesus' victory by their faithful witness and sacrificial death rather than by engaging in military violence.[29] "If you are to be taken captive, into captivity you go; if you kill with the sword, with the sword you must be killed. Here is . . . the endurance and faith of the saints" (13:10).[30] In oth-

29. Bauckham, *Revelation*, 77.

30. The omitted words ("a call for") do not occur in the Greek text.

er words, if Revelation narrates the divine drama and calls the Christian church to have a part in this drama, it is the part of faithful witness, or *active pacifism*, even in the face of an evil empire. This role may startle us; Revelation, as we have seen, is full of paradoxes and surprises.

## The Nations and their Inhabitants

The faithful are not, of course, the only humans on the stage of cosmic and political conflict. The word "nations" appears nineteen times in Revelation, and various groups of people are portrayed as either collaborators (kings of the earth and merchants—depicting lovers of political and economic power, respectively; 18:3), and victims ("human lives," perhaps slaves; 18:13) in Babylon. The judgments enacted by God seem to call for repentance, but evidence for actual repentance in Revelation is difficult to find. The final assize does not look good for the fornicating kings of the earth (19:18–21) or for average people facing God's judgment (20:12–15; 21:8)—even including some who think they are among the faithful (2:5, 16, 23; 3:3, 5, 16).

Despite this dramatic tension in the book, it is clear that the ultimate divine goal is for the salvation of humanity and the healing of the nations (21:22–27). It appears that even some of the former Babylonian conspirators will be redeemed ("the kings of the earth"; 21:24). God and the Lamb will be with them, reigning rightly as Lord of all (15:3–4).

## Summary

In this chapter we have sketched the main acts of the drama that unfolds in Revelation, and examined the chief characters in the drama, with special attention to the unholy trinity and to the church. We are now prepared to consider the visions of judgment and of salvation, paying more attention to theological than to merely exegetical concerns.

**Questions for Reflection and Discussion**

1. How might considering Revelation as a drama with characters enhance our reading and performance of the text?

2. How do you explain the perennial fascination with 666 and the antichrist? Where do you see Babylon-like and antichrist powers at work today?

3. What are some of the specific ways the church can bear witness against such powers for the benefit of the world?

4. What are some practical ways Christians who are not poor or persecuted can develop a greater connection with those who are?

# 8

## Visions of the Judgment of God

## (Revelation 6–20)

When most people hear or use the word "apocalypse," they think of total and final destruction, the result of divine judgment on the world gone awry. "There is an unremitting movement toward judgment in Revelation," writes one interpreter.[1] This is certainly true, but if we read Revelation carefully and responsibly—which in this regard means especially as symbolic and narrative literature—we will come to a more nuanced understanding of apocalypse, and of divine judgment. The main contentions of this chapter, all closely interrelated, are four[2]:

- Revelation's visions of judgment do not ultimately conflict with the central and centering vision of God and the Lamb in chapters 4 and 5.

- Revelation's visions of judgment on evil—especially the evil of imperial idolatry and oppression—should be understood as *symbols*, rather than *depictions*, of divine activity.

- Revelation's visions of judgment symbolize God's *penultimate* (next-to-last) rather than *ultimate* (final) activity in human history. That is, judgment is a means to an end; the goal being eschatological salvation, the creation of a new heaven and new earth in which

---

1. Schnelle, *Theology of the New Testament*, 770.
2. See also Boring, *Revelation*, 112–19.

humanity realizes its true *raison d'être* as reconciled peoples flourishing together in the presence of God and the Lamb.

- Revelation's long, detailed visions of judgment are not intended primarily for "Babylon," but for the church. John is projecting high-definition images, with the volume fully turned up, proclaiming, "Babylon is doomed! Nothing is more certain." As in all rhetoric, the repetition is for emphasis, and the message is one of both promise and warning.

Before we look rather briefly at the actual texts in Revelation that describe the judgment of God—space does not permit any more than that—we need to make one observation and then consider the first claim listed above.

First, the observation: sometimes, at least, God's judgment in Revelation takes the form of imperial practices themselves, or the consequences of such practices. War, famine, pestilence, death, injustice in the marketplace, and rebellion are all portrayed in chapters 6 through 20, and all are human evils rather than cosmic events.[3]

Second, the theological issue raised by the first claim: if we take Revelation 4 and 5 as the book's core vision, an apparent conflict emerges when considering the topic of divine judgment. We saw earlier (at the end of chapter 6) that Revelation does *not* contain two competing Christologies and theologies—one of power and one of weakness—symbolized by the Lion and the Lamb, respectively. Rather, Revelation presents Christ as the Lion who reigns *as* the Lamb, not *in spite of* being the Lamb. This means also that Revelation presents God as the one who reigns *through* the Lamb, not *in spite of* the Lamb. "Lamb power" is "God power," and "God power" is "Lamb power." If these claims are untrue, then Jesus is not in any meaningful way a faithful witness. More importantly, the book's central affirmation that Christ is worthy of divine worship is incoherent, because Christ is fundamentally different from—and other than—God.

3. Richard (*Apocalypse*, 86) even claims that the more cosmic plagues of the trumpets and bowls are not "natural" disasters, but "direct consequences of the structure of domination and oppression" and "the agonies of history that the empire itself causes and suffers . . . by its very idolatry and lawlessness." Today, he says, they are "the disastrous results of ecological destruction, the arms race, irrational consumerism, the idolatrous logic of the market, and the irrational use of technology and of natural resources."

All of this means that judgment by God/Christ in Revelation must be an expression of divine identity that is not in conflict with Lamb power. The judgment of the world originates in its failure to believe and be faithful to this God. When it creates its own deities, it suffers the natural consequences of deifying the non-divine. In this sense, judgment proceeds from the throne of God and from the Lamb (6:16–17) because the rejection of the divine gift of life carries with it inherent deadly consequences. It is not, therefore, because imperial power and Lamb power co-exist in God that wrath descends from God's throne, but because when humans reject Lamb power they experience it as imperial disaster—disordered desire, death, and destruction.

We will return to, and amplify, these points—and the other basic claims about divine judgment in Revelation—after considering some aspects of the visions themselves. We will devote the most attention to Revelation 17–18.

## Visions of Judgment in Revelation

As the outline of the book presented in chapter 2 suggests, Revelation portrays the judgment of God in groups of seven scenes: seven seals (6:1–8:1); seven angels with trumpets (8:2–11:19); and seven angels with bowls (15:1—16:21, with the seventh bowl extended and then celebrated, as the finale, in 17:1—19:10). This is not really the finale, however, as Christ appears in judgment on his white horse as the Word of God and as King of Kings and Lord of Lords, crowned with many diadems and clothed in a blood-dipped robe, to make war with the sword in his mouth (19:11–21). However, this is not the finale either, because following the 1,000 years of Satan's binding (20:1–6), the *final* finale occurs: the final judgment, when the unholy trinity (devil, beast, false prophet), the unrepentant, Death, and Hades all meet their fate (20:7–15).

The visions of judgment account for approximately half of the book and are to be taken seriously for that reason, if for none other. Furthermore, the theme of judgment—of the churches as well as the world—appears outside of these seven-part visions, foreshadowed in the opening vision of Christ (1:16, which notes the sharp, two-edged sword that proceeds from his mouth), and including shorter visions, hymn texts, and other items in chapters 6 to 20.[4]

4. For judgment (or the threat thereof) of the churches, see 2:5, 16; 3:3, 18. Cf.

These visions are symbolic, not literal. Regarding 19:1–9, for example, Bruce Metzger says that this is

> symbolism at its highest . . . Never shall we see the "white horse," or the sword projecting from the mouth of the conqueror, or the birds gorged with the flesh of fallen warriors (19:21). The descriptions are not descriptions of real occurrences, but of symbols of the real occurrences. The message that John conveys through this symbolism is that evil will surely be overthrown. Here that message is presented in apocalyptic pictures of almost repellent realism.[5]

We might well wonder what the function of such vivid symbolism is. Taken individually or together, these visions of judgment create a literary, rhetorical, and emotional experience of shock and awe. Their primary purpose, however, is not to instill fear but to provide a wake-up call for those who are sleeping, not merely through life, but through empire.

### Seven Seals, Four Horsemen

The justly famous four horsemen of the Apocalypse (6:1–8), the first four of the seven seals in the scroll opened by the Lamb, seem to represent a chain of events that human history has known all too well: conquest, the breakdown of peace, death in war, economic injustice, famine and disease. "[T]his first tidal wave of violent imagery expresses the apocalyptic insight that the world's suffering is *allowed* by God, but is more fundamentally a result of *sin*."[6] We would of course be misguided not to see these also as divine punishment, similar to the snowball effect of sin unleashed in the world according to Paul in Rom 1:18—32.[7] The question "human sin or divine punishment?" presupposes a false dichotomy and asks for an unnecessary choice; the answer is of course, "both." But it is clear that sin precedes judgment, and is not the will of God.

Thus war and its aftermath as divine judgment do not justify humans, especially not Christians, taking up arms. Commenting on the second horse, the red horse, Eugene Peterson therefore writes:

---

1 Pet 4:17: "For the time has come for judgment to begin with the household of God; if it begins with us, what will be the end for those who do not obey the gospel of God?"

5. Metzger, *Breaking the Code*, 92.

6. Howard-Brook and Gwyther, *Unveiling Empire*, 142.

7. So also Rowland, "The Book of Revelation," 530.

> For a time, writ large in the headlines, war is perceived as an
> evil, and there are prayers for peace. But not for long, for it is
> quickly glamorized as patriotic or rationalized as just. But war is
> a red horse, bloody and cruel, making life miserable and horrid.
> . . . The perennial ruse is to glorify war so that we accept it as a
> proper means of achieving goals. But it is evil. It is opposed by
> Christ. Christ does not sit on the red horse, ever.[8]

### Seven Trumpets, Seven Bowls

Revelation 8:6—9:21 and 16:1–21 both draw on historical events and
cultural realities to depict the coming judgment of God. Most obvious as
sources are the plagues narrated in the book of Exodus, but other biblical accounts of judgment (such as the locusts in Joel) also factor into the
imagery. In addition, the ongoing fear of natural disaster in the form of
destruction by earthquakes, and of manmade disaster in the form of destruction by invaders (especially the Parthians from the east) feed these
visions. "The poet puts unlikely images alongside one another and lets
them work in our imaginations, as cross-fertilizing metaphors."[9] In the
trumpets and bowls, writes Richard Bauckham, John has

> taken some of his contemporaries' worst experiences and worst
> fears of wars and natural disasters, blown them up to apocalyptic
> proportions, and cast them in biblically allusive terms. The point
> is not to predict a sequence of events. The point is to evoke and to
> explore the meaning of the divine judgment which is impending
> on the sinful world.[10]

The most significant difference between the trumpets and the
bowls is the scope of the latter (e.g., all sea creatures die in 16:3, not just
one third, as in 8:9), indicating the finality of this judgment. Among the
seven bowls is the famous sixth one, with its reference to Harmagedon
(NRSV) or Armageddon (16:12–16). Despite the vast amount of speculation regarding the time and location of this battle, Revelation mentions it only in passing. The place name means "mountain of Megiddo,"
a city where numerous battles had taken place in the Old Testament.

8. Peterson, *Reversed Thunder*, 77.

9. Peterson, *Reversed Thunder*, 98.

10. Bauckham, *Theology*, 20.

It is a logical setting for a symbolic battle of cosmic proportions—and nothing more.

### Parousia on a White Horse, Judgment on a White Throne

The multi-crowned,[11] multi-named (Faithful and True, Word of God, King of kings and Lord of lords) rider on the white horse of victory in 19:11–21 is clearly Christ. Like a Roman general in appearance, he comes to wage war and to rule, to capture and punish the two beasts, and to host a banquet where the beast's clients and others constitute the meal. It is an ugly and disturbing scene. Some believe it is the actual battle of Armageddon that is only hinted at in chapter 16.[12] In any event, "[t]hough the armies had assembled for a battle, it turned out to be an execution."[13] There is no battle.

Nevertheless, Tim LaHaye and other dispensationalists believe that this scene depicts a warrior-Christ who will return in power, joined by literal warriors, to wage a literal war. But there are two details that suggest that the second coming of Christ will not occur like that. First, his titles show that he rules by being the Word of God and the Faithful and True one; that is, by his word (19:15, 21) and his faithful death. The second detail bolsters the first: his robe is dipped in blood (19:13) *even before he engages his enemies*. The blood, therefore, is his own.[14] Christ's victory over his enemies, as elsewhere in Revelation, transpires through his death. The symbolism of war and a meal may be graphic, but neither can become the governing image; that belongs to the Lamb, implicitly present here, in these two details.

The final judgment at God's white throne (20:11–15) also suggests victory, indeed, ultimate victory. Preceded by the final defeat of the unholy trinity (20:7–10), this scene focuses not only on the judgment of all humans but also the defeat of Death and Hades. Humanity's final enemies have been vanquished.

11. Alluded to in the hymn "Crown Him with Many Crowns."

12. See, e.g., Witherington, *Revelation*, 241–45.

13. Witherington, *Revelation*, 244.

14. This interpretation is debated, but I find it most convincing in light of the book as a whole, as do many other interpreters.

## *The Interludes*

Interpreters of Revelation often refer to the breaks in the action (that is, the visions of judgment) as interludes. Interpreters differ on what to call an interlude, but the following texts are good candidates: 7:1–17; 10:1—11:13; 14:1–20; 19:1–10; 20:1–6. Whatever their specific rhetorical functions, such as giving the audience some respite from the intensity of the judgment scenes, the interludes are not superfluous placeholders. As we saw in the previous chapter, two of the texts most often identified as interludes (chapters 7 and 14) are in fact essential to Revelation's presentation of the church. Indeed, one principal function of the interludes is to reassure the faithful that God will execute judgment, that they will be preserved through tribulation even if they are killed; and that they will be rewarded for their faithfulness. Moreover, the interludes even carry along the judgment theme (see 7:2–3; 11:5–6, 13; 14:6–20; 19:2–3).

One text that should be classified as an interlude is 20:1–6, the famous passage about the millennium, the 1,000–year reign of Christ and his martyr-saints. It is incredible to some interpreters, myself included, that so much ink and theology have been devoted to one paragraph of the Apocalypse, but "the pursuit of the millennium"[15] has occupied interpreters since the second century. Entire theological systems are constructed around the words "premillenial," "postmillenial," and "amillenial."[16] Like John, however, we do not need to say much about the millennium.

Hope for a temporary messianic age on earth, before the final judgment and the permanent new age, was a concept already known in Jewish apocalyptic.[17] The primary function of this blissful interlude in Revelation is to reassure the church that its martyrs will be victorious, and thereby to reinforce the church's faithful witness. In effect, the scene creates (or, better, recognizes) a special class of faithful witnesses who have suffered the ultimate fate and therefore deserve—and will receive—special recognition by God as co-regents with Christ even before the

---

15. The title of a book by Norman Cohn.

16. See, e.g., Clouse, *Meaning of the Millennium* and "Christian Hope Thru History." A handy overview in table format is Reddish, *Revelation*, 391.

17. References may be found in most commentaries.

New Jerusalem. Those judged and oppressed by Babylon will now rule and judge.[18]

## Revelation 17–18: A Theological Account of Empire ("Babylon") and its Fate

In the previous chapter we considered the harlot of Babylon as an actor in the great cosmic drama. We now turn to this figure again, to reflect on the account of her judgment in Revelation 17–18. These two chapters, best understood as an expansion of the seventh bowl of judgment from chapter 16, are a two-part theological account of empire (principally chapter 17, lampooning it as a harlot) and its fate (principally chapter 18, taunting the demise of the harlot-empire and those who lament it). That fate is divine judgment and, therein, termination—unexpected and quick (18:8, 10, 17, 19). Much of what we find in chapters 17 and 18 has been anticipated by earlier chapters, but here it is presented in more graphic detail as the fall of Babylon (17:5; 18:2, 10, 21; cf. 14:8; 16:19), the "great city" (16:19; 17:18; 18:10, 16–21). These chapters are deeply rooted in the prophetic critiques of the original Babylon and of Tyre (Isaiah 23–24, 27; Jeremiah 50–51; Ezekiel 26–28) for their idolatry, violence, and lavishness. To first-century Jewish and Christian ears, "Babylon" would have meant Rome, as we saw in the previous chapter.

Ironically, however, although Revelation 17 has some of the most explicit references to Rome and Rome's emperors in the book (e.g., the "seven hills" in vv. 9–11; the vast extent of the empire in v. 18), its immediate and particular referents create a remarkable space for both identifying "Babylon" as empire more broadly and for laying the foundation for its critique. Seven features of empire emerge in this chapter[19]:

1. Empire is a system of domination that both seduces the powerful, partly with the promise of more power, and intoxicates common people with its alluring wine, perhaps the false promise of security

18. For a similar view, see, e.g., Blount, *Revelation*, 359–68, and Bauckham, 107–8.

19. Howard-Brook and Gwyther (*Unveiling Empire*, 162–84) show that the images in Revelation 17–18 demonstrate Rome's infidelity and seduction ("whore"), coercion and violence ("murderer"), economic exploitation (lavish dress and accessories), and imperial arrogance. Its fall is characterized by the images of desolation, nakedness, occupation by unclean beings, disease, burning and smoke, and the absence of culture (177–78).

that supposedly comes from increasing prosperity and power (17:2, "kings of the earth . . . inhabitants of the earth").

2. Empire is by definition both territorially grand and ideologically expansive, creating a kind of pseudo-ecumenism of politics and religion, and blasphemously self-promoting its own (alleged) grandeur, making claims about itself that are rightly made only about God (17:3–5).

3. Empire self-presents as aesthetically pleasing and full of benefactions to its subjects, both great and small, but in fact this appearance masks many "abominations," which constitute the essence of the imperial character (17:4). Among these abominations are practices that use, abuse, and oppress defenseless human beings, treating them like commodities. Contemporary examples include human trafficking, sweat shops, abortion without restraint—and many more abuses of power.

4. Despite its claims to divine status—sanction, mission, protection, etc.—empire is always ultimately opposed to the true God and those who represent the true power of God that is manifested in the life and death of Jesus. Empire will eventually resort to anything necessary, including lethal violence, to silence the powerful pro-God, counter-imperial witness of the faithful (17:5, 14).

5. Empires grow, in part, because the conquered acquiesce (17:13).

6. Empires often eventually die of a self-inflicted wound; their subjects revolt and destroy the very thing that has empowered them, and this reversal may be seen in a real sense as the judgment of God (17:16–17).

7. Empires (plural), that is, the particular historical realities, are in fact simply short-term manifestations, or incarnations, of something much more powerful and permanent that we may call Empire.

For what, we may ask, is Babylon, or Empire, judged? Essentially, for multiple forms of idolatry and injustice, the two fundamental charges brought against humanity throughout the Bible, from the prophets to Jesus to Paul through to Revelation. Babylon is guilty of sins against God, people, and the earth. It engages in a sort of corporate corruption of covenantal obligations.

Babylon makes promises, demands, and claims that are appropriate only for God to make. It sacralizes, even divinizes, its own power, and then it requires absolute allegiance to that power. The progression of this course, as Revelation 18 makes especially clear, is the pursuit of luxury and the neglect of the poor, first by Babylon itself, then by its clients, then by its everyday citizens. One inevitable result is the treatment of certain human beings as goods to be traded (18:13), and the elimination of others for their failure to offer absolute allegiance. Another is violence and war, death and destruction, hunger and famine (ch. 6). The final inevitable result is the destruction of the earth without fear of consequences, temporal or eternal (11:18).

Chapter 18 is a celebratory dirge that expands on some of these points, especially the nature of Empire's abominations and the scope of those who participate in them. John calls a spade, a spade, as the British chieftain Calgacus also famously did, labeling the Romans "robbers of the world." "To plunder, butcher, steal, these things they misname empire; they make a desolation and they call it 'peace.'"[20] But Revelation 18 above all shows that Empire is judged and therefore doomed, and that despite centuries of growth in its size and power, its theopolitical megalomania (18:7)—especially manifested in its structures of greed and violence—will end in a flash.[21] The certainty of that swift and certain end constitutes the litany of chapter 18 (see vv. 10, 17, 19), which concludes in 19:1–10 with the great "Hallelujah" choruses. This promised end has given hope to oppressed believers for centuries, as one spiritual attests:

### Babylon's Falling

Pure city, Babylon's falling to rise no more
Oh, Babylon's falling, falling, falling
Babylon's falling to rise no more.

If you get there before I do
Babylon's falling to rise no more
Tell all my friends I'm coming too.

20. Quoted in Tacitus, *Agricola* 30.4–5.

21. On the importance of commerce and idolatrous consumerism in Revelation, see especially Kraybill, *Imperial Cult and Commerce*; Bauckham, *Climax*, 338–83; and deSilva, *Seeing John's Way*.

## Babylonian Vocations and other Economic Practices

It would be a mistake, however, to think that the judgment of Babylon applies only to "them." The summons to "come out" (18:4) presupposes our existence "within," that is, within Babylon. I am quite sure, however, that neither John nor Jesus would object to our never having gone in (figuratively speaking), so that we do not then have to come out. Thus the corollary to "come out" is "don't enter," and the likely consequence of going or remaining in is sharing in Babylon's judgment, along with the fornicators, idolaters, and others named in 21:8 and 22:15.

Assuming that many of us, in certain ways, have in fact entered Babylon, what might it mean to come out? One aspect of "coming out" that is central to Revelation 18 is economic, which can be considered on the individual, family, and congregational levels. Economic faithfulness has to do, minimally, with how we earn our money and what we do with it once we have earned it. Gilbert Desrosiers suggest that the two beasts of chapter 13 can be interpreted as capitalism and consumerism, and David deSilva reminds us that "John understood that a person cannot share in the profits of domination without also sharing in its crimes."[22] If Christians should not engage in sex in the same kinds of ways as "the Gentiles who do not know God" (1 Thess 4:5), then neither should we engage in commerce as if we were non-believers.

Since at least the time of Tertullian, in the late second century, the church has grappled with which vocations might be inappropriate for Christians, even idolatrous. Tertullian raised questions about a host of occupations, including teaching (for promoting secular values and polytheism, or idolatry) and the military (for engaging in idolatry and violence). Touched by God's amazing grace, John Newton (1725–1807) knew he had to cease buying and selling slaves. But apart from outright illegal jobs like prostitution and drug-dealing, the church today seldom discourages any career path considered by young people or undertaken by adults. In my own United Methodist denomination, for example, a video on "vocation" for youth mentions a career in the military in the same breath as vocations in social work, medicine, the church, and so on.

While few Christians today would question the appropriateness of teaching in secular schools as a vocation, perhaps, at the very least,

22. Desrosiers, *Introduction*, 93; deSilva, *Seeing Things John's Way*, 47.

Christian teachers should question and "come out" from some of the values and practices inscribed in many secular—and even Christian—forms of education. I am thinking here, not of topics like evolution, but of even larger worldview issues, such as nationalism and consumerism, to name just two. As for the military, many Christians cannot even imagine a reason why a career in the military might be anything less than an honorable Christian vocation, much less engage in a serious discussion about it. But this is a topic in need of discussion, especially for those who live in or near Babylon. There is something amiss when a Christian youth can go to summer camp one month and sing "Blessed Be the Name of the Lord," and then go to Marine boot camp the next month and chant "We can kill." But it happens.

It would be easy to assume that most careers and day-to-day practices are exempt from critique, but Revelation will not allow us to be so naïve. If it involves buying or selling goods, Revelation subjects it to question. Is this a business that directly or indirectly promotes the rich and exploits the poor? Does it harm the earth or other human beings? If so, then Revelation 18 addresses it. Churches, too, need to consider carefully the sources and means of their income, whether local "fundraising" techniques, such as flea markets or silent auctions or fashion shows, or larger issues such as investing.

Revelation 18 also raises questions about how we spend the money we have earned. Like the economy judged in Revelation 18, many contemporary economies are based on lust (material and sexual), dominion, and exploitation, even human trafficking (cf. Rev 18:13). We may live in just such an economy, where more is always better and sex consistently sells, and we may inadvertently support other economies, where the poor are exploited or even traded. Alternatively, we might turn a blind eye to the existence of economic injustice, whether nearby or far away.

As individuals, families, and churches, we are shaped in the West by consumerist, anti-God, and anti-human values that oppose the very essence of the gospel. Do our ways of spending benefit the least, the last, and the lost? Do they promote justice and the healing of the nations? Do they reflect our convictions about the reign of God and the Lamb? Or do they reflect the values and practices of Babylon, of those who do not know God? Revelation 18 prompts us to think through these sorts of issues, and to do something explicitly, perhaps even radically, Christian, about them.

It should be noted that the judgment comes upon the city, but not only the city; the "kings of the earth" (17:12, 18; 18:3, 9), nations (18:2), and merchants (18:3, 11, 15) with whom it does business mourn; and the elite who cooperate with, and benefit from, it suffer judgment, too (6:15–17; see also 17:1–6; 18:1–3, 9–13). John the Seer, like all biblical prophets, holds the nations accountable for injustice.

## Interpreting the Visions of Judgment Carefully—and Theologically

We have now given a theological account of the judgment of Babylon, which is described clearly but not in gory detail. However, the larger question of Revelation's judgment scenes, particularly their violence and destruction, remains. These scenes of judgment have, of course, been the main source of criticism of the book of Revelation. "[T]here is far too much destroying in the Apocalypse. It ceases to be fun."[23]

Many readers will likely share that sentiment. So what are we to make of these visions?

New Testament scholar Warren Carter describes the visions of judgment in Revelation as "imaginary violence" and "a sustained fantasy of violent revenge."[24] Many would agree. But Carter also rightly points us to the fact that Revelation draws on traditions about judgment from the Hebrew Bible and the teachings of Jesus, and he indicates several ways in which Revelation qualifies the violence. "Much more is happening," he writes, "than God's unmitigated revenge."[25] Specifically, according to Carter, there are seven significant qualifications to the book's apparent vengeful violence:[26]

1.  As noted above, "empire brings about its own demise," meaning that justice, not merely revenge, is at work.

2.  In the seven trumpets, mercy "tempers the destruction," which is partial rather than total and is intended to bring about repentance.

---

23. Lawrence, *Apocalypse*, 135.
24. Carter, *Roman Empire*, 124.
25. Carter, *Roman Empire*, 124.
26. Carter, *Roman Empire*, 124–28.

3.  In the figure of the slaughtered Lamb—himself the victim of imperial violence—raised by God we see God's life-giving, nonviolent, counter-Roman means of triumph.

4.  The Lamb's final conquest comes not in the form of military action but in "revealing, persuading, and judging" words from one who did not kill but died for others.

5.  Divine judgment ensues only when people refuse to repent.

6.  The "overarching agenda seems to be salvation, not vengeful destruction."

7.  God's people are not called to overthrow Empire violently but to resist it by nonviolent faithful living.

Building in part on Carter's important insights about the role of divine judgment within the symbolic and narrative world of Revelation, we may now offer some additional theological perspectives on the meaning and function of divine judgment in Revelation.

According to Revelation and the biblical witness generally, the judgment of the world, like salvation, is the responsibility and privilege of God and the Lamb alone; it is one of their "reserved powers," so to speak. During this life, it is *not* the mission of humans, whether inside or outside the church. The role of human beings in history—at least those who are part of the people of God—is to announce this judgment prophetically, but not in any sense to execute it.[27]

Paradoxically, however, divine judgment may be manifested in history through secular human agents, that is, the not-people-of-God forces in the world. This is certainly the witness of the Hebrew Scriptures that shape the book of Revelation; one thinks even of the original Babylon. The manifestation of divine judgment through human agents, and specifically unrighteous ones, results in part from the fact that evil is inherently self-destructive, and that by its very existence it invariably invites others to participate in its destruction.

Judgment can also be manifested in, or at least symbolized by, cosmic events, and this is of course the way in which apocalyptic literature in general, and Revelation in particular, portrays divine judgment. But

---

27. I have qualified this discussion of the (lack of a) human role in judgment ("During this life"; "in history") because there are biblical texts that suggest the participation of God's "holy ones" in the eschatological judgment.

like apocalyptic's numbers, colors, and other symbols, cosmic signs should be understood less as literal events than as symbols of the distress and dis-ease generated by human evil. It is therefore not inappropriate to see, for example, today's ecological crisis as a form of divine judgment inasmuch as human greed, injustice, and misuse of the world's resources have caused cosmic distress and dis-ease. We might refer to this as *indirect* divine judgment.

On the other hand, it would be theologically irresponsible to interpret every earthquake or tsunami or epidemic as an act of divine judgment for at least two fundamental reasons. First of all, to do so is once again to misinterpret symbolic, apocalyptic language literally. Secondly, and more importantly, correlating specific disasters with intentional divine wrath and judgment is tantamount to claiming an intimate knowledge of the mind of God, and that is an act of incredible hubris, if not idolatry. Human beings—apart perhaps from a very few specially inspired biblical prophets and seers—have not been granted insider information about the ways of God in executing the reserved power of judgment.

This leads us to further consideration of the symbolic language of the visions of judgment in Revelation, the vehicle of Revelation's revelation, so to speak. The language and images of death and destruction symbolize—in comprehensible, if disturbing, idiom—the *universality* and *finality* of God's ultimate eradication of evil *rather than the means by which God brings about that eradication*. As the omnipotent One who spoke creation into existence, God hardly needs to resort to literal violence to effect the cessation of evil.[28] In fact, the idea of such literal violent destruction, whether executed by God or by divinely approved cosmic forces or by humans, actually "ridding the world of evil" is—upon serious contemplation—preposterous. Instead, Revelation should be understood as portraying *symbolically* what God does *actually* with a divine performative utterance, an effective word not unlike the word that spoke creation into existence. It is a word of *new* creation. Revelation's symbolic language uses the only kinds of realities known to humans to approximate the universality and finality of God's eschatological dealing with evil. What, after all, is more comprehensive and permanent in human experience than total destruction?

---

28. This is true whether we understand evil as the absence of good or the presence of a malevolent power.

One modern image of total and universal destruction might be the scene of Hiroshima. But if a contemporary writer used the mushroom cloud as a symbol of divine judgment, would we really be forced to believe that God was literally about to cause humans to instigate a nuclear war to execute divine judgment and eradicate evil? Hardly. The scene corresponds to the *effect* of divine judgment on evil, not the *means* of judgment.

This truth that the language of judgment in Revelation symbolizes God's effectively speaking evil into non-existence is perhaps most sharply represented by the vision of Jesus' victorious appearance as the Word of God on the white horse, with a sword in his mouth (19:11–16, 21).[29] This signifies the effective word of God's judgment—the wrath of God and the Lamb—that needs no literal sword, and which a literal sword could never accomplish. Moreover, this Jesus comes dressed in a robe dipped in blood (19:13)—his own blood—because the battle has already been fought and won in his death. The judgment he executes is his word so that the effects of his saving death may be fully realized in God's work of renewal.

Finally, in the book of Revelation, divine judgment is not an end in itself. It is God's "Plan B" when humanity persists in evil rather than repenting. It then becomes a means—a necessary means, to be sure, but still only a means—to the fulfillment of God's plan to heal the nations and create a space for all people to flourish in harmony with one another before God. This space is the new heaven and new earth, whose principal distinction from human history as we experience it is that evil is nowhere to be found. In fact, God will not permit evil to be present there; indeed, God will have permanently eradicated it by making all things new. Thus evildoers must either repent and participate in the renewal of all things, or be excluded from that space. The decision is theirs, and theirs alone. Bruce Metzger wisely comments on 14:1–20:

> [T]his picture of wrath and hell means nothing more or less than
> the terrible truth that the sufferings of those who persist in reject-
> ing God's love in Christ are self-imposed and self-perpetuated.
> The inevitable consequence is that if they eternally persist in such

---

29. This scene echoes a similar image that appears twice in the early chapters of Revelation (1:16; 2:26).

READING REVELATION RESPONSIBLY

rejection, God will never violate their personality. Whether any soul will in fact eternally resist God, we cannot say.[30]

Another way to say that judgment is a means rather than an end is also to recognize that God's judgment is not fundamentally about God's *power* but about God's *persistence*. Or we might say it is about God's *mission*, the *missio Dei*. Nothing can or will thwart the purposes of God to liberate, save, and redeem the world.[31] Judgment, or what we might call divine exclusion,[32] serves that purpose, carrying forth the mission of God and the Lamb as an unfortunate but necessary—given the reality of free will—means to the ultimate end.

The corollary of judgment as a means rather than an end is that God's judgment is also meant to call people to repentance. Judgment also involves mercy. God would prefer that the perpetrators of evil and the unfaithful repent. That is the explicit message to the churches (2:5, 16, 21–22; 3:3, 19) and the implicit summons in the judgment visions—though its success is not yet apparent (9:20–21; 16:9, 11).

Some may object and argue that Revelation clearly depicts God and the Lamb on a mission to judge evildoers and eventually to wipe out evil—and to do so at least in part through human agents, now in the course of history as well as at some future time of final judgment. Something like this motive leads some people to try to "rid the world of evil," and it is a common interpretation, for instance, of "The Battle Hymn of the Republic," based in part on Rev 14:14–20 and 19:11–20: "Mine eyes have seen the glory of the coming of the Lord / He is [now, already] trampling out the vintage where the grapes of wrath are stored / He hath loosed the fateful lightning of His terrible swift sword."

One very important observation about Revelation speaks against this kind of interpretation. In Revelation there are at least five occasions in which preparations for a kind of "final battle" are made, the last of which is the battle of Christ on the white horse, marked by his own (not his enemies') blood. At this battle, as in all the other battles, however, *no*

---

30. Metzger, *Breaking the Code*, 79.

31. Cf. Reddish (*Revelation*, 318): "The various plagues in Revelation are John's pictorial way of saying that God has not abandoned creation nor ignored the pain, suffering, and evil that have taken root in that creation."

32. In his excellent book *Exclusion and Embrace*, Miroslav Volf speaks of the necessity of exclusion after all means have been exhausted to bring someone into the reconciling embrace of a community. The same can be said of God.

*actual fighting occurs!* As noted above, we learn the fate of the enemies of God, but this is more of a battle summary or report of casualties (e.g. Rev 19:20–21). To repeat: there is no actual final battle in Revelation. Why? Because the images of battle are supposed to suggest to us the *promise* and *reality* of God's defeat of evil, but they are not the *means* of that defeat. There is no literal battle, no literal war of the Lamb for those present at the second coming to join in (as the "Left Behind" series imagines it), no literal pre-Parousia campaign conducted by human soldiers, Christian or otherwise, on behalf of God. "[I]n the cataclysmic battle of Revelation 19, what do the heavenly armies do? *Nothing.* . . . All the actions belong to Christ,"[33] and his only weapon is the "sword" of his word.

To read Revelation otherwise—for example, finding justification for wars conducted by superpowers against people and systems deemed evil—is not merely to make a theological decision that offends the sensibilities of pacifist Christians; rather, this approach completely misreads the book's symbolism and plot. Yes, the slaughtered Lamb fights for God and will act on behalf of God to rid the world of evil, but he does so with only his own blood and a sword in his mouth (19:15), not with a sword in his hand to literally shed the blood of his enemies.

The integrity and witness of the church depend, in part, on realizing this truth. The war of the Lamb is not what humans have been fighting all these centuries.

## The Cries for Justice and the Celebration of Divine Judgment

Before concluding this chapter, we need to address one final issue. For many people, two very disturbing and closely related aspects of Revelation are the cries for divine judgment and justice, and the celebration of the same when it occurs. We see these dimensions of the book in texts like the following:

> When he opened the fifth seal, I saw under the altar the souls of those who had been slaughtered for the word of God and for the testimony they had given; they cried out with a loud voice, "Sovereign Lord, holy and true, how long will it be before you judge and avenge our blood on the inhabitants of the earth?" They were each given a white robe and told to rest a little longer, until

33. Koester, *Revelation and the End of All Things*, 177 (emphasis added).

the number would be complete both of their fellow servants and of their brothers and sisters, who were soon to be killed as they themselves had been killed. (Rev 6:9–11)

" . . . Rejoice over her [fallen Babylon], O heaven, you saints and apostles and prophets! For God has given judgment for you against her." . . . After this I heard what seemed to be the loud voice of a great multitude in heaven, saying, "Hallelujah! Salvation and glory and power to our God, for his judgments are true and just; he has judged the great whore who corrupted the earth with her fornication, and he has avenged on her the blood of his servants." Once more they said, "Hallelujah! The smoke goes up from her forever and ever." And the twenty-four elders and the four living creatures fell down and worshiped God who is seated on the throne, saying, "Amen. Hallelujah!" (Rev 18:20, 19:1–4)

The sentiment "How long?" is not only a normal human reaction to injustice—"a question with a long history"[34]—it has biblical precedent, especially in the Psalms (see, e.g., 13:1–2; 74:9–10; 94:3; 119:84). Nevertheless, it can seem vengeful. Moreover, the "Hallelujah" (19:1), apparently elicited by the angelic voice, seems like gloating. Can either this radical questioning or apparent gloating be a mark of a faithful and Christlike church? To answer this question, three observations are in order.

First, sentiments like those expressed here should be seen not only as expressions of normal human emotions, but also as cathartic and God-centered alternatives to the more base sentiment of "taking justice into our own hands." The cry for judgment here is "established in its proper context, the act of worship."[35] By expressing, in worship, first their anger and then their gratitude, the saints affirm the basic theological and ethical stance of Revelation: that the role of the church is to pray for and bear witness to God's justice, not to take up arms against injustice. This is *not* the same as inaction, much less apathy. Indeed, it is action that got those who are speaking in these texts where they are—into heaven by means of martyrdom.

Second, these are not really cries for, or celebrations of, vengeance. Vengeance is self-centered: "I'm going to get even." But these texts are

34. Peterson, *Reversed Thunder*, 136.
35. Peterson, *Reversed Thunder*, 144.

ultimately centered on God and on others, especially on a world that has been greatly harmed by the injustice of the imperial perpetrators. The lines that follow the angel's invitation to rejoice in chapter 18 are especially relevant:

> Then a mighty angel took up a stone like a great millstone and threw it into the sea, saying, "With such violence Babylon the great city will be thrown down, and will be found no more . . . for your merchants were the magnates of the earth, and *all nations were deceived by your sorcery.* And in you was found the blood of prophets and of saints, *and of all who have been slaughtered on earth.*" (Rev 18:21–24; emphasis added)

Here we see that the angel's indictment of Babylon is due, not only to her having murdered prophets and saints, but to her having deceived "all nations" and having "slaughtered" many who were *not* prophets or saints. In other words, the murder of God's people is just a subset of a larger, international network of injustices perpetrated by Babylon. Indeed, it is likely that it was the witness of these prophets and saints *to* the justice of God and *against* the broader injustices of Babylon that led to their murder. That is to say, then, that the desire for, and the celebration of, divine judgment for the murderers of God's people is fundamentally grounded in a concern for the mistreatment of others and a profound desire to see God's will for the earth—"the healing of the nations" (Rev 22:2)—come to pass. It is not about vengeance.

It is, however, about God's justice and integrity. In 6:10 the martyrs call God "holy and true." If God is true in the biblical sense of the word, God will act appropriately by executing the justice that the holiness of God requires. A permanent state of injustice would mean that God is neither true nor just, and in the narrative world of Scripture as a whole, that simply cannot be.

Third, it is very important for those who have little or no direct experience of injustice not to criticize those who cry out for, and then celebrate, the justice of God. The South African pastor, theologian, and anti-apartheid activist Allan Boesak wrote a moving interpretation of Revelation from his perspective, where "How long?" was a common cry:

> [T]here has hardly been a place where the police and the army have not wantonly murdered our children, piling atrocity upon atrocity for the sake of the preservation of apartheid and white privilege. And as they go from funeral to funeral, burying yet

another victim of law and order or yet another killed by govern-
ment-protected death squads, the cry continues to rise to heaven:
"How long, Lord?"[36]

What some of us need is not to question the cries of the oppressed but to
feel more fully the realities of injustice, especially when it is perpetrated
by the Babylons of our own day. As J. Nelson Kraybill writes in commenting on the strong and desperate cry for justice in Revelation:

> Perhaps what the Christian church in the West today needs is
> more anger, not less. We may need Revelation to jolt us out of our
> slumber, to open our eyes to see the idolatry and injustice that
> pervade globalization and empire today. Something beastly is at
> work, for example, in a world where people starve to death or die
> of preventable disease while nations spend billions on weapons
> and leisure.[37]

## Final Victory

It is tempting to read the visions of judgment and (symbolic) destruction
as the activity of an angry God and/or the ranting of an angry people;
many have been unable to resist the temptation. But in the end, we have
argued, God is portrayed in Revelation, not as uncontrollably angry,
but as inexorably just. God's faithfulness to the creation, all humanity,
and the church leads to the divine war against evil, Empire, and their
lies, represented by the unholy trinity and named "Babylon." The three
members of that unholy triumvirate together meet their final fate, along
with those who ultimately refuse the mercy of God, as well as Death and
Hades themselves (20:10, 14–15). In other words, God wins: "It is done!"
(16:17; 21:6). The new creation inaugurated in the death and resurrection of the Lamb can now be completed. "It is done" means also "Let's
begin! I am making all things new!" The church celebrates the victory it
has longed for only because the judgment of Babylon means the salvation of the world.

36. Boesak, *Comfort and Protest*, 69–70.

37. Kraybill, *Apocalypse and Allegiance*, 137.

**Questions for Reflection and Discussion**

1.  What new perspectives about divine judgment and about Revelation have you gained from reading this chapter? Are there parts of the chapter with which you disagree?

2.  What questions or concerns remain for you about the judgment of God and/or the scenes of judgment in Revelation?

3.  How might Christian churches begin to raise and address the issue of "Babylonian" vocations and other economic practices? the problem of apathy about injustice?

4.  If God did not deal with evil, would God be just? Would God be God?

# 9

## Final Vision, Hope Fulfilled:
## New Heaven, New Earth, New City

## (Revelation 21–22)

It would be difficult to imagine a more fitting conclusion to Revelation—indeed to the New Testament as a whole and to the entire Bible—than Revelation 21–22. The role of triple terminus played by these two chapters is unique to this biblical book.

The last two chapters of Revelation closely parallel its first chapter. The prologue (1:1–6) and the epilogue (22:6–21) create apocalyptic, prophetic, epistolary, liturgical, and theopolitical bookends. Similarly, the opening vision of the majestic Christ present among the seven urban churches (1:9–20) foreshadows the presence of God and the Lamb in the new city (21:1—22:5). The One who promised to come has in fact come,[1] and the promises to the churches addressed in chapters 2–3 and to the martyrs in chapter 7—promises drawn from chapters 21–22—have been realized in the new Jerusalem. The way of the Lamb (with those who follow in it) has been vindicated, the way of the beast (with those who follow in it) condemned. Moreover, the unholy triumvirate of Satan, the beast from the sea, and the beast from the land has been defeated, along with the idolatry and evil they perpetrate on the human race in the name of the divine. The harlot of Babylon—the supposedly eternal empire,

---

1. That is, in the narrative sequence of the visions, though of course in actual history the coming is still future; hence the prayer, "Come, Lord Jesus" (22:20).

*Roma Aeterna*, the *Imperium Aeternum*—is gone, replaced by the Lamb's bride, the new Jerusalem, which will actually last forever.

As the climax of the New Testament, Revelation 21–22 shows us that the incarnation of God in Jesus the Jew from Nazareth is now permanently reprised as God and the Lamb dwelling with humanity forever. The reign of God that was inaugurated in the coming, life, death, and resurrection of Jesus—and narrated throughout the New Testament—has arrived in its fullness, as symbolized in the throne of God and the Lamb.

Genesis and Revelation constitute the Bible's two bookends, comprising the canon's own alpha and omega. The grand narrative that began with creation now ends in new creation, as promised by the prophets along the way. The original garden that became a source of curse and death because of human disobedience is now an urban garden, the place where millennia of human civilization come to fulfillment and nations finally live in peace, where blessing and life replace the original curse and death. "Hallelujah!" is the only appropriate response.

## Some Highlights of the Final Vision

Revelation's stunning final vision (21:1—22:5), full of scriptural images and allusions, impresses the reader with its magnificence, beauty, and scope, not to mention its vivid sense of human flourishing before God, of true healing and life.[2] It draws on some of the greatest texts of hope in the Jewish tradition, many found in the latter parts of Isaiah (especially chapters 54, 60, and 65–66), but also on images from texts about the Temple and its priests, including the hope of a new Temple envisioned in Ezekiel 40–48.

The promise of new creation is most famously found in Isaiah 65 and 66 (cf. Isa 43:18–19):

> For I am about to create new heavens and a new earth; the former things shall not be remembered or come to mind. But be glad and rejoice forever in what I am creating; for I am about to create Jerusalem as a joy, and its people as a delight. I will rejoice in Jerusalem, and delight in my people; no more shall the sound of

---

2. "Life" is mentioned in the vision in 21:6, 27; 22:1, 2 and then in the epilogue in 22:14, 17, 19. For the scriptural echoes, see the table in Howard-Brook and Gwyther, *Unveiling Empire*, 186.

> weeping be heard in it, or the cry of distress. (Isa 65:17–19; cf. 54:11–14)

> For as the new heavens and the new earth, which I will make, shall remain before me, says the Lord; so shall your descendants and your name remain. From new moon to new moon, and from sabbath to sabbath, all flesh shall come to worship before me, says the Lord. (Isa 66:22–23)

In Revelation, the new Jerusalem is identified with the Lamb's bride, the people of God, the faithful ones who have conquered (21:1–10; 22:3–4). Instead of an actual temple, God and the Lamb *are* the temple (21:22).

This city stands in stark contrast to the idolatrous, oppressive city of Babylon portrayed in chapters 17–18, the city that is fallen and judged.[3] The new Jerusalem is "God's alternative to Rome's empire"[4]—and to subsequent incarnations of Babylon. One way Revelation portrays the New Jerusalem as God's alternative to Babylon is by its very size: 12,000 stadia (1,500 miles) in length, width, and height means that the city "has a footprint approximately equal in size to the entire land mass of the Roman empire"; it is "large enough to encompass . . . the world as John knew it."[5] It is probably depicted as square because the ancient ideal of perfection, especially for a city, was a square; indeed, Babylon was remembered as a square (Herodotus, *History* 1.178). But Revelation goes a dimension further and portrays the city as a cube, because the Holy of Holies was a cube (1 Kings 6:20), and the victorious children of God are a community of royal priests (Rev 1:6; 5:10; 20:6).

The size of the new Jerusalem also indicates the fullness of its inhabitants. Revelation's final vision is the climax of a series of images in the book that serve as a "counterpart" to the judgment scenes, "universalistic accents which are among the finest pages in the Bible."[6] From the visions of a multinational gathering (5:9; 7:9) to the promise of all nations coming to worship (15:4), Revelation moves toward a vision of a

---

3. For an instructive table of comparisons, see Prévost, *How to Read the Apocalypse*, 110.

4. Carter, *Roman Empire*, 63.

5. Kraybill, *Apocalypse and Allegiance*, 177, 212.

6. Prévost, *How to Read the Apocalypse*, 63.

redeemed humanity (21:24, 26; 22:2). The current community of believers is the first fruits of God's salvation (14:4), not the entire harvest.[7]

What is particularly striking about this final urban vision is not only its size or who and what is present, but also what is absent from the city:

- no sea, symbol of chaos and evil (21:1);

- no death (21:4; cf. Rev 20:14; 1 Cor 15:26; Isa 65:25);

- no tears, mourning, or crying (21:4; cf. Isa 25:8; 35:10; 65:19);

- no evil, unclean, or accursed things/persons (21:8, 27; 22:3);

- no temple, because "its temple is the Lord God the Almighty and the Lamb" (21:22);

- no sun, moon, or other luminaries, and yet no night (21:23, 25; 22:5; cf. Isa 60:19–20); and

- no closed gates (21:25; cf. Isa 60:11).

These omissions both accord with prophetic visions and, as we will see, have theological significance.


## The Theological Significance of the Final Vision

In light of these highlights, we may now offer the following synthetic interpretive comments about Revelation 21:1—22:5.[8]

1. To emphasize what was said at the beginning of the chapter: this vision—or, rather, this coming reality—is the *climax of the book of Revelation, the New Testament, the entire Bible, the whole story of God, and also the story of humanity*. As such, it is aesthetically, literarily, and theologically satisfying.

2. The vision of a "new heaven and new earth" does not mean the destruction and replacement of the material world but its transformation, especially the transformation of human existence within that

---

7. This does not make John a universalist, as 21:8, 27; 22:3 make clear. But the primary rhetorical function of these texts is to elicit repentance, not restrict salvation. Even 1:7 ("all the tribes of the earth will wail" at the Parousia) cannot, therefore, mean that anyone is permanently excluded unless they wish to be.

8. See also Reddish, *Revelation*, 412–17.

material world.[9] The culture of the beast has been replaced by the culture of the Lamb; a culture of death by a culture of life; a culture of insecurity and fear by a culture of peace and trust. The new heaven, new earth, and new city are not, therefore, some kind of ethereal mist, but very real. This eschatological reality is not an *escape* from the materiality of existence but the very *fulfillment* of material existence. In Revelation 21–22, we "are immersed in materiality from start to finish."[10] Paradise, the original creation depicted in Genesis, has been restored, not abandoned or destroyed.

Eugene Peterson complains that "new heaven and new earth" is usually reduced to "heaven" and then completely misunderstood: "The frequency with which St. John's vision of heaven is bloated by make-believe into an antibiblical fantasy is one of the wonders of the world."[11] N. T. Wright concurs, rightly calling Revelation 21–22 "the marriage of heaven and earth . . . the ultimate rejection of all types of Gnosticism, of every worldview that . . . [separates] the physical from the spiritual. . . . It is the final answer to the Lord's Prayer [thy kingdom come]."[12]

3.   Paradise restored or regained cannot ignore the millennia of human civilizations that have transpired. Thus this "paradise" is not just a garden but an urban garden or, even better, a *garden-city*. This tells us that it is not civilization/culture/the city itself that is evil, but the distortion of city/culture/civilization caused by evil people and powers. As Richard Bauckham puts it:

> In the beginning God had planted a garden for humanity to live in (Gen 2:8). In the end he will give them a city. In the New Jerusalem the blessings of paradise will be restored, but the New Jerusalem is more than paradise regained. As a city it fulfills humanity's desire to build out of nature a human place of human culture and community.[13]

The new Jerusalem is the antithesis of Babylon. Babylon is the great harlot, a beast; it is infested with demons; it is drunken and murder-

9. See Bauckham, *Theology*, 47–51, and most commentators.

10. Peterson, *Reversed Thunder*, 170.

11. Peterson, *Reversed Thunder*, 171.

12. Wright, *Surprised by Hope*, 104.

13. Bauckham, *Theology*, 135.

ous. It is a culture of death. Jerusalem is the bride of the Lamb, full of the presence of God; it provides healing and is lacking all pain, tears, and death. It is a culture of life.

4.   In this eschatological reality, the boundary between heaven and earth—God's reality/abode and ours—is permanently removed. Eschatological life is marked by God's *perpetual perceptible presence*— a state of permanent incarnation, so to speak. This is, in fact, the most significant characteristic of the New Jerusalem: divine presence in all its fullness and glory (21:3, 22; cf. Ezek 37:26–27).

5.   The necessary correspondence to the absolute divine presence is the absence of all that is anti-God. The series of negations ("no this, no that") used to describe the eschatological reality in Revelation 21–22 does not imply something essentially negative or unpleasant, much less something incomplete. On the contrary, this series of negations means the *removal of all that prevents human flourishing in community before God* and the *presence of all that permits and promotes that flourishing*. In this reality, people have all that they need, expressed in the concrete realities of light and water.

  Bernd Wannenwetsch has described this eschatological reality as a "negative political theology" marked by "'the presence of the absence.'" Cultural hubris, civil religion, greed, and war are all gone; the city is appropriately desacralized and secularized because all honor is given to God and the Lamb, who rightly receive the glory that humans instinctually (but inappropriately) offer to their cities, countries, and cultures—often in the temples dedicated to their deities. The absence of such temples is the necessary corollary to the omnipresence of God and the Lamb. In anticipation of that day, the church bears witness to the inclusive, non-civic worship of God in the present.[14]

6.   The reading of parts of Revelation 21–22 at funerals is perfectly understandable and appropriate. Yet we must not permit this appropriation of the Bible's culminating vision to limit our interpretation of it. Yes, it promises the individual's hope of deliverance from tears and death; yes, it implies a reunion with "all who have gone to

14. See Wannenwetsch, "Representing the Absent in the City" (quotations come from 172).

their rest in the hope of rising again." But it is much more than this. God's eschatological reality is ultimately about *reconciliation among peoples*—the "healing of the nations" (Rev 22:2)—and not just individual salvation. This corporate reconciliation takes place when people from every tribe and tongue and nation center their lives on God and the Lamb. Revelation is, like the rest of the Bible, about the creation of a people, a people living in harmony with God, one another, and the entire creation.

7. This eschatological reality is *not a fantasy but a certain hope*, guaranteed by the faithful and true God and by the death, resurrection, and exaltation of the slaughtered Lamb, the faithful and true witness. Its certainty *inspires us to four things*, by God's grace:

    a. *worship*: giving honor and praise to God and the Lamb for the present and future salvation offered to us and all the world;

    b. *mission*: embodying the values and practices of the eschatological reality now, remaining faithful and true even, if necessary, to the point of death;

    c. *prophecy*: naming and speaking against values and practices that are at odds with those of God's coming new creation, whether they occur among God's people or in the wider world; and

    d. *hope*: recognizing that this new creation cannot be achieved by human effort or even prayer, for it is foreshadowed now only by grace, and it will come in fullness only in God's good time and after God's final defeat of all the powers arrayed against both God and humanity: evil, Empire and its culture of death, and death itself.

For this reason, the worshiping, missional, prophetic, hopeful church is inspired by Revelation to pray, with John, "Come, Lord Jesus." It is the hope of the Lord's coming and of the new creation, nurtured in worship, that enables the church's faithfulness and resistance. This spirit is eloquently captured in the words of the hymn "How Can I Keep from Singing"[15]:

---

15. There are actually several versions of this hymn, which was originally written in 1868 by Baptist minister Robert Wadsworth Lowry but both supplemented and altered thereafter. I have included only two, original stanzas, plus the refrain.

My life flows on in endless song:
Above earth's lamentation,
I catch the sweet, tho' far-off hymn
That hails a new creation.

*Refrain*
No storm can shake my inmost calm,
While to that refuge clinging;
Since Christ is Lord of heaven and earth,
How can I keep from singing?

Through all the tumult and the strife
I hear the music ringing;
It finds an echo in my soul—
How can I keep from singing?

8.   Finally, if there was ever any doubt that Revelation really does engage in the christological reconfiguration of God, especially prominent in chapters 4–5, the end of Revelation confirms this interpretation. Here the city's temple is "the Lord God the Almighty and the Lamb" (21:22), "the glory of God is its light, and its lamp is the Lamb" (21:23), and the throne of God we have seen since the first chapter (1:4) is explicitly "the throne of God and of the Lamb" (22:1, 3; cf. 7:17). This may be further ratified by the epilogue, if the first of the three "I am coming soon" sayings (22:7, 12, 20) is intended to be spoken by the Lord God (see 22:6–9 in light of 1:8). The Alpha and Omega of the prologue is clearly God (1:8), but by the time the reader reaches the epilogue, the Alpha and Omega has become, or has also become, the Lord Jesus (22:13).

The book of Revelation ends with an epilogue (22:6–21), a series of brief sentences summarizing the various aspects of the book. We hear words of assurance, blessing, and hope. We also hear words of warning. But the dominant chord struck in these closing verses is one of invitation and promise. The invitation is a double invitation, and the promise a double promise. The church invites Jesus to come (22:20), and he promises to do so (22:7, 12, 20). In addition, the church in the Spirit invites others to come, and those who respond are promised the gift of life (22:17). This is the message of Revelation: *the loving, liberating, life-giving Lamb who is Lord invites any and all to become part of his community of disciples, his faithful bride, and thus enter into God's new creation. Revelation is, at its core, an evangelical book, a word of good news, an invitation to follow the Lamb into the new creation.* The contemporary worship song "All Who are Thirsty," noted in chapter 1, echoes this message: "All who are thirsty, all who are weak / Come to the fountain / Dip your heart in the stream of life."

This is not an invitation to a superficial private spirituality but to a deeply rooted public discipleship of faithfulness, hope, and love in the middle of a sometimes hostile world that follows after other lords and gods. The stakes in this endeavor are high, but the rewards are greater still.

## Final Vision and Present Witness:
## Revelation and the Mission of the Church

Before concluding this chapter we must address one final criticism of Revelation: that it promotes a "pie-in-the-sky" hope that makes people "so heavenly minded that they are no earthly good." Does Revelation really promote ethical apathy?

Unfortunately, there has been a powerful and persistent tendency in many branches of the Christian church to view eschatology as a means of future escape *from* this world, with a corresponding flight from present responsibility *to* this world. This escapist eschatology and (non-) ethic has been met in some circles by a pendulum swing in the opposite direction, with the effect that eschatology gets reduced to human effort. Human activity will somehow usher in Utopia, the kingdom of God, justice for all, ecological sanity, or whatever the latest cultural preoccupation may be.

These two opposite tendencies may be seen especially in the way Christians read Revelation. Many "traditional" readings, as well as more modern dispensationalist perspectives (the "Left Behind" series, for example), are inclined to see Revelation's portrayal of the new heaven and earth as a reality in the distant future without serious consequences for how we live now, except that we should be prepared to give an account of "why God should let me into heaven." In reaction to this sort of approach, however, some Christians have argued that eschatology is now, since God expects us to end Empire's death-dealing and injustice, to create a new world of life and justice through our own efforts. Taken to its extreme, this reaction can eliminate the eschatological dimension of Revelation and of Christian hope more generally. One sees this to varying degrees in certain liberationist and ecological interpretations of Revelation.

Such readings of Revelation are certainly understandable, especially as reactions against the irresponsibility of other approaches. Ultimately, however, the eschatology-now approach is not theologically coherent. In fact, it is a kind of corporate Pelagianism—belief in salvation by human effort. That is, it wrongly assumes that human effort can bring about the kingdom of God, thereby failing to take the power of individual and corporate sin with sufficient seriousness. This kind of approach also demonstrates obliviousness to centuries of failed attempts to establish with human hands that which only God can establish.

So is there a middle way between escapist future-oriented interpretations of Revelation and unrealistic interpretations of Revelation's promises as a fully realizable, this-worldly Utopia created by human hands? The answer is "Yes," and it centers on the word "witness" that is so important in Revelation. Christian churches and individuals are called to bear witness to God's present transcendent reality and reign, as well as God's future eschatological renewal and final victorious rule in which there will be true life, peace, and justice for all. Adela Yarbro Collins puts it this way:

> The destiny of the world and even of the church is beyond human control. But people can discern the outlines of that destiny and ally themselves with it. They can avoid working against it. And they can embody its values in witness to the world.[16]

Christians bear this witness in both word and deed, proclaiming and demonstrating alternative ways of life that reflect the present and future divine reign of God and the Lamb revealed in Revelation. Revelation is, in other words, a *missional* text. (We will return to this in the next chapter.)

As communities of uncivil worship and witness, Christians seek to practice the ways of peace, justice, reconciliation, evangelism, and earth care that are implied in the vision of the new heaven and new earth

16. Collins, *Apocalypse*, 150.

given to us in Revelation 21–22. In visionary, truthful worship we have been caught up into God's own plan for the re-creation of the world, and we long to share that vision by witnessing to it in concrete practice. For example, a God who plans on the healing of the nations and who "passionately wants the nations to stop learning war can never be at home in a world where livings are made from war and destruction . . ."[17] Neither can we.

This is done, not with the false, crusading dream that such activity will eventually bring the nations to faith in Christ, defeat all corporate sin, end all Empire, and make all things new. Rather, because Christians have the true hope that *God* will in fact do all those things, and because they have experienced the early signs of that future, complete transformation in their own lives and communities, they attempt, with the Spirit's power, to live as an alternative community shaped both by the reality of the new creation and by the promise of the *fullness* of that new creation in God's future. Such an eschatological witness avoids the escapist irresponsibility of some interpretations of Revelation without positing a theological error that is no less misguided.

To summarize: John's visions in chapters 21–22 are "proleptic glimpses"[18] into God's future that summon us to bear concrete witness to them now.[19] This future is not primarily about "going to heaven when we die," although the martyrs and other saints are indeed currently with God in the heavenly realm. Ultimately, however, the conclusion of Revelation is not about going to heaven, whether by way of death or via rapture. In fact, the hope of Revelation is not about rapture or going to heaven but about what Barbara Rossing calls a "rapture in reverse," the descent of God to us![20] This is not to deny the existence of heaven in the present but to place the eschatological (future) emphasis where Revelation places it: on heaven and earth being transformed into one unified, merged reality, the new-heaven-and-new-earth.[21]

17. Boesak, *Comfort and Protest*, 130.

18. I owe this vivid and accurate phrase to my Duke student Katherine Smith.

19. Such glimpses may be found elsewhere, such as in 7:9–17.

20. Rossing, *The Rapture Exposed*, 141–58.

21. That is, the "marriage of heaven and earth" (Wright, *Surprised by Hope*, 104–6). Even the current reality called heaven is not fundamentally an escape from this world or from responsibility. For the faithful deceased, heaven is a place of active praise and prayer. For those living on earth, it "is not another life but the transcendent depths of

## Revelation 21–22 as Script for Christian Mission

Revelation does not lead to apathy about the present or future of the world. It compels its readers, rather, to be a missional community that bears witness to the coming of God and the fullness of God's kingdom among humanity.

What would it mean if Revelation were taken as a book of Christian mission, even as the *key* to a missional hermeneutic? If Revelation reveals the goal of the divine, biblical narrative and thus the goal of human existence (salvation), then what we see at the end of the end—that is, in Rev 21:1—22:5 (and related texts)—gives us both a picture of the *telos* and the contours of Christian mission: bearing witness in the present to the future, the *telos*. Revelation 7, one of the most important but under-appreciated New Testament texts, briefly depicts the

> great multitude that no one could count, from every nation, from all tribes and peoples and languages, standing before the throne and before the Lamb, robed in white, with palm branches in their hands. They cried out in a loud voice, saying, "Salvation belongs to our God who is seated on the throne, and to the Lamb!" (Rev 7:9–10)

This perpetual multinational liturgy embodies the universal salvation brought in Christ: the reconciliation of the peoples of the earth to one another and to their creator and redeemer. Both aspects of their reconciliation are witnessed by their loud voice and common praise.

We have already noted in Rev 21:1—22:5 additional images and promises of this salvation: the presence of God, the absence of suffering and evil, the lush urban garden with beautiful walls and streets, and trees that have perpetual fruit and leaves for the healing of the nations.

What does it mean to bear witness, in advance, now, to this salvation? That is the first, urgent missional question that we must face. The answer will by necessity be both "vertical" and "horizontal." That is, it will involve human-to-God and human-to-human relationships. And it will mean witnessing to the physicality and the beauty of the new creation, which has already begun (cf. 2 Cor 5:17).

I spent part of my time writing this book in eastern Cameroon, on the outskirts of the region's capital city of Bertoua. I was giving lectures

---

our history that make us lead this present life differently" (González, *Out of Every Tribe and Nation*, 75).

in a seminary full of bright and dedicated students who learn Hebrew and Greek—and everything else—without the aid of textbooks. In Cameroon most of the people are poor and suffering, often from a lack of basic necessities, but also sometimes from various sorts of spiritual pressures and persecutions. The Christians there are certainly not the arrogant elite of Laodicea, but much more like the poor and powerless yet faithful believers of Smyrna or Philadelphia.

Bertoua, the main city in a region of dense, vibrant forests, is no heavenly (or even earthly) Jerusalem. There are no streets paved with gold; in fact, there are only three or four streets paved with anything. The quarter-million people who call this city home see no brightly colored precious stones. The only things that sparkle are the zinc roofs on top of the mostly dull houses made of deep-red mud bricks, mud and straw, wood, or (occasionally) barely painted concrete. In addition to the timber, there are diamonds, and perhaps gold, to be mined in Cameroon, but evidence of the country's natural wealth is not yet found in any of its cities or thatched-roof villages. The countryside is gorgeous, with lush vegetation and plenty of sources of natural water, but in the city water is hard to come by; some people have tap water in their homes, but many must trek to one of the wells dug by Kiwanis International or some other humanitarian organization.

So the image of a lovely city, an urban garden for all, like that described in Rev 21:22—22:5, has a powerful appeal and promise when considered from this vantage point. The hope of a beautiful city here on earth is not an opiate for the poor, or an irresponsible middle-class reduction of the gospel to a ticket to heaven. Rather, it is the legitimate hope for liberation from poverty and oppression, and for the fullness of life as God intended it to be. In Cameroon, for example, the 2008 worldwide economic crisis—the temporary collapse of imperial dominance and stability with remarkable parallels to Revelation 18—made life in that besieged nation even worse. Perhaps only the poor, the underdeveloped, the oppressed can *truly* appreciate that city of hope. It has been the source of true hope for many Christians in difficult circumstances throughout the last 2,000 years, not least those who sang spirituals of hope—for both this life and the next—after being kidnapped from places not far from Cameroon:

### We'll Soon Be Free

We'll walk de golden street (*three times*)
Where pleasure never dies.
My brudder, how long (*three times*)
'Fore we done sufferin' here?
We'll soon be free (*three times*)
When Jesus sets me free.
We'll fight for liberty (*three times*)
When de Lord will call us home.

Those who live in better circumstances than these faithful sisters and brothers dare not criticize them for having such hope. Indeed, all who believe are offered the same hope, for it is hope not just for oneself, but for the family of nations and the entire cosmos.

At the same time, such a hope does not relieve our responsibilities to and for others now. In Bertoua there is a place called the Maranatha Spiritual Center, a site for retreats and spiritual direction.[22] By virtue of its name, one might think that it would be removed from the pain of everyday life, its people merely praying for, and eliciting hope in, the second coming. But precisely the contrary is the reality, for those associated with the Maranatha Spiritual Center are also deeply involved in ministering to people's daily physical needs and working with others—government officials, healthcare workers, and so on—for the development of the Cameroonian people, so that they may have a life with God and with one another that is at least less of a contradiction of their eschatological reality.

Thus hope in the coming of the Lord does not give believers either the duty or the right to do nothing except passively wait. Hope separated from faith is blind, self-help optimism, the heresy of Pelagianism. But hope separated from love is narcissism, the error of antinomianism (abandonment of ethical responsibility). It is effectively a rejection of the Christian faith.

The Maranatha ("Come, Lord Jesus!") prayer and hope of Rev 22:20 should therefore be read as a short form of the Lord's prayer and its clarion call to the Christian community. To pray for the coming of the kingdom, the coming of the Lord, is to commit oneself and one's com-

22. "Maranatha" is Aramaic for "Our Lord, come" (see 1 Cor 16:22).

munity to embody the values and practices of that kingdom—*now*—in whatever circumstances we find ourselves. The (relatively unknown) 20th-century hymns "For the Healing of the Nations" by Fred Kaan and "O Lord You Gave Your Servant John" by Joy Patterson both try to capture this dynamic relationship between vision and mission, without assuming that we can effect the kingdom of God on our own. Kaan's 1965 hymn begins, "For the healing of the nations, Lord, we pray," and includes the line "All that kills abundant living, let it from the earth be banned." Patterson wrote in 1988: "You gave Your servant John a vision of the world to come / A radiant city filled with light . . . . Our cities wear shrouds of pain . . . . Come, Lord, make real John's vision fair / Come dwell with us, make all things new / We try in vain to save our world / Unless our help shall come from You."

The script present in Revelation 21–22 cannot, however, be reduced to a vision of social justice apart from God and apart from the salvation of individuals. Revelation will not allow that common mistake any more than it permits an escapist eschatology. Rather, the final vision is deeply pastoral, spiritual, evangelical, and liturgical, as well as social. The healing of the nations requires peoples to worship God and the Lamb together. Hope for the salvation of the world means also salvation for each individual; God wipes away human tears one at a time. As we saw in chapter 1, looking at the origins of the choral anthem "E'en So Lord Jesus, Quickly Come," the hope of Jesus' coming comforts those who experience personal pain and loss, even as it comforts the politically oppressed.

The missional church—the *fully* missional church—constitutes a foretaste of the future we see displayed in Revelation 21–22: a Spirit-enabled partial and proleptic actualization of, and witness to, God's new creation for each and for all. "Heaven," writes Eugene Peterson, "is not a purple passage tacked onto the end of the Apocalypse to give a flourish to the rhetoric, but an immersion in the realities of God's rule in our lives that has the effect of reviving our obedience, fortifying us for the long haul, and energizing a courageous witness."[23]

This is nothing other than another form of faithful witness, of faithful resistance, for to resist Empire and its effects in the world is to live according to the empire (reign, kingdom) of God, and vice versa. This takes place only by the power of the Spirit and only in the realiza-

23. Peterson, *Reversed Thunder*, 173.

tion that God alone can bring the kingdom in its fullness. Moreover, the church-in-mission must always be prepared to become the church under siege, as John warned his churches. Mission and suffering will, in fact, often go hand in hand. Both because the church's missional activity is always only a foretaste of the end and because the church universal always lives under the threat of persecution, the witnessing-suffering church is therefore always the hopeful church that never ceases to pray, "Come, Lord Jesus."

### Questions for Reflection and Discussion

1. In what ways does Revelation 21–22 conclude the book of Revelation, the New Testament, and the entire Christian Bible?

2. In your experience of the church, has it leaned more toward escapist apathy or corporate Pelagianism? How does the church maintain an appropriate missional balance without committing either of these errors?

3. How might the final chapters of Revelation help shape the mission of your particular Christian community?

4. In what sense is Revelation a book both for and about the oppressed? How can readers who are not among the oppressed nonetheless read and heed Revelation?

# 10

## Following the Lamb: The Spirituality of Revelation

Throughout this book we have said that although Revelation is many things, it is not a detailed forecast of the events at the end of the world. It is, however, a spiritual writing. Some people may have a difficult time connecting Revelation and spirituality. But the word spirituality in a Christian context simply means the lived experience of Christian faith,[1] that is, life for God and God's kingdom, life in Christ, life empowered by the Spirit. We turn in this final chapter to a synthesis of all that has gone before, focusing on the lived experience of Christian faith that is both presupposed in and advocated by Revelation. What kind of church and what kind of Christian is the Spirit who speaks in Revelation aiming to form?

### The Message of Revelation: A Brief Summary

How can we summarize what we have said about the book of Revelation and its message? We have called Revelation a theopoetic, theopolitical, pastoral-prophetic writing. It is above all a community-forming document, intended to shape communities of believers in Jesus as the Lamb of God into more faithful and missional communities of uncivil worship and witness.[2] The primary agenda of John the Seer is to increase covenant faithfulness in the church universal—then and now. To use the

1. See McGinn and Meyendorff, eds., *Christian Spirituality: Origins to the Twelfth Century*, xv.

2. As elsewhere in this book, by "uncivil" I mean "not-civil-religion."

language of Revelation itself, the agenda of its author is to form *victori-ous* communities, communities that do conquer and will conquer. And by "conquer," Revelation means remaining faithful, even to death, in order to experience glorious, everlasting life with God, the Lamb, and all the redeemed in God's new heaven and earth.

If that sounds like what some Christians (especially certain Protestants) label "works righteousness," it is time for us to stop worry-ing about this concern and start realizing the seriousness of the call to covenant faithfulness in the Scriptures, including Revelation. Revelation sees death all around, especially in the evils of imperial cultures (wheth-er ancient or modern) that promise life but deliver its opposite. The New Testament offers rescue from this culture of death in all its forms, but its offer of salvation is an offer of liberation from death *for a new way of life*. That is, salvation in the New Testament is as much about faithfulness (fidelity) as it is about faith (assent and trust).[3]

This is not, however, "works righteousness," for we do not earn our salvation—the Lamb did that for us by his death. The question becomes, rather, what exactly salvation is, and the book of Revelation, like the rest of the New Testament, makes it clear that salvation consists in a faithful covenantal relationship with God and others made possible by the death of Christ, the activity of the Spirit, and the encouragement of other faith-ful witnesses, living and dead.

In other words, according to Revelation, we have been redeemed *from* a culture of death *by* the death of the Lamb *for* faithfulness to death—all of which is, paradoxically, life itself. It is also victory itself. It is conquering the temptation to give up or give in, even in the face of all that the culture of death can do.

## The Spirituality of Revelation

What kind of spirituality emerges when we read Revelation as a theo-poetic, theopolitical, pastoral-prophetic writing focused on the reign of God and the slaughtered Lamb, through which the Spirit still speaks to the churches—rather than as a script about the end of history? It is a *theopolitical liturgical and missional* spirituality, a spirituality of *uncivil worship and witness*. By its very nature this is not a private or merely

---

3. For a full discussion of salvation in the NT and the Bible as a whole, see Middleton and Gorman, "Salvation."

inner spirituality; instead, it is embodied in the world—"performed." Faithful readers are faithful performers of the theopolitical drama and song that is Revelation. "Interestingly," writes Richard Hays, "Revelation opens with a blessing on those who are to 'perform' it [1:3]. . . . For this work to have its full effect, it must be read aloud; that is the sort of text that it is, like the script for a play—a play in which the readers now find themselves the performers."[4]

This performative or narrative spirituality has the following main elements:

- worship;
- discernment, vision, and imagination;
- faithfulness and prophetic resistance (to idolatry and injustice);
- self-criticism;
- cruciform, courageous nonviolent warfare;
- embodied communal witness and mission, including evangelization; and
- hope.

It is not, in other words, a spirituality for the faint of heart.

## Worship

Revelation summons us to worship God the creator and redeemer, the Alpha and Omega, who reigns. It summons us to worship Jesus the redeemer, the slaughtered Lamb, the Alpha and Omega, who is Lord. The reign of God is not merely future or past but present. The summons to worship is therefore inseparable from allegiance. God in Christ both offers all and demands all. When a community publicly worships this God, abandoning the idolatrous and false claims of political entities, cultural ideologies, and anything else that claims ultimate credence and allegiance, two things happen. First, the community—as a whole and as individuals—will be caught up, like John himself (1:10) in the Spirit of God, becoming a sacred space in which their imaginations and lives can be increasingly converted into the image of the Lamb. Second, others will take notice. They will witness the community's faithful witness to

4. Hays, *Moral Vision*, 184.

the Faithful Witness. Some will be drawn in, while others will be indifferent, suspicious, or even hostile.

It is not accidental that Revelation, as a book of worship, is filled with songs, or that so many Christians through the centuries have composed hymns and songs based on Revelation. Those who follow the Lamb are a singing people. Our praise is joyful, but also serious, because singing something like "Worthy is the Lamb" is "a political act, and the political power of the act is greater because it is sung, for others can join the chorus and fix it in aural memory."[5]

Because the liturgical spirituality of Revelation is about allegiance and life, not just ritual and song, those who worship God and the Lamb must be deliberate in their refusal to engage in anything approaching idolatry, especially the syncretistic nationalism that permeates so many churches (churches that may disagree, ironically, on many other matters). According to Revelation, in the church's worship we should remember and honor prophets and martyrs, not veterans and fallen warriors; faithful witnesses, not loyal patriots; the One who was slain to secure our true freedom, not the ones who killed and were killed to preserve (so it is claimed) our freedom. *That this self-evident truth about worship seems so odd, so radical, simply demonstrates how comfortable the church has become in bed with the beast.*

In some churches, what should be unthinkable has become normal, even expected. In some, not to celebrate a national holiday, especially one that memorializes warriors, is a sin greater than skipping Maundy (Holy) Thursday and Pentecost. Such holidays become civil-religion versions of Good Friday, since the deaths of the fallen are treated as Christlike sacrifices: "Greater love has no one than this: that a man lay down his life for his friends" (John 15:13; RSV) is inappropriately transformed from a statement about discipleship to Christ into a militarized mantra about service to country.

In Revelation, faithfulness is portrayed *positively* as following the Lamb (14:4) and being marked with God's seal of ownership and protection (7:3). It is also portrayed *negatively* as not following the beast or receiving the mark of the beast (13:16–17; 14:9, 11; 16:2; 20:4). Together, these two images of faithfulness demonstrate that we cannot have it both ways: beast and Lamb, imperial power and Lamb-power, civil religion mixed with worship of God and the Lamb. *This is an either-or proposi-*

5. Hays, *Moral Vision*, 184.

*tion with very serious consequences.* There is no synthesis, no syncretism permitted here. The "uncivil" call of Revelation is to forsake the idolatrous worship of secular power and to worship God alone.

Most of us do not like such either-or propositions when it comes to "religion." We especially do not like choosing between "civil religion" and "Christian discipleship." It is easier to have it both ways. What makes the "both-and" approach especially attractive is that it seems so right, so noble, so pious. Why is it so seductive? Because, according to Revelation, it is the deliberate, deceitful, demonic work of the propaganda mechanisms of the idolatrous imperial powers (19:20; 20:3). Nationalistic allegiance or devotion, especially when dressed in religious garb, may not feel like idolatry, but Revelation makes us face the issue head on (13:4, 8, 12, 15; 14:9, 11; 16:2; 19:20).

For most readers of this book their Babylon will not be a totalitarian regime engaged in overt oppression and persecution, or threatening to do so. But that is precisely the point. Revelation offers a vision of the church for *ordinary* empire. We fall short of Revelation's vision for the church in many ways. In worship, we hear the Spirit speaking through song, Scripture, sermon, and one another. An essential part of worship, as we see in the messages to the churches, is repentance. Certainly that word is a fundamental aspect of what the Spirit is saying to us who gather for worship today, too.

I was recently inspired by the way in which a brand-new pastor I know, preparing to lead his first worship service—on Sunday, July 4— met with the church's lay leadership the day before to discuss their plans for a service that would include patriotic songs and even the pledge to the American flag. He gently said to them, "This is a day to express pride in our country, but not during worship. Here we focus on Jesus, and that's especially important to me on my first Sunday. Can we do that, and remove the patriotic elements from worship?" "Even the red, white, and blue formatting of the hymn texts we will project on the screen?" asked a lay leader. "Yes, even them, if it's not too late." "You're the pastor," replied the lay leader. "We will do it." And they did.

### Discernment, Vision, and Imagination

Worship offers us an alternative vision of God and of reality that unveils and challenges Empire. We need the Spirit's wisdom and guidance to perform this vision well. It is crucial that the church not withdraw from life in the world but only from that which is anti-Lamb. How can it know what to withdraw from, and what to participate in, without the Spirit's gift of discernment? How can it know what its alternative life should look like without the vision that the Spirit gives to those who hear what the Spirit is saying to the churches?

It is important to stress again that Revelation does not call for the wholesale rejection of culture and of engagement with the world; rather, it calls for discernment. It is one thing, in other words, to live in an empire or superpower, to live in the shadow of the beast, trying to avoid participating in the evils of idolatry while bearing witness to another empire, the kingdom of God, and thereby working for the good of the world as salt and light. It is quite another to unconditionally endorse that empire—or any culture—or to sacralize it. Yet that is what many Christians and churches have done; they have baptized their country and/or culture into the name of the triune god of political, economic, and military power, wrongly thinking that this is the power of God.

The eternal gospel of the slaughtered Lamb unveils the flawed character of this undiscerning baptism. But because civil religion in the West borrows heavily from the symbols and texts of Christian faith, it is nearly impossible for many Christians and churches to recognize the problem before us. Syncretism is a powerful, subtle device. It makes sense. But the "moral strategy of the Apocalypse . . . is to destroy common sense as a guide for life."[6]

Thus the vision required for discernment does not make Christian faith anti-Rome, anti-American, or anti-culture in some general, all-encompassing sense. Rather, it calls us to rely on the discerning Spirit to distinguish the good (and the neutral) from the bad in order to remain *in* Babylon but not *of* it. We learn where we can say "yes," and where we must say "no." Then the church's mission can go forward in faith and in faithfulness.

### Faithfulness and Prophetic Resistance

The negative fruit of discerning vision is the ability to say "no." The Christian church is easily seduced by Empire's idolatry and immorality because these claims and practices are often invested with religious

6. Meeks, *The Moral World of the First Christians*, 145.

meaning and authority. In the context of "civil religion," the church is called to "come out," to withdraw. For "mainline" Christians and others who are used to being part of the status quo, this will be very difficult, and many will resist the very idea of resistance.

But Revelation calls all Christians to refuse participation in acts that express allegiance and devotion to the gods of power and might, whether military, political, social, or economic. In the midst of Empire, the church is called to resistance in word and deed as the inevitable corollary of faithfulness to God, a call that requires the prophetic spiritual discernment provided by God's Spirit in true worship. It means speaking truth to power. And it is, as we know from Revelation, a vocation that may result in various kinds and degrees of suffering.

## Self-Criticism

An apocalyptic spirituality like that in the book of Revelation carries several inherent dangers, chief among them hubris. Talk of identifying idolatry and Empire, of resistance and speaking truth to power, can easily lead an individual or a church to a place of self-assurance that may stand in need of correction—sometimes radical correction. Yet apocalyptic, with its "either-or" categories, does not appear to lend itself easily to self-criticism.

Yet self-criticism is nonetheless needed.[7] Apocalyptic visionaries do not see, much less live, flawlessly. Even John apparently made a significant mistake on two occasions, trying to worship an angel (19:9–10; 22:8–9). And we are not John, much less one of the revelatory angels or multi-eyed creatures before the throne of God. The call for repentance in Revelation is addressed to the church as much as the world; five of the seven churches received criticism from Jesus. "There are no grounds for complacency—only watchfulness (3:3) and the constant endeavoring to keep one's robes clean (22:4)."[8]

---

7. See Charry, "'A Sharp Two-Edged Sword,'" 351–53, 357–60.
8. Rowland, "The Book of Revelation," 523.

## Cruciform, Courageous Nonviolent Warfare

The resistance (discerning, imaginative, and self-critical) required of Christians can be likened to warfare in search of victory. But because this victory is that of the victorious slaughtered lamb, Christian resistance to Empire conforms to the cruciform pattern of Jesus Christ and of his apostles and saints: faithful, true, courageous, just, and nonviolent. Revelation depicts in 3-D visions and at length what Ephesians 6 says in less fully developed but still powerful images:

> For our struggle is not against enemies of blood and flesh, but against the rulers, against the authorities, against the cosmic powers of this present darkness, against the spiritual forces of evil in the heavenly places. Therefore take up the whole armor of God [see vv. 14–17], so that you may be able to withstand on that evil day, and having done everything, to stand firm. (Eph 6:12–13)

It is important here to emphasize how Revelation conveys a spirituality and ethic of nonviolence, as we have seen in earlier chapters. There are three very closely related points to be made.

First, in his faithful and suffering death, Jesus has already demonstrated both how God deals with evil and how God's people are to deal with evil. His death dealt the final blow to evil and to death itself, not in a show of violent power but in a paradoxical and subversive act of not confronting evil on its own terms. His death liberates from evil, death, and violence all those who embrace him and his death as the apocalyptic revelation of God in the world.

Second, Revelation knows that true spiritual existence is warfare, but it defines victory in the cosmic battle as faithfulness. Neither the Lamb nor his followers fight in any other way than faithfulness, even to the point of suffering and death.

Third, since the defeat of evil is already in principle accomplished by the death of the Lamb as a nonviolent speech-act of faithful resistance, its final defeat will be finally accomplished in the same kind of way. This is the *modus operandi* of the Lamb: he comes on the white horse of victory bearing his own blood, reminding us that he will defeat the powers of evil *as the Lamb*, not with a sword in his hand but with a sword in his mouth. Just as it was the speech-act of faithful resistance to evil incarnate—the cross—that began the process of destroying evil, so also will the Word of God, the eternal gospel, kill death and de-create evil when the same Christ returns. Once again, the word of the Lord will not return to God void (Isa 55:11); it will accomplish its mission, but in God's way, the way of the Lamb.

It is this *modus operandi* of faithful, nonviolent action and speech, rooted in the life and witness of the Lamb, that is the way offered to, and ultimately required of, the Lamb's followers. The false cult of civil religion entails the nationalization (or tribalization), and even militarization, of worship. In the true cult of God and the Lamb, however, worship is universal and peaceful. Its warfare is conducted with words, not weapons. Even the cry for justice is an expression of this kind of warfare, a verbal affirmation of God's faithfulness with a corollary, uncivil pledge of nonviolence. *This combination of a cry for justice and a commitment to nonviolence may be the most significant feature of Revelation's liturgical theology and spirituality.*

Richard Hays echoes these conclusions:

> A work that places the Lamb that was slaughtered at the center of its praise and worship can hardly be used to validate violence and coercion. God's ultimate judgment of the wicked is, to be sure, inexorable.... But these events [of judgment in Revelation] are in the hand of God; they do not constitute a program for human military action. As a paradigm for the action of the faithful community, Jesus stands as the faithful witness who conquers through suffering. ... Those who read the battle imagery of Revelation with a literalist bent fail to grasp the way in which the symbolic logic of the work as a whole dismantles the symbolism of violence.[9]

### Embodied Communal Witness and Mission

Revelation is not primarily a book to be dissected but to be lived; that is the nature of resistance literature. Christian resistance, like warfare, is not passive but active. It consists of the formation of communities and individuals who pledge allegiance to God alone; live in nonviolent love toward friends and enemies alike; leave vengeance to God but bear witness to God's coming judgment and salvation; create, by God's Spirit, mini-cultures of life as alternatives to Empire's culture of death; and invite all who desire life with God to repent and worship God and the

9. Hays, *Moral Vision*, 175.

Lamb. The will of God is for all to follow the Lamb and participate in the present and coming life of God-with-us forever. A community that takes the spirituality of Revelation seriously will therefore be unashamedly evangelical, that is, proclaiming in word and deed "the eternal gospel" (14:6) and inviting others into the communion of the saints. Revelation offers us a missional spirituality.

The notion of a *missional* spirituality may seem odd at first, especially in light of Revelation's summons to "Come out of her [Babylon], my people" (18:4). This would seem to curtail any conversation about mission before it even begins. However, as we saw in our study of Revelation 21–22, "come out" is not a summons to escape, and the spirituality of Revelation is not an escapist spirituality. The withdrawal is not so much a physical exodus as a theopolitical one, an escape from civil religion and the idolatry of power-worship, as we have argued throughout the book. It is a creative, self-imposed but Spirit-enabled departure from certain values and practices.[10] This is the necessary prerequisite to faithful living *in* the very Babylon from which one has escaped. That is, the church cannot be the church *in* Babylon until it is the church *out of* Babylon.

Revelation says "yes" as well as "no" to the world. The church that is both in and out of Babylon will not be able to sit still. Perceiving idolatry leads us to evangelize. Perceiving injustice leads us to action. "No one can enter imaginatively into the world narrated by this book and remain complacent about things as they are in an unjust world."[11] Both are needed, and both are rooted in Revelation's final, hopeful vision.

In other words, a spirituality of uncivil worship and resistance does not mean that the church is uninterested in the "welfare of the city" (Jer 29:7). Quite the opposite. But its missional activity in the interest of the city's welfare is shaped, not by the values and agenda of the city, but by the gospel. The faithful church expresses its commitment to the city—to the "inhabitants of the earth"—only in ways that are true to the gospel and to Christians' identity as followers of the Lamb. This means that the

10. This does not rule out a geographical move and may entail it for some. I am thinking here of the work of John Perkins in practicing and advocating Christian relocation, reconciliation, and redistribution, and of the New Monasticism's commitment to moving into places "abandoned by Empire."

11. Hays, *Moral Vision*, 183. He continues: "this means that Revelation can be read rightly only by those who are actively struggling against injustice. If Revelation is a resistance document, its significance will become clear only to those who are engaged in resistance." See also Schüssler Fiorenza, *Revelation: Vision of a Just World*, 139.

church will above all serve, and that service will be Lamb-like, cruciform. It will neither sacralize nor seek secular power, whether economic, political, or military. It disavows, in other words, Christendom in favor of Christ.

## Hope

God the creator and Christ the redeemer take evil and injustice seriously, and soon will both judge humanity and renew the cosmos. We hope and long for the wiping away of everyone's tears and for the healing of the nations. We anticipate the day when those nations will worship God and the Lamb. We bear witness in word and deed to that certain future. But we know that only God can bring that final, future reality to earth, so we constantly pray, "Come, Lord Jesus."

The beauty of hope in Revelation is that it is both personal and global, even cosmic. It can comfort us at times of personal loss, as in the death of a loved one, and at times of global loss, as in a natural disaster or in times of great evil, such as war or genocide. At the end of the day—at the end of the Bible—the book of Revelation is a book of hope.

## Conclusion

Revelation is obviously not the only book in the Bible, and its spirituality cannot stand alone, any more than the spirituality of any other book or writer can replace the entire biblical witness. Revelation must be a conversation partner with the rest of the canon. But without attending to its apocalyptic-prophetic voice, we may not be prompted to ask the hard questions that no other biblical book poses so sharply, and we may not perceive things that no other book reveals so clearly. Moreover, seeing God and life through the eyes of Revelation will help us recover the message of the prophets, Jesus, and Paul in ways that our cultural blinders—whatever they may be—otherwise hinder or even prevent.

**Questions for Reflection and Discussion**

1. What does the characterization of Revelation's spirituality as "a theo-political liturgical and missional spirituality, a spirituality of uncivil worship and witness" mean to you? What are some particular ways that your Christian community can embody Christian discipleship versus civil religion while still affirming the good aspects of the culture in which is located?

2. Are you convinced that a life of nonviolence is central to the book of Revelation? To Christian discipleship? Why or why not?

3. In what ways is Revelation a hopeful book?

4. How might the interpretation of Revelation offered in this book affect the church's practices of evangelization?

# Postlude:
# Reading Revelation Responsibly (Reprise)

To read Revelation responsibly, we have argued, is to read it not as a script for the future but as a script for the church. We need to be clear what this means in the sharpest terms possible: *we have just turned the approach taken by many, if not most, readers of Revelation topsy-turvy*. (Not that this book is the first, or only, to do so, as the many quotes and notes testify.) Furthermore, we have argued that Revelation itself upsets the apocalyptic apple cart, so to speak, that many take for granted. It is my conviction and hope that the approach offered in this book is both more faithful to John and more salutary for the church—and the world.

So how do we perform this uncivil, theopoetic, theopolitical, non-violent, missional, prophetic script "on the ground"? Throughout the book, I have tried to provide at least some ideas and examples. Revelation itself offers us, I think, three highly relevant final pairs of words—and a fourth single word, making (of course) a total of seven.

The first pair of words would be *Look and Listen*. This is a book of visions and auditions. It invites us to cast our eyes on the Lamb that was slaughtered. It calls us to see in him both the way *to* God and the way *of* God. We meditate on the atoning character of his death but also on his faithful witness in that death. We open our ears, individually and corporately, to the Spirit who is constantly speaking to the church.

The second pair of words would be *Worship and Witness*. This is a book of hymns and liturgies. So we offer our praise to God and to the Lamb, night and day. We pledge our allegiance to the one who alone is worthy of it. We allow our praise, and the vision of God and the Lamb that inspires it, to infect and affect everything we think, say, and do. And we tell others about that One who alone is worthy of their worship and allegiance, too. Our witness consists of action, not just words.

The third pair of words would be **Come out and Resist**. This is a book of prophetic challenge and uncomfortable demands because most of us understandably like what Empire claims to offer: security, purpose, victory, control of history, sacred honor, duty, and blessing, and we are willing to offer our minds, hearts, and bodies in return. With our vision corrected by the Lamb and our focus on him, we seek next to disengage our minds, hearts, and bodies from all that promises life but delivers death. We need to resist the seduction of normalcy and of civil religion, and engage the world in new ways and on new terms. We do not accept or participate in the sacralization of secular power: political, military, economic, or any other form. Rather than placing rapture bumper stickers on our cars—"In case of rapture, this vehicle will be unmanned"—we announce, with words and deeds (and maybe even a few bumper stickers) that we follow the Lamb.

The last word, then, would simply be **Follow**. We follow the Lamb. *Vicit Agnus Noster, Eum Sequamur*—"Our Lamb has conquered; let us follow him"—said the Moravians and John Howard Yoder. We seek to follow him *out of* Empire into the new creation, but also, paradoxically, *into* empire: into the dark corners of empire, those places where the vision of God and the Lamb is most needed; where death needs to be replaced with life; where we can bear witness in word and deed to the coming new creation; where there will be life-giving water for all, the end of pain and tears, and healing for individuals and nations. We follow him into a new heaven and new earth liberated from the effects of our sin and even from sin itself, alive with the perpetual presence of the living God, in whom we can be both lost and found in eternal wonder, awe, and praise. Living faithfully in light of that vision is no small challenge.

Revelation concludes the canon; it completes God's story. Perhaps it would not be too bold to suggest that if the church of Jesus Christ is to be faithful to its vocation in the 21st century, the book of Revelation—especially its vision of the slaughtered, victorious, and coming Lamb—must become more central to our worship, our spirituality, our practices. Perhaps, in a profound way, the last book of the Bible needs to become the church's first book.

*Worthy is the Lamb! Amen. Come, Lord Jesus!*

# Bibliography

Abrams, M. H., general editor. *The Norton Anthology of English Literature.* 3rd ed. Vol. 2. New York: Norton, 1974.

Aune, David. "The Influence of Roman Imperial Court Ceremonial on the Apocalypse of John." *Biblical Research* 18 (1983) 5–26.

———. *Revelation.* Word Biblical Commentary 52 A–C. 3 vols. Waco, TX: Word, 1997–98.

———. "Revelation." In *The HarperCollins Bible Commentary*, rev. ed., edited by James L. Mays, et al., 1187–1202. San Francisco: HarperSanFrancisco, 2000.

Barr, David R. "John's Ironic Empire." *Interpretation* 63 (2009) 20–30.

Bauckham, Richard. *The Climax of Prophecy: Studies on the Book of Revelation.* London: T. & T. Clark, 1993.

———. *Jesus and the God of Israel: God Crucified and Other Studies on the New Testament's Christology of Divine Identity.* Grand Rapids: Eerdmans, 2008.

———. *The Theology of the Book of Revelation.* New Testament Theology. Cambridge: Cambridge University Press, 1993.

Beale, G. K. *The Book of Revelation.* New International Greek Testament Commentary. Grand Rapids: Eerdmans, 1999.

———. *John's Use of the Old Testament in Revelation.* Journal for the Study of the New Testament Supplement Series 166. Sheffield, UK: Sheffield Academic, 1998.

Beasley-Murray, George R. *The Book of Revelation.* New Century Bible. Grand Rapids: Eerdmans, 1974.

Blount, Brian K. *Revelation: A Commentary.* New Testament Library. Louisville: Westminster John Knox, 2009.

Boesak, Allan A. *Comfort and Protest: The Apocalypse from a South African Perspective.* Philadelphia: Westminster, 1987.

Bonhoeffer, Dietrich. *Discipleship.* Translated by Barbara Green and Reinhard Krauss. Dietrich Bonhoeffer Works 4. Minneapolis: Fortress, 2001.

Boring, M. Eugene. *Revelation.* Interpretation. Louisville: John Knox, 1989.

Boxall, Ian. *The Revelation of Saint John.* Black's New Testament Commentaries. Peabody, MA: Hendrickson, 2006.

Boyd, Gregory A. The *Myth of a Christian Nation: How the Quest for Political Power is Destroying the Church.* Grand Rapids: Zondervan, 2005.

Boyer, Paul S. *When Time Shall Be No More: Prophecy Belief in Modern American Culture.* Cambridge, MA: Belknap, 1992.

Carey, Greg. "The Book of Revelation as Counter-Imperial Script." In *In the Shadow of Empire: Reclaiming the Bible as a History of Faithful Resistance*, edited by Richard A. Horsley, 157–76. Louisville: Westminster John Knox, 2008.

Carter, Warren. *Matthew and Empire: Initial Explorations.* Harrisburg, PA: Trinity, 2001.

———. *The Roman Empire and the New Testament: An Essential Guide.* Nashville: Abingdon, 2006.

Charry, Ellen T. "'A Sharp Two-Edged Sword': Pastoral Implications of Apocalyptic." In *Character and Scripture: Moral Formation, Community, and Biblical Interpretation,* edited by William P. Brown, 344–60. Grand Rapids: Eerdmans, 2002.

Chesterton, G. K. *Orthodoxy.* Centennial Edition. Nashville: Sam Torode Book Arts, 2009 [1908].

Clouse, Robert G. "Christian Hope Thru History." [Mar 3, 2004] http://www.presence .tv/cms/christianhope_clouse.shtml.

———, editor. *The Meaning of the Millennium: Four Views.* Downers Grove, IL: Inter-Varsity, 1977.

Clouse, Robert G., Robert N. Hosack, and Richard V. Pierard. *The New Millennium Guide: A Once and Future Guide.* Grand Rapids: Baker, 1999.

Cohn, Norman. *The Pursuit of the Millenium: Revolutionary Millenarians and Mystical Anarchists of the Middle Ages.* Rev. and enl. ed. Oxford: Oxford University Press, 1970.

Collins, Adela Yarbro. *The Apocalypse.* New Testament Message. Collegeville, MN: Liturgical, 1990 [1979].

———. "Introduction: Towards the Morphology of a Genre." *Semeia* 14 (1979) 1–20.

Crossan, John Dominic. *God and Empire: Jesus against Rome, Then and Now.* San Francisco: HarperSanFrancisco, 2007.

Daniels, T. Scott. *Seven Deadly Spirits: The Message of Revelation's Letters for Today's Church.* Grand Rapids: Baker Academic, 2009.

Davis, Ellen F. *Scripture, Culture, and Agriculture: An Agrarian Reading of the Bible.* Cambridge: Cambridge University Press, 2009.

deSilva, David A. *Seeing Things John's Way: The Rhetoric of the Book of Revelation.* Louisville: Westminster John Knox, 2009.

Desrosiers, Gilbert. *An Introduction to Revelation: A Pathway to Interpretation.* London: Continuum, 2000.

Ewing, Ward. *Power of the Lamb: Revelation's Theology of Liberation for You.* Eugene, OR: Wipf & Stock, 2006 [1990].

Friesen, Steven J. *Imperial Cults and the Apocalypse of John: Reading Revelation in the Ruins.* New York: Oxford University Press, 2001.

González, Justo L. *Out of Every Tribe and Nation: Christian Theology at the Ethnic Roundtable* Nashville: Abingdon, 1992.

Gorman, Michael J. *Elements of Biblical Exegesis: A Basic Guide for Students and Ministers.* Rev. and exp. ed. Peabody, MA: Hendrickson, 2009.

———. *Reading Paul.* Cascade Companions. Eugene, OR: Cascade Books, 2008.

———. "A 'Seamless Garment' Approach to Biblical Interpretation?" *Journal of Theological Interpretation* 1 (2007) 117–28.

Harink, Douglas. *Paul among the Postliberals: Pauline Theology beyond Christendom and Modernity.* Grand Rapids: Brazos, 2003.

Hays, Richard B. *The Conversion of the Imagination: Paul as Interpreter of Israel's Scripture.* Grand Rapids: Eerdmans, 2005.

———. *The Moral Vision of the New Testament: A Contemporary Introduction to New Testament Ethics; Cross, Community, New Creation.* San Francisco: HarperSanFrancisco, 1996.

Hill, Craig C. *In God's Time: The Bible and the Future.* Grand Rapids: Eerdmans, 2002.

Horsley, Richard. *Revolt of the Scribes: Resistance and Apocalyptic Origins.* Minneapolis: Fortress, 2010.

Howard-Brook, Wes, and Anthony Gwyther. *Unveiling Empire: Reading Revelation Then and Now.* Bible and Liberation Series. Maryknoll, NY: Orbis, 1999.

Hughes, Richard T. *Myths America Lives By.* Urbana: University of Illinois Press, 2003.

Jewett, Robert. *Mission and Menace: Four Centuries of American Religious Zeal.* Minneapolis: Fortress, 2008.

Jewett, Robert, and John Shelton Lawrence. *Captain America and the Crusade Against Evil: The Dilemma of Zealous Nationalism.* Grand Rapids: Eerdmans, 2003.

Johns, Loren L. *The Lamb Christology of the Apocalypse of John: An Investigation into Its Origins and Rhetorical Force.* Wissenschaftliche Untersuchungen zum Neuen Testament 2/167. Tübingen: Mohr Siebeck, 2003.

Johnson, Luke Timothy. *The Writings of the New Testament: An Interpretation.* 3rd ed. Minneapolis: Fortress, 2010.

Koester, Craig R. "On the Verge of the Millennium: A History of the Interpretation of Revelation." *Word & World* 15 (1995) 128–36.

———. *Revelation and the End of All Things.* Grand Rapids: Eerdmans, 2001.

———. "Revelation's Visionary Challenge to Ordinary Empire." *Interpretation* 63 (2009) 5–18.

Kovacs, Judith, and Christopher Rowland. *Revelation: The Apocalypse of Jesus Christ.* Blackwell Bible Commentaries. Malden, MA: Blackwell, 2004.

Kraybill, J. Nelson. *Apocalypse and Allegiance: Worship, Politics, and Devotion in the Book of Revelation.* Grand Rapids: Brazos, 2010.

———. "Apocalypse Now." *Christianity Today* 43/12 (Oct. 25, 1999) 30–40.

———. *Imperial Cult and Commerce in John's Apocalypse.* Journal for the Study of the New Testament Supplement Series 132. Sheffield, UK: Sheffield Academic, 1996.

Krodel, Gerhard A. *Revelation.* Augsburg Commentary on the New Testament. Minneapolis: Augsburg, 1989.

LaHaye, Tim. *Revelation Unveiled.* Grand Rapids: Zondervan, 1999.

Lawrence, D. H. *Apocalypse and the Writings on Revelation.* New York: Penguin, 1980 [1931].

Lindsey, Hal. *There's a New World Coming: An In-Depth Analysis of the Book of Revelation.* Irvine, CA: Harvest House, 1984 [1973].

Luther, Martin. "Preface to the Revelation of St. John [I]." In *Luther's Works: Word and Sacrament,* vol. 35, edited by E. Theodore Bachmann, 398–99. Philadelphia: Fortress, 1960.

———. "Preface to the Revelation of St. John [II]." In *Luther's Works: Word and Sacrament,* vol. 35, edited by E. Theodore Bachmann, 399–411. Philadelphia: Fortress, 1960.

Maier, Harry O. *Apocalypse Recalled: The Book of Revelation after Christendom.* Minneapolis: Fortress, 2002.

Mangina, Joseph L. *Revelation.* Brazos Theological Commentary on the Bible. Grand Rapids: Brazos, 2010.

Matera, Frank J. *New Testament Theology: Exploring Diversity and Unity.* Louisville: Westminster John Knox, 2007.

McGinn, Bernard. *Antichrist: Two Thousand Years of the Human Fascination with Evil.* San Francisco: HarperSanFrancisco, 1994.

McGinn, Bernard, and John Meyendorff, editors, with Jean Leclercq. *Christian Spirituality: Origins to the Twelfth Century*. World Spirituality 15. New York: Crossroad, 1985.

Meeks, Wayne A. *The Moral World of the First Christians*. Library of Early Christianity 6. Philadelphia: Westminster, 1986.

Metzger, Bruce M. *Breaking the Code: Understanding the Book of Revelation*. Nashville: Abingdon, 1993.

Middleton, J. Richard, and Michael J. Gorman. "Salvation." In *New Interpreter's Dictionary of the Bible*, edited by Katharine Doob Sakenfeld, et al., 5:45–61. Nashville: Abingdon, 2009.

Müller-Fahrenholz, Geiko. *America's Battle for God: A European Christian Looks at Civil Religion*. Grand Rapids: Eerdmans, 2007.

Murphy, Francesca Aran. "Revelation, Book of." In *Dictionary for Theological Interpretation of the Bible*, edited by Kevin J. Vanhoozer, et al., 680–87. Grand Rapids: Baker Academic, 2005.

Okoye, James Chukwuma. "Power and Worship: *Revelation* in African Perspective." In *From Every Nation: The Book of Revelation in Intercultural Perspective*, edited by David M. Rhoads, 110–26. Minneapolis: Fortress, 2005.

Olson, Carl E. *Will Catholics Be "Left Behind": A Catholic Critique of the Rapture and Today's Prophecy Preachers*. San Francisco: Ignatius, 2003.

Peterson, Eugene H. *Reversed Thunder: The Revelation of John and the Praying Imagination*. San Francisco: HarperSanFrancisco, 1991 [1988].

Pippin, Tina. *Death and Desire: The Rhetoric of Gender in the Apocalypse of John*. Literary Currents in Biblical Interpretation. Louisville: Westminster John Knox, 1992.

Prévost, Jean-Pierre. *How to Read the Apocalypse*. Translated by John Bowden and Margaret Lydamore. New York: Crossroad, 1993.

Price, S. R. F. *Rituals and Power: The Roman Imperial Cult in Asia Minor*. Cambridge: Cambridge University Press, 1984.

Reddish, Mitchell G. *Revelation*. Smith & Helwys Bible Commentary. Macon, GA: Smith & Helwys, 2001.

Resseguie, James L. *The Revelation of John: A Narrative Commentary*. Grand Rapids: Baker Academic, 2009.

Richard, Pablo. *Apocalypse: A People's Commentary on the Book of Revelation*. Maryknoll, NY: Orbis, 1995.

———. "Reading the *Apocalypse*: Resistance, Hope, and Liberation in Central America." In *From Every Nation: the Book of Revelation in Intercultural Perspective*, edited by David M. Rhoads, 146–64. Minneapolis: Fortress, 2005.

Rossing, Barbara R. *The Rapture Exposed: The Message of Hope in the Book of Revelation*. Boulder, CO: Westview, 2004.

Rowe, C. Kavin. *World Upside Down: Reading Acts in the Graeco-Roman Age*. New York: Oxford University Press, 2009.

Rowland, Christopher C. "The Book of Revelation: Introduction, Commentary, and Reflections." In *The New Interpreter's Bible*, edited by Leander E. Keck, et al., 12:501–736. Nashville: Abingdon, 1998.

Russell, D. S. *The Method and Message of Jewish Apocalyptic 200 BC–AD 100*. Philadelphia: Westminster, 1964.

Sanders, Jack T. *Ethics in the New Testament: Change and Development*. Philadelphia: Fortress, 1975.

Schnelle, Udo. *Theology of the New Testament*. Translated by M. Eugene Boring. Grand Rapids: Baker Academic, 2009.

Schüssler Fiorenza, Elisabeth. *Revelation: Vision of a Just World*. Proclamation Commentaries. Minneapolis, MN: Fortress, 1991.

Scofield, C. I., editor. *The Scofield Reference Bible*. Oxford: Oxford University Press, 1917 [1909].

Sittser, Gerald Lawson. *A Cautious Patriotism: The American Churches and the Second World War*. Chapel Hill: University of North Carolina Press, 1997.

Standaert, Michael. *Skipping Towards Armageddon: The Politics and Propaganda of the Left Behind Novels and the LaHaye Empire*. Brooklyn: Soft Skull, 2006.

Stark, Rodney. *The Rise of Christianity: How the Obscure, Marginal Jesus Movement Became the Dominant Religious Force in the Western World in a Few Centuries*. San Francisco: HarperSanFrancisco, 1997.

Stott, John. R. W. *What Christ Thinks of the Church: An Exposition of Revelation 1–3*. Grand Rapids: Baker, 2003 [1958].

Sweet, J. P. M. *Revelation*. Westminster Pelican Commentaries. Philadelphia: Westminster 1979.

Talbert, Charles H. *The Apocalypse: A Reading of the Revelation of John*. Louisville: Westminster John Knox, 1994.

Thompson, Leonard L. *The Book of Revelation: Apocalypse and Empire*. New York: Oxford University Press, 1990.

Tuck, William Powell. *The Left Behind Fantasy: The Theology Behind the Left Behind Tales*. Eugene, OR: Resource Publications, 2010.

Tuveson, Ernest Lee. *Redeemer Nation: The Idea of America's Millennial Role*. Chicago: University of Chicago Press, 1968.

Wainwright, Arthur W. *Mysterious Apocalypse: Interpreting the Book of Revelation*. Nashville: Abingdon, 1993.

Wall, Robert W. *Revelation*. New International Biblical Commentary. Peabody, MA: Hendrickson, 1991.

Walvoord, John F. *The Revelation of Jesus Christ*. Chicago: Moody, 1966.

Wannenwetsch, Bernd. "Representing the Absent in the City: Prolegomena to a Negative Political Theology According to Revelation 21." In *God, Truth, and Witness: Engaging Stanley Hauerwas*, edited by L. Gregory Jones, et al., 167–92. Grand Rapids: Brazos, 2005.

Wesley, John. *Explanatory Notes on the New Testament*. Grand Rapids: Baker, 1986 [1755]. Online: http://www.ccel.org/ccel/wesley/notes.titlepage.html.

Wilson, Mark. *Charts on the Book of Revelation: Literary, Historical, and Theological Perspectives*. Grand Rapids: Kregel, 2007.

Wilson-Hartgrove, Jonathan. *To Baghdad and Beyond: How I Got Born Again in Babylon*. Eugene, OR: Cascade, 2005.

Wink, Walter. *Engaging the Powers: Discernment and Resistance in a World of Domination*. Minneapolis: Fortress, 1992.

Witherington, Ben, III. *Revelation*. New Cambridge Bible Commentary. Cambridge: Cambridge University Press, 2003.

Wright, N. T. "Farewell to the Rapture." *Bible Review* 17:4 (2001) 8, 52. Also available at http://www.ntwrightpage.com/Wright_BR_Farewell_Rapture.htm.

———. *Following Jesus: Biblical Reflections on Discipleship*. Grand Rapids: Eerdmans, 1994.

## Bibliography

———. *The New Testament and the People of God*. Minneapolis: Fortress, 1992.

———. *Surprised by Hope: Rethinking Heaven, the Resurrection, and the Mission of the Church*. New York: HarperCollins, 2008.

Volf, Miroslav. *Exclusion and Embrace: A Theological Exploration of Identity, Otherness, and Reconciliation*. Nashville: Abingdon, 1996.

Yoder, John Howard. *The Politics of Jesus: Vicit Agnus Noster*. 2nd ed. Grand Rapids: Eerdmans, 1994.

# Subject and Name Index

christology (*continued*)
139–40, 142, 143, 154–55, 160,
167, 183
*See also* Faithful Witness (Christ);
Lamb (Christ); reign, of God/
the Lamb.
christophany, 102–15
church. *See* ecclesiology.
cities of Revelation 2–3, xii, 26–27,
42–43, 81–101, 117, 124
civil religion, xv–xvi, 12, 31–34, 40–56,
59–60, 68, 75–78, 99, 125, 135,
165, 176 n. 2, 179–87, 190
American, 48–56, 180
Collins, Adela Yarbro, 169
Collins, John, 14, 20 n. 16
colors, 78, 98, 139 n. 3, 147–49
conflict. *See* drama.
consumerism, 78, 98, 139 n. 3, 147–49
*See also* economic injustice.
contemporary-historical interpretive
approach. *See* preterist
interpretive approach.
correspondence, in interpretation, 37–
38, 63–64, 68, 71
courage, 55, 76, 100, 132, 174, 178,
183–84
creation. *See* new heaven and earth.
Crossan, John Dominic, 2
cruciform interpretive strategy, 77–80
cruciformity, 75, 76, 77–80, 84, 178,
183–84, 186
culture, 25 n. 30, 47, 48, 50, 56, 75, 76,
95, 99, 115, 117, 118, 134, 145 n.
19, 164–66, 177, 181, 184, 187
Daniels, T. Scott, 97–98
Darby, J. N. D, 65
date of Revelation, 27–29
date of second coming, xii–xiii, xvi
Davis, Ellen, 22
decoding interpretations, 37, 63–67
deSilva, David, 25 n. 30, 120, 147 n. 21,
148
discernment, 76, 79, 169, 178, 180–83
discipleship, xv, 11, 12, 34–37, 39, 72, 73,
76, 77, 79, 82–84, 97, 168, 179,
180, 187

dispensationalism, 22–23, 65–66, 67,
71, 79–80, 84–85, 98–101, 143,
168–69
Domitian, 24, 28–29, 41–42, 124, 128
dragon. *See* Satan.
drama, Revelation as, 37–38, 109 n. 13,
116–37, 145, 178
and characters, 37, 109 n. 13, 119–36
and conflict, 37–38, 109 n. 13, 116,
123, 136
and plot, 109 n. 13, 117–119
dualism, apocalyptic, 15–16, 50
Dürer, Albrecht, x, 6, 7, 129
Dylan, Bob, 103
ecclesiology, 38, 52 n. 52, 55, 68, 76, 79,
81–101, 122, 130–36, 144–45,
148–50, 155, 156, 158, 159, 165–
75, 176–77, 179–82, 185–86,
189–90
economic
faithfulness, 148–50, 159
injustice, 33, 44–47, 55, 91, 96–97,
99, 123, 141, 145 n. 19, 149
power, 44–47, 55, 92–93, 94, 96–97,
99, 123, 136
*See also* consumerism.
Ellul, Jacques, 67 n. 14
Emperor, cult of. *See* imperial cult.
empire, 11–12, 15, 17, 33, 40–48, 68, 73,
75, 76, 83, 85, 125, 136, 139 n. 3,
141, 145–47, 150–51, 158, 166,
169, 170, 174, 180, 181–82
contemporary, 21, 33, 40–48, 158,
181
critique of/alternative to, 33, 40–48,
55–56, 59, 180, 183–85, 190
Roman, 12, 21, 25, 33, 40–48, 91,
103, 124–25, 160–62
*Epistle to Digonetus*, 134
escapism, xii, xvi n. 9, 72, 79–80, 95 n.
15, 164, 168–70, 174, 175, 185
eschatology, xii, xiii, 13, 10, 22, 65, 74,
168–69, 174
*See also* hope; new creation; second
coming.
ethics, Revelation and, 25, 111–12

*See also* discipleship; faithfulness;
nonviolence; spirituality.

evil, 11, 12, 15–16, 17, 20, 24, 33, 38,
50, 66, 68, 75, 76, 116, 117, 120,
121–22, 123–30, 138, 139, 141,
142, 151–55, 158, 159, 160, 163,
164, 166, 171, 177, 181, 183–84,
186

*See also* judgment; suffering.

evangelization, 167–74, 178, 184–87

exceptionalism, American, 48–50

Faithful Witness (Christ), xv–xvi, 26, 32,
55, 76, 97, 108, 119, 120–22, 131,
178–79, 184, 189

faithfulness, xv, 12, 17, 19, 24–25, 32–33,
34, 37, 38, 39, 55, 59–60, 68,
73–76, 78–79, 82, 83–84, 87,
88–90, 93–97, 99, 100, 109, 112,
116, 117, 118, 121, 122, 130–32,
133, 135, 136, 140, 144, 146, 148,
151, 156, 162, 166, 168, 172–74,
176–85, 190

*See also* discipleship; Faithful
Witness (Christ); John, author of
Revelation; witness.

Fiorenza, Elisabeth Schüssler, x, 11, 67

form, of Revelation. *See* genre.

four horsemen, 1, 141–42

Friesen, Steven J., 41 n. 20

funerals and Revelation, 165–66

futurist interpretive approach. *See*
predictive interpretive approach.

genre, of Revelation, 10–30

God, doctrine of. *See* theology proper
(doctrine of God); theophany.

Gorman, Michael J., xiv n. 4, 112 n. 22,
177 n. 3

Handel, G. F., x, 5, 6, 112, 113

Harink, Douglas, 16

Harmagedon. *See* Armageddon.

Hays, Richard B., x, 8, 67, 108, 178, 184,
185 n. 11

heaven, new, and new earth. *See* new
creation.

Hill, Craig, 73

hope, xv, 4, 10, 11, 12, 15–16, 20, 21,
32–33, 35, 55, 59–60, 69, 72,

74, 75, 79, 82–84, 144–45, 147,
160–75, 178, 185, 186, 187

Horsley, Richard, 15

Howard-Brook, Wes, and Anthony
Gwyer, x, 11, 33, 42 n. 25, 43, 45,
67, 145 n. 19, 161 n. 2

hybrid. *See* genre, of Revelation.

hymns,
civil-religion, 52–53, 154
in Revelation, 34–35, 37, 58, 102–15,
116, 140, 189
with text from Revelation, x, 4–6,
20–21, 39 n. 16, 100, 112–14,
143 n. 11, 154, 166–67, 174, 179
*See also* worship.

idealist interpretive approach. *See*
theopoetic interpretive approach.

idolatry, xv–xvi, 18, 24, 33–34, 54, 55–
56, 75, 76, 78–79, 88–91, 93–99,
103, 117, 118, 120, 122–125, 128,
130, 138–39, 145–47, 148, 152,
158, 160–61, 162, 178–82, 185

imperial cult, 20, 27, 31–33, 40–44, 56,
82, 91, 92, 93, 96, 103, 106, 124

imagination, 4, 6–8, 21–22, 28, 69–70,
142, 178, 180–81

injustice, 16, 33–34, 67, 76, 120, 139,
141, 146, 150, 152, 156–59, 169,
178, 185, 186

*See also* economic injustice.

interludes, 57–58, 144–45

intertextuality, 23 n. 28

*See also* Scripture.

Irenaeus, 28, 65

Jerusalem. *See* new Jerusalem.

Joachim of Fiore, 6, 65

John, author of Revelation, 27–28, 62,
81, 96, 117, 131

Johnson, Andy, 46 n. 40

judgment, xvi, 1, 3, 11, 15, 16, 17, 19,
23–25, 33, 35–38, 57–58, 62,
76, 77, 79, 85, 91 n. 11, 108, 109
n. 15, 110–11, 115, 116, 118,
119–20, 130, 133, 136, 138–159,
162, 184, 186

last, 23, 76, 109 n. 15, 143

*See also* evil; vengeance; violence;
wrath.

# Scripture Index

∾

# New Testament

☙

## Other Ancient Sources